WHAT'S COOKING IN OUR NATIONAL PARKS

by

National Park Service Western Regional Office
Cookbook Committee

This collection of recipes has been compiled by the Cookbook Committe, National Park Service, Western Region, with the cooperation of employees from all areas administered by the National Park Service, Western Region.

COMMITTEE MEMBERS

Catherine Hjort   David Hughes

Charles Adams   Ronald Replogle

Milton Kolipinski   Harry Sloat

Peggy Rolandson, Chairlady

FRONT COVER – Looking out on the beauty of Rocky Mountain National Park, these campers cook a hearty breakfast. (Photo by Mike Hallacy, Denver, Colorado.)

Your support of this cookbook helps provide scholarship loans to family members of National Park Service employees and alumni. Five percent of all sales are added to an Education Trust Fund, administered by the Employees & Alumni Association of the National Park Service. Membership in the Association is available to present and past National Park Service employees; write to the address above.

Library of Congress Cataloguing-in-Publication Data

What's cooking in our national parks / by National Park Service,
Western Regional Office, Cookbook Committee.
      p.   cm.
  Includes index.
  ISBN 0-89646-081-9
     1. Cookery. 2. National parks and reserves--West (U.S.)--Description and travel--Views. I. United States. National Park Service. Western Regional Office. Cookbook Committee.
TX714.W46 1989
641.5--dc20   89-8541
                                         CIP

Published and distributed by

VISTABOOKS
0637 Blue Ridge Road,
Silverthorne, CO 80498-8931

ISBN 0-89646-081-9

DEDICATION

When this book was first published in 1973, it was dedicated to the National Park Service Family with all proceeds from the sales going to the National Park Service 's Employee and Alumni Association's Education Fund. Starting with a printing of 2,000 copies, book sales have far surpassed our most exaggerated hopes. Thus, as visitors to their national parks have expressed an interest in cooking they also have made an investment in the future of many young Americans. There will never be an end to the good that has come from such a modest beginning.

Howard H. Chapman
former Western Regional Director,
National Park Service

Appreciation is expressed to the following parks, individuals, and offices:

ARIZONA
Arizona Arheological Center, Tucson
Casa Grande Ruins National Monument
Chiricahua National Monument
Coronado National Monument
Fort Bowie National Historic Site
Grand Canyon National Park
Montezuma Castle National Monument
Organ Pipe Cactus Natonal Monument
Petrified Forest National Park
Saguaro National Monument
Tonto National Monument
Tumacacori National Monument
Tuzigoot National Monument
Walnut Canyon National Monument

CALIFORNIA
Cabrillo National Monument
Channel Islands National Monument
Death Valley National Monument
Fort Point National Historic Site
Golden Gate National Recreation Area
John Muir House National Historic Site
Joshua Tree National Monument
Lassen Volcanic National Monument
Muir Woods National Monument
Pinnacles National Monument
Point Reyes National Seashore
Redwood National Park
Sequoia and Kings Canyon National Park
Western Regional Office, San Francisco
Whiskeytown-Shasta-Trinity National Recreation Area
Yosemite National Park

HAWAII
City of Refuge National Historic Site
Haleakala National Park
Hawaii Group, Honolulu
Hawaii Volcanoes National Park

NEVADA
Lake Mead National Recreation Area
Lehman Caves National Monument

WASHINGTON, D.C.
The Director's Office

SPECIAL THANKS TO:Ronald H. Walker, Director, National Park Service
Fred R. Bell, Visual Information Specialist, NPS
Howard H. Chapman, Director, Western Region, NPS
Forrest M. Benson
Charles F. Adams
Catherine and Frank Hjort
David and Cora Hughes
Milton and Donna Kolipinski
Dorothea Miehle
Shelley Momii
Harry Sloat
Teresita Smith
Marilyn Treabess
Ron and Mary Alice Replogle
Peggy and Gordon Rolandson

OLYMPIC NATIONAL PARK, WASHINGTON, SPORTS THE LARGEST RAIN FOREST OUT-SIDE OF THE TROPICS. (NPS photo).

MOLTEN LAVA POURING INTO THE SEA AS PART OF VOLCANIC ACTIVITY IN 1969-60 DISPLAYS FROM KILAUEA CRATER IN HAWAII VOLCANOES NATIONAL PARK. (NPS photo.)

A PIECE OF OUR BEAUTIFUL EASTERN SHORE IS PRESERVED IN ACADIA NATIONAL PARK, MAINE. (NPS photo by Richard Frear).

THE FIREHOLE RIVER MEANDERS THROUGH THE MIDWAY GEYSER BASIN IN YELLOWSTONE NATIONAL PARK.
(NPS photo by George Grant).

Appetizers
Beverages

VIEW OVERLOOKING THE TIMELESS WONDER OF THE GRAND CANYON IN GRAND CANYON NATIONAL PARK, ARIZONA. (NPS photo by Cecil W. Stoughton).

APPETIZER

1/2 c. mayonnaise	2 beaten eggs
2 T. flour	1/2 c. milk

Combine above ingredients; mix until blended.

1 2/3 c. drained crabmeat (7½ oz. can) optional	1 pkg. (8 oz.) natural Swiss cheese, sliced and diced
1/3 c. sliced green onions	

Combine with first ingredients and pour into unbaked pastry line Quiche pan. Bake at 350 degrees for 40 to 45 minutes. (Unbaked pastry can be used in a pie dish.)

PASTRY RECIPE

1 c. flour	1 t. salt
1/2 c. shortening (Crisco)	3 to 4 T. cold milk

Mix and let set for 2 minutes. Serves 10 to 12.

Dagmar Robinson
Channel Islands NM

CHEESE ROLLS

3 pkg. (3 oz.) cream cheese	1/4 t. Accent
1/2 lb. very sharp cheese	1/2 t. Worcestershire sauce
1/2 lb. pimiento cheese	Dash of Tabasco sauce
1/4 c. mayonnaise	2 crushed garlic buds

Mix thoroughly; chill; form into two rolls. Roll 1 in chili powder and the other roll in paprika. Use as spread on crackers.

Shirley Mae Johnson
Regional Office

DEVILED EGGS

4 eggs, hardboiled

Slice eggs lengthwise. Set halved whites on a dish, and place yolks in small bowl. Mash till smooth and crumbly. Add and combine the following ingredients:

1 T. vinegar	1 t. prepared mustard
1 t. garlic salt	1 T. minced onion
1/4 t. cayenne pepper	1½ t. dry onion soup mix
1/2 t. dry mustard	1 t. Worcestershire sauce

Add enough mayonnaise to moisten. Whip until creamy. Drop small spoonfuls of yolk mixture into whites. Sprinkle tops with paprika.

Elaine Hounsell
Lake Mead NRA

CRABMEAT AND GRUYERE TREATS

1 c. crabmeat
1/4 c. Gruyere cheese, grated
1 T. Chablis wine
1/2 t. salt
1 T. mayonnaise

Mix all ingredients together. Pile high on rounds of white bread that have crusts removed and toasted on one side. Bake in 450 degree oven until hot. Makes about 50 treats. Serve warm.

Heidi Kobayashi
Regional Office

DELICIOUS SNACK

2 small cans chopped
   mushrooms, drained
1 small can chopped black
   olives
1 small can chopped chili
   peppers
1/2 lb. Tillamook or Cheddar cheese

Chop all fine or put through a grinder. Add 1 small can of plain tomato sauce, a dash of garlic powder. Put on rye bread rounds cut in 1/2 and crusted. Bake at 400 degrees until bubbly.

Chuck and Irene Adams
Regional Office

CHIPPED BEEF SPREAD

1 pkg. (8 oz.) cream cheese
2 T. milk
1/2 c. sour cream
1/2 t. garlic powder
3/4 T. prepared horseradish
4 oz. dried chipped beef, chopped
Dash of pepper
1/2 c. chopped pecans
2 T. butter

Combine all ingredients except pecans and butter; mix well and put in heatproof serving dish. Saute pecans in butter and sprinkle over cream cheese mixture. Bake in 350 degree oven about 15-20 minutes until warm but not runny. Serve with corn chips. A cocktail party favorite.

Mary Alice Replogle
Regional Office

OLIVE CHEESE BITES

25 pitted olives
1/2 c. sifted flour
1/8 t. dry mustard
1/4 t. black pepper
3 T. melted butter
green onions (or pieces of
   mushrooms)
1/8 t. salt
1/8 t. paprika
1 c. grated Cheddar cheese (sharp)
1 t. milk

Stuff olives with onions or mushroom pieces. Sift all dry ingredients and blend well. Mix with cheese. Stir in butter and milk. Using fingers, mold a rounded teaspoon of dough around each olive, covering completely. Place on baking sheets and bake in hot oven (400 degrees) for 15 minutes or until lightly browned. Serve warm. Makes 25 bites.

Peggy Rolandson
San Francisco Office

GUACAMOLE

2 medium size onions
4 medium size tomatoes

1 clove garlic, peeled
2 small hot chili peppers

Grind all the above ingredients together. Just before serving, add 4 mashed avocados, 1 tsp. lime juice and salt and pepper to taste.

Marilyn J. Scott
Kings Canyon NP

CHEESE BALL

1 (8 oz.) jar cream cheese
1 jar Old English cream cheese

1/4 jar Blue Cheese
1/2 medium grated onion
1 scant t. garlic powder

Blend with fork. Chill cheese for several hours until firm. Shape into ball and roll in chopped pecans and chopped parsley. Place on compote or plate, surround by crackers and serve.

Chuck and Irene Adams
Regional Office

CHUTNEY DIP

1/2 pt. whipping cream
18 oz. cream cheese
1/4 c. chopped cashews

3 T. chutney juice
1 pkg. curry mix from Uncle
   Ben's curry rice
OR 1 T. curry

Whip cream and beat cream cheese, until fluffy. Blend in chutney and curry seasoning. Fold in whipping cream and sprinkle cashews.

Bunny Chew
Lake Mead NRA

SESAME CHICKEN WINGS

3 lb. chicken wings
2 T. flour
1/4 c. cornstarch
1/4 c. mochicko flour
1/4 c. sugar
1 T. salt
1 qt. peanut oil

1/4 t. MSG
1/4 c. soy sauce
1 T. oyster sauce
2 eggs, beaten
1/4 c. chopped green onion
2 c. sesame seeds

Disjoint chicken; discard tips. In a large mixing bowl, combine first 6 ingredients. Mix in the next 4 ingredients. Dip chicken into batter; coat well. Heat oil in a large skillet. Sprinkle chicken with sesame seeds. Fry 6 to 8 minutes or until done. Makes 6 servings.

Adele Fevella
Haleakala NP

HAPPY HOUR DOGS

1 c. catsup
1 c. chili sauce
1 T. vinegar (cider)

1 T. mustard (prepared)
1/4 c. brown sugar
1/2 t. garlic, minced

Heat and simmer till well mixed; if too thick, add a little water. Before serving, add: 1 pkg. wieners, cut into 5 pieces. (10 wieners to a pkg. or 50 pieces.) When hot, turn into chafing dish—with picks on side to spear pieces.

Chuck and Irene Adams
Regional Office

HOT COOKIES (To be served with cocktails)

1/2 lb. Old English cheese
2 sticks oleo or butter
2½ c. sifted flour

1 c. finely chopped nuts
1/2 to 2 t. red pepper
1 t. salt

Grate cheese; combine with soft oleo. Mix with hands. Work in flour, salt, pepper; add nuts. Mold into 3 rolls. Chill overnight. Slice thin; bake at 350 degrees till light brown. Serve warm.

Mary and Forrest Benson
Regional Office

MARINATED ARTICHOKE HEARTS

1 pkg. frozen artichoke hearts
1/4 c. champagne vinegar
1/2 c. olive oil
1 clove minced garlic

1 T. parsley, chopped
1 T. red onion, chopped
Salt and pepper to taste

Cook artichoke hearts as directed; drain. Mix and marinate for 4 hours. Marinade also good using eggplant cubes, cauliflower, or green beans.

Marilyn J. Scott
Kings Canyon NP

STUFFED MUSHROOMS

Remove stems and with a teaspoon gently remove some pulp from caps. Chop stems and pulp very fine. Saute one large clove garlic in butter. Add mushroom pulp.

Add: Fine bread crumbs and a little white wine. Melt butter and a little white wine in a shallow baking dish. Stuff mushroom caps and place in dish. Sprinkle with Parmesan cheese. Bake 15 to 20 minutes at 350 degrees.

Chuck and Irene Adams
Regional Office

MARINATED BEANS

1 can garbanzo beans
1½ c. oil
1/2 c. wine vinegar
1/4 c. capers

1/4 c. chopped green onions
1/4 c. chopped stuffed green olives
1/4 c. chopped parsley

Drain beans. Combine all ingredients and chill thoroughly.

Dave and Josephine Jones
San Francisco Office

COCKTAIL FRANKS

1 jar (4 oz.) French's mustard
1 jar (4 oz.) grape jelly

2 lb. franks, cut in chunks

Heat mustard and jelly; add franks. Heat thoroughly. Serve in chafing dish; spear with toothpicks.

Tom Doyle
Regional Office

CHEESE BALL

1 jar (6 oz.) Roquefort
  cheese, softened
1 jar (10 oz.) sharp cheese
  spread, softened
1 jar (10 oz.) cream cheese, softened

2 T. onion, grated
1 t. Worcestershire sauce
1 c. pecans, ground
1/2 c. parsley, finely chopped

Combine cheeses, onion, Worcestershire sauce. Blend well. Stir in 1/2 cup pecans and 1/4 cup parsley. Shape into ball. Place in bowl lined with waxed paper. Chill overnight. About 1/2 hour before serving, roll ball in mixture of remaining nuts and parsley.

Mary and Forrest Benson
Regional Office

CHEESE CRISP

Flour tortillas
Shredded cheese

Butter
Hot sauce

Butter the tortillas; cover with shredded cheese; slip under broiler until cheese starts to melt—watch carefully—serve with hot sauce. May use large tortillas and cut into individual servings.

HOT SAUCE FOR CHEESE CRISP

1 can stewed tomatoes
1 can diced green chili
1 onion, chopped very fine

1 t. salad oil
1 t. vinegar
Salt, pepper, garlic salt to taste

Put all ingredients into bowl and squash together with hand until very soupy. May be used on shredded lettuce in Mexican dishes.

Kathleen DeWitt
Death Valley NM

HAILSTONES

One pint jars with lids (one for each adult in party). Put 3 ounces of bourbon, 1 sprig of mint, 2 tablespoons of sugar into each jar; fill with crushed ice; put lids on and shake until a frothy mess forms. Let each shake their own jar. Sip slowly and commune with nature. Wonderful refresher after a hike or at beach parties and the like.

Nick Weeks
Regional Office

MARGARITAS

2 oz. Triple Sec liqueur
4 oz. Tequila

6 oz. can frozen lemonade
Crushed ice to make 36 ounces

Mix in blender until "slushy". Serve in 8 oz. glasses with salted rims.

Salted Rims: Wet rim by running lemon around it and dip rim lightly into bowl with salt in it. Knock lumps off rims.

Peter and Karla Allen
Lake Mead NRA

SANGRIA—MEXICAN PUNCH

1 c. strawberries, halved
1 peach, peeled and sliced
2 T. sugar
2 bananas, peeled and sliced

Juice and grated rind of 1 lemon
3/4 t. cinnamon
1 c. orange juice
2 bottles red wine

Mix ingredients; let stand at room temperature at least 1 hour. Just before serving, add 15 ice cubes and soda water if desired.

Chuck and Irene Adams
Regional Office

CHRISTMAS WINE PUNCH

3 fifths red currant wine
1 T. caraway seeds
1 cinnamon stick

1 fifth rose' wine
1 T. cloves

Set wine and spices approximately 1/2 hour. Then bring almost to a boil, slowly. Serves 30 cups.

Dagmar Robinson
Channel Islands NM

CRANBERRY PUNCH

1 qt. 7-Up
2 c. orange juice
1 qt. pineapple sherbet

1/4 c. lemon juice
2 bottles cranberry juice
(15 oz. size)

Combine all ingredients into large punch bowl. Serves about 25.

Joy Gifford
Point Reyes NS

GLUG

1 gal. claret or burgundy wine	Raisins
1 fifth (or a little less) bourbon	Almonds (blanched)
1 small bottle glaced fruit	Cinnamon sticks (4 or 5)
Few cloves	

Boil everything except bourbon. Then add bourbon and bring to boil again and serve. Can be served warm or cold.

Shirley Mae Johnson
Regional Office

DANDELION WINE

To 8 quarts of dandelion blossoms, add 2 gallons of hot water and let stand a day and a night. Then squeeze out blossoms and boil liquid for 5 minutes. Add 2 pounds sugar and the juice of 4 lemons. Bottle and set to ferment.

(Recipe from my grandmother's recipe book written at the time of her marriage in 1881.)

Susie Cahill
Haleakala NP

LIME PUNCH

2 cans (46 oz. size) "Citrus Cooler" drink	1 large bottle Quinine Water or Tonic
Vodka to own discretion	

Float a large chunk of ice in punch bowl. Add a few slices of fresh limes to ingredients in the bowl and serve.

Tom Doyle
Regional Office

HOT SPICE PUNCH

8 c. boiling water	1 c. sugar
1 lge. frozen can orange juice	1 whole clove
Juice of 1 lemon	1 cinnamon stick

Break cinnamon stick into pieces. Place clove and cinnamon in 1 cup of hot mixture and steep for 10-15 minutes. Strain into hot punch. Serve at once. A good holiday drink.

Genevieve Dalley
Lake Mead NRA

DIRTY BIRD

After skiing - shake up: with ice, add 1½ ounces each vodka, Kahlua coffee liqueur, and heavy cream; strain and serve. This "Dirty Bird" recipe appeared in the February issue of ENGINEERING AND MINING JOURNAL.

Anonymous
Regional Office

APRICOT EGG NOG

1 qt. egg nog
2 (12 oz. size) cans apricot nectar
2 c. milk
1 T. lemon juice

1/16 t. salt
1 c. brandy
1 c. heavy whipping cream
Nutmeg

Have all ingredients well chilled. Combine egg nog, nectar, milk, lemon juice, salt and brandy. Beat heavy whipping cream to moderately soft peaks and fold into other mixture just before serving. Sprinkle with nutmeg. Makes about 2½ quarts. Variation: Omit brandy and add 1/2 teaspoon almond extract. This recipe appeared in the Hawaiian "Garden Island". Very good.

Mike and Ruth Yoshinaka
Regional Office

LIME-FROSTED PARTY PUNCH

3¼ to 4 c. pineapple-
    grapefruit drink, chilled
2/3 c. fresh lemon juice
2 qt. cold water

3½ oz. envelope unsweetened
    lemon-lime soft drink powder
    (Kool Aid)
2 c. sugar
2 pt. lime sherbet
4 bottles (7 oz.) 7-Up, chilled

In punch bowl, combine chilled pineapple-grapefruit drink, lemon juice, cold water, soft drink powder and sugar. Stir till soft drink powder and sugar are completely dissolved. Top punch with large dips of lime sherbet. Resting bottle on rim of punch bowl, carefully pour in 7-Up. Serve some sherbet with each cup of punch. Serves 30-35.

Anne Lewis
Sequoia NP

HOT WASSAIL

1 qt. (1 can) unsweetened
    pineapple juice
1 bottle cranberry juice cocktail
2 qt. apple juice
    OR 1 can apricot nectar

6 sticks cinnamon
1 t. whole cloves
Dash of nutmeg
4-6 whole oranges

Combine ingredients in large pan except oranges and whole cloves. Heat to boiling; reduce heat and simmer 20 minutes. Stud oranges with cloves. Remove pan from heat. Strain. Pour into large serving bowl, using oranges for decoration. Remove cinnamon sticks or it will get too strongly spiced. Pour 1 shot of rum into the mugs for those desiring it. Serve hot or cold. Yields 20 (8 oz.) servings. This is very good to have at the holiday season.

Peter and Karla Allen
Lake Mead NRA

MEXICAN CHOCOLATE

Heat 1 quart of milk to boiling with 1 stick cinnamon and 3 tablespoons strong coffee. Add 2 squares chocolate or 4 tablespoons cocoa dissolved in boiling water. Heat again to boiling. Remove from fire. Add 1/2 teaspoon vanilla, 1/2 teaspoon nutmeg and 1/2 teaspoon salt. Beat with egg beater until foamy. Serve at once in tall chocolate cups. Sweeten to taste.

Nick Weeks
Regional Office

GLOGG — (PUNCH)

2 qt. burgundy wine
1/2 to 3/4 lb. sugar
1/2 t. cardamom (whole)
1 stick cinnamon

1/2 t. cloves (whole)
1/2 t. ginger (whole)
A small piece candied orange peel
Vodka to taste

Add sugar and spices to wine and heat, stirring frequently. Do not boil. Add vodka to individual taste (1/2 cup to pint per recipe). Can be made in larger quantities and stored in bottles and heated as used. Serve very warm with a few raisins and almonds in punch glasses.

Chuck and Irene Adams
Regional Office

TETON TEA

1 qt. strong tea
1 qt. pkg. each Wyler's Lemonade
   and orange drink mixes
1½ qt. water
Whole cloves, cinnamon sticks

Lemon slices
1/2 gal. red wine (burgundy
   or Chianti)
1 pt. dark rum
1 pt. brandy
2 c. sugar or to taste

Brew tea; add ingredients through cinnamon (spices to taste). Simmer 10 to 15 minutes and add liquors. Heat but do not boil. Serve in mugs with lemon slices, cinnamon sticks in each mug.

Carla Martin
Tuzigoot NM

DIXIE FRUIT SPARKLE

5 bananas, mashed
Juice of 5 oranges and 5 lemons

5 c. sugar
7 c. water

Mix thoroughly and freeze. When ready to serve, fill large glasses about 1/3 full of frozen mixture. Finish filling glasses with flavor choice of soda. Garnish with mint and cherry. Makes about 35 glasses.

Helen Koch
Joshua Tree NM

DRIED FRUIT CORDIALS

(Sip golden colored apricot cordial; then eat the wine-saturated fruit.)

1 lb. dried apricots, prunes
   with pits, pears, or peaches
1 c. brandy

1 bottle (4/5 qt.) or 3 1/3 cups dry
   white wine
2 c. sugar

In a glass, ceramic, or stainless steel container, combine dried fruit with wine, brandy, and sugar, stirring well. Cover tightly and set aside at room temperature for at least a week to allow flavors to develop. Stir occasionally for the first few days until the sugar is dissolved.

After one week, the apricots, prunes, and pears have the texture of poached fruit and are ready to eat; the peaches will be comparatively firmer. The fruit taste in the wine reaches its maximum intensity in three or four weeks. After about six weeks, the fruit may become softer than you like and, if so, should be removed; the wine keeps indefinitely.

To serve, offer a piece of fruit with some of the wine; sip the wine and each the fruit. Or serve separately. This mixture can also be put up into canning jars—sterilized—sealed and used as token gifts at the holiday time. (Makes about 10 half-pint jars.)

Jayne Ramorino
Regional Office

CREAM SICKLE

Shake with ice: 1 ounce each lemon juice, orange juice, vodka, gin and creme de cacao; strain or serve on the rocks. This concoction is served at "Ma Bell's" in Shubert Alley (between 44th and 45th), New York City. Recipe appeared in February issue of ENGINEERING AND MINING JOURNAL.

Anonymous
Regional Office

THE SERENE WINTER WILDERNESS OF SHENANDOAH NATIONAL PARK, VIRGINIA IS BECOMING MORE POPULAR WITH HIKERS. (NPS photo by Richard Frear).

THE FAMOUS HALF-DOME OVERLOOKING THE MERCED RIVER IN YOSEMITE NATIONAL PARK. (NPS photo).

**Soups
Salads
Vegetables**

LIGHTHOUSE AT CAPE HATTERAS NATIONAL SEASHORE, NORTH CAROLINA. (NPS photo by Ralph Anderson).

ZUPA GRZYBOWA ZE SMIETANA (Polish Cream of Mushroom Soup)

1 lb. mushrooms	10 c. chicken stock
6 T butter	1 c. whipping cream
1 lemon	1/2 c. dry vermouth
6 T. flour	Salt and white pepper

Wash and slice mushrooms into large pieces. In a deep kettle (preferably neither black iron nor aluminum, since metal discolors mushrooms) melt three tablespoons butter. Add the mushrooms, three to four drops of freshly squeezed lemon juice and a little salt. Lower the heat, cover the mushrooms loosely with aluminum foil and allow them to sweat for at least fifteen minutes, stirring occasionally to keep them from scorching or discoloring. Remove from the heat and place mushrooms in one bowl and the liquid in another bowl. In the kettle, melt three tablespoons butter, add 6 tablespoons flour stirring well with a whip. Gradually add ten cups of chicken stock. Blend completely. Return the soup to the heat and stir constantly until it boils. Then reduce heat and allow to simmer. Stir every so often to prevent a skin from forming. Just before serving, carefully add one cup whipping cream, one-half cup dry vermouth and season highly with salt and white pepper. Do not boil after adding the whipping cream and vermouth. Serves from eight to ten guests.

(Adapted from "Creme Champignon Suppe" Le Champignon Gourmet School of Marin.

Murph and Donna Kolipinski
Regional Office

ALBONDIGAS SOUP

Combine in kettle:

5 c. bouillon	1 can (15 oz.) stewed tomatoes

Mix together in bowl:

1 med. onion, chopped	1/4 t. sage
1 can (2 oz.) diced green chili	1/4 t. savory
1/4 t. chili powder	1/4 t. ground cloves
	1/4 t. thyme

Add half of the preceding mixture to bouillon in kettle and bring to a boil. Add to remaining half of mixture:

1 lb. ground beef	Crumbled saltines or bread
1 egg	crumbs for proper consistency
Salt and pepper to taste	

Mix well. Form into balls 1 inch in diameter. Drop into boiling liquid and simmer 10-15 minutes. Add 3 cups rice (precooked separately) to mixture and serve hot.

Myrna Keeling
Chiricahua NM

LEEK SOUP

1 lb. thick white leeks	1/2 pt. milk
1/4 lb. potatoes	Salt and pepper
1/2 oz. butter	1/8 c. cream (optional)
1 pt. stock or water	1 egg yolk (optional)

Slice and chop leeks. Melt butter and cook leeks for 10 minutes. Keep lid on pan and shake it from time to time. Boil stock and add to leeks along with potatoes. Simmer until vegetables are tender. Put in blender until smooth. Or work through sieve. When reheating, add the cream and egg yolk if desired. Season with salt and pepper; top with chopped chives.

Dorothea Miehle
Regional Office

LENTIL SOUP (An Original)

Stage 1:

Several soup bones with marrow	Salt and pepper
1/2 lb. beef	2 onions, cut in halves
2 or 3 qt. water to cover	1 bay leaf

Simmer 2 hours. Then to Stage 2: Remove bay leaf and bones. Skim off congealed fat. Stage 3: Reheat with:

1 pkg. lentils	6 hot dogs, cut up
1 c. cut up celery	Cut up cooled beef
1 c. cut up carrots	

Simmer all together for 2 hours and add water to thin as it cooks. Add some thyme and salt to taste. Stage 4: Eat it!

Doug and Fifi Cornell
Golden Gate NRA

VEGETABLE SOUP

3 lb. beef shank or beef bones	2 bay leaves
6 c. water	1 c. celery
1 med. can tomatoes	1 c. sliced carrots
1/4 to 1/2 c. chopped onion	1 c. diced potatoes
1 T. salt	1 c. chopped cabbage
2 T. Worcestershire sauce	1/4 t. chili powder, if desired

Cook meat (or brown) in water, tomatoes, onion and seasonings. Simmer 2 hours—covered. Remove meat from bones and cut into small pieces. Set broth overnight in refrigerator and remove excess fat—if time permits; if not, drop a few ice cubes into kettle to solidify the fat and remove. Add vegetables; simmer 1 hour or until they are tender. Remove bay leaves before serving. Serves 8.

Mary Benson
Regional Office

BUSBEE'S NAVY BEAN BROTH

2 c. Navy beans
1½ lb. butt-end ham
3 qt. water
1/2 t. celery salt

2 t. salt
1/8 t. pepper
1 t. Accent
1 med. onion, minced
Dried parsley flakes

Soak beans in water to cover overnight. Prepare soup stock by simmering ham in the 3 quarts of water for 2 hours; add beans, celery salt, pepper, salt and Accent. Slow boil until beans are tender. Take out ham and grind; add onions and simmer until soup begins to thicken (approx. 1/2 hour); add ground ham and serve hot. Sprinkle each serving with parsley flakes and Parmesan cheese croutons, cut into diamond shapes. To prepare croutons: spread toast with butter and sprinkle Parmesan cheese on top. Place on pan and toast in oven.

Heidi Kobayashi
Regional Office

MINESTRONE SOUP

1/2 c. olive or salad oil
1 clove garlic, minced
2 c. chopped onion
1 c. chopped celery
4 T. chopped parsley
1 can Hunt's tomato paste
1 (10½ oz.) can beef bouillon
    undiluted
9 c. water

1 c. chopped cabbage
2 carrots, sliced thin
2 t. salt
Dash of sage
1/4 t. pepper
1 (1 lb.) can kidney beans
1 zucchini squash, sliced
1 c. green beans or peas
1 c. elbow macaroni
Grated Parmesan cheese

Heat oil in large heavy pot. Add garlic, onion, celery and parsley. Cook until soft. Stir in tomato paste and next 7 ingredients. Mix well. Bring to boil. Lower heat, cover and simmer slowly for 1 hour. Add remaining ingredients, except cheese. Cook 10-15 minutes more or until macaroni is tender. Serve with cheese. Makes 8 servings.

Ruth Uzar
Regional Office

CREAM OF PEANUT SOUP

1 onion, chopped
1/2 c. celery, chopped
1/4 c. margarine

1 T. flour
2 qt. chicken stock
1½ c. crunchy peanut butter
2 c. light cream (can use milk)

Saute onion and celery until soft, not brown. Stir in flour until well blended. Add stock and bring to boil. Remove from heat then puree in blender. Return to heat and add cream and peanut butter. Do not boil. Serve when heated. Also good served iced.

Marilyn J. Scott
Kings Canyon NP

MEATBALL VEGETABLE SOUP

1 qt. water
1½ c. chopped onions
2 T. butter or fat
1 clove garlic, minced
1 can consomme
1 bay leaf

10 peppercorns
1 can (No. 2½) tomatoes
1 c. chopped celery
2 c. chopped carrots
2 c. chopped zucchini
Salt to taste

Meatballs:

1 lb. ground beef
1/2 t. garlic salt
1 T. dried parsley
1/2 c. boiling water

1½ t. seasoned salt
1 T. grated onion
1 egg
1 slice bread
Dash of pepper

Cook all vegetables and broth till vegetables are tender. Make meatballs and shape with a teaspoon. Drop into boiling soup. Cook 15 minutes longer.

John and Janet Sage
Regional Office

RASPBERRY JELLO SALAD

1 pkg. raspberry jello
3/4 c. boiling water
1 c. crushed pineapple with juice

1 pkg. frozen raspberries
1 envelope Dream Whip

Prepare Dream Whip first and set aside. Dissolve jello in boiling water; add crushed pineapple and raspberries (broken into chunks). Mixture will begin to thicken as you stir—if not, place in refrigerator for a few minutes—when thick, do not let set. Fold in Dream Whip. Return to refrigerator until firm.

Genevieve Dalley
Lake Mead NRA

SAUERKRAUT SALAD

2 cans (1 lb.) sauerkraut,
  undrained
1 green pepper, chopped
1 carrot, finely chopped

1 onion, thinly sliced
1 c. celery, chopped
1 jar (2 oz.) chopped pimiento
1 c. sugar

Mix together all ingredients except sugar. Sprinkle sugar on top of mixture; cover and refrigerate at least 24 hours. Stir well before serving. Serves 6 - 8.

Marilyn J. Scott
Kings Canyon NP

LENTIL SALAD IN PAPAYA BOATS

2 Hawaiian papayas
1 c. lentils
2 c. water
1 t. salt
1 bay leaf

2 T. green pepper
2 T. chopped green onion
6 cherry tomatoes, sliced
2 T. chopped parsley

Dressing:

1/4 c. olive oil
2 T. cider vinegar
1/2 t. salt

1/8 t. dry mustard
1/8 t. pepper

Chill papayas. Simmer lentils in salted water with bay leaf for 20 minutes. Drain and cool. Place dressing ingredients in covered jar and shake vigorously. Toss the lentils with the dressing and add tomatoes, pepper, onions and parsley. Toss again. Halve and seed papayas. Fill hollows with lentil salad. Makes 4 servings. (Recipe appeared in Food Section of "The Garden Island".)

Mike and Ruth Yoshinaka
Regional Office

SPICED CABBAGE

1/2 c. sugar
1/4 c. vinegar
Salt to taste

1/2 head grated cabbage
Optional: grated carrot, celery
    and green pepper

Combine sugar, vinegar and salt; pour over grated cabbage. Chill thoroughly. The addition of grated carrot, celery and/or green pepper adds extra zing and color.

Carol Reigle
Lake Mead NRA

MEXICALI SALAD

1/2 c. pitted ripe olives, sliced
2 tomatoes, cut into wedges
1/4 c. chopped green onions
1 c. corn chips

1 can tuna
1/2 c. shredded Cheddar cheese
1/2 head lettuce

Break lettuce into chunks and add tuna, tomatoes, onions and corn chips. Pour on dressing. Toss lightly. Sprinkle with cheese and decorate with additional ripe olives.

Dressing:

1/2 c. mashed ripe avocado
1 T. lemon juice
1 c. dairy sour cream
1/3 c. salad oil

1/2 t. sugar
1/2 t. chili powder
1/4 t. salt
1/4 t. Tabasco sauce

Beat with electric beater until smooth.

Catherine Hjort
Regional Office

GAZPACHO

4 c. diced tomatoes	1/2 c. lemon juice
1½ c. chopped green pepper	1/4 c. olive oil
3/4 c. chopped onion	1 T. paprika
1 clove garlic	1/2 c. diced cucumber
2 c. beef bouillon	1 T. salt
	Pepper

Combine all ingredients. Let stand at room temperature for 2 hours.
Stir and chill. Serve with sour cream or croutons.

Murph and Donna Kolipinski
Regional Office

FIVE CUP SALAD

1 c. crushed pineapple	1 c. miniature marshmallows
1 c. fresh or canned drained	1 c. shredded coconut
orange sections	1 c. sour cream

Combine and mix well; refrigerate several hours or overnight. Serve
on crisp lettuce leaves or as a dessert. Makes 6 to 8 servings.

Dorothy Ruse
Regional Office

VINEYARD SALAD MOLD

2 pkg. (3 oz.) strawberry gelatine	2 pkg. (10 oz.) frozen straw-
1½ c. boiling water	berries, thawed
1½ c. California rose' wine	1 can (8½ oz.) crushed
1 c. sour cream	pineapple, undrained

Dissolve gelatine in boiling water. Stir in rose' wine, strawberries, and
undrained pineapple. Pour half of mixture into large mold. Refrigerate
until set. Spread sour cream over top. Spoon on or carefully pour on remaining gelatine over top. Refrigerate until set. Unmold on salad greens.

Murph and Donna Kolipinski
Regional Office

GAZPACHO

1 c. finely chopped peeled tomatoes	2 - 3 T. tarragon wine vinegar
1/2 c. each finely chopped green	2 T. olive oil
pepper, celery and cucumber	1 t. salt
1/4 c. finely chopped onion	1/4 t. ground black pepper
2 t. snipped parsley	1/2 t. Worcestershire sauce
1 t. snipped chives	2 c. tomato juice
1 clove garlic, minced	

Combine in glass or stainless steel bowl. Chill at least 4 hours.

Chuck and Irene Adams
Regional Office

PETE'S POTATO SALAD

3 or 4 med-large potatoes
2 T. butter or margarine
1/4 c. French or Italian dressing
1 small onion
3 hard-cooked eggs

1/2 c. salad dressing
Spices to taste (green pepper,
  salt, pepper)
1 t. bac-onions
Dash of salt

Cook potatoes. When soft, drain and immediately break into chunks with fork (don't mash into chunks, too small). Dot with butter. Let cool. When cooled (not cold), toss gently with fork to mix in butter. Dump dressing over potatoes and toss lightly with fork. Let marinate overnight in refrigerator. Just before time to serve, add onion, chopped fine. Add eggs, chopped fine. Add salad dressing and toss gently. It should spoon-up and hold its shape. Season to taste after adding salt and bac-onions. Serves 6 - 8.

Peter and Karla Allen
Lake Mead NRA

CHRISTMAS SALAD

1/2 lb. fresh mushrooms, sliced
1 basket cherry tomatoes
1 pt. fresh Brussels sprouts,
  OR 1 pkg. (10 oz.) frozen, slightly cooked

Salad dressing (French, Italian
  or Russian)
Salad greens

Combine mushrooms, tomatoes, sprouts and salad dressing; chill several hours. Serve on greens. Makes 4 - 6 servings.

Mary Alice Replogle
Regional Office

CUCUMBERS WITH ZEST

Alternate layers of a thinly-sliced large cucumber and a thinly-sliced large onion in a bowl. Pour dressing over this and chill for 8 hours. Serve as a salad.

Horseradish Dressing:

1/2 c. mayonnaise
1 c. sour cream
2 t. sugar
1/2 t. salt
1/4 t. paprika
1/4 t. dry mustard

1/4 c. prepared horseradish
1/4 t. prepared mustard
1/2 t. Worcestershire sauce
Dash of cayenne pepper
Dash of hot pepper sauce
1/4 c. vinegar

In small mixing bowl or blender, combine all ingredients; mix until smooth. Serves 6.

Elaine Hounsell
Lake Mead NRA

CURRIED CRAB STUFFED PAPAYAS

4 Hawaiian papayas	2 t. apple cider vinegar
3 c. cooked brown rice	1/4 c. raisins
6 T. mayonnaise	1/4 c. chopped nuts
1½ to 2 t. curry powder	1/4 c. chopped parsley
1 t. salt	1/2 lb. crabmeat, cleaned and flaked (or 1 can [8 oz.] drained)

Cut papayas in halves. Scoop out seeds. Combine cooked rice with mayonnaise, stirring lightly with a fork. Add curry powder to taste. Add remaining ingredients; mix lightly and chill. Fill hollows with salad mixture and put halves together, wrapping tightly in plastic wrap. Chill. When ready to serve, slice papayas across in 1 inch slices. Arrange slices on plate, garnish with watercress. Makes 6 servings. This recipe was taken from Food Section "The Garden Island".

Mike and Ruth Yoshinaka
Regional Office

DELICIOUS BEAN SALAD

1 can garbanzo beans	1 chopped green pepper
1 can red kidney beans	2/3 c. salad oil
1 can green beans	1 c. vinegar
1 can wax beans	1½ c. sugar
1 onion, chopped	2 t. salt
	1 t. pepper

Drain all beans, then rinse. Combine with onion and green pepper. Heat remaining ingredients together until sugar dissolves. Cool; pour over beans and allow to marinate 24 hours or more. Serves 10 to 12.

Adele Fevella
Haleakala NP

SAUERKRAUT SALAD

2 c. sauerkraut	1 med. onion, chopped
2 c. chopped celery	1/2 c. red pepper or
1/2 c. chopped green pepper	pimientos, chopped

Drain and cut sauerkraut with scissors. Combine all ingredients. Serve with Dressing.

Dressing:

1 c. sugar	1/2 c. oil
1/2 c. vinegar	

Shake dressing in a jar until blended. Mix salad with dressing. Refrigerate at least overnight.

Catherine Hjort
Regional Office

VEGETABLE JELLY SALAD

1 T. granulated gelatin
2 T. cold water
1¼ c. tomato juice
Bit of bay leaf

1 slice onion
1 t. sugar
1/2 t. salt
1/4 c. chopped celery
1 t. finely grated carrot

Soak gelatin in the cold water. Heat tomato juice, bay leaf, onion, sugar and salt. Add gelatin; stir until dissolved and strain. Cool and add celery and carrot. Pour into individual molds that have been dipped into cold water. Chill and serve on shredded lettuce. Garnish with cream cheese balls. Yields 2 portions.

Virginia Duckett
Regional Office

RED AND WHITE FRUIT SALAD

1 can fruit cocktail (2 c.)
1 pkg. each of lemon and
   red jello
1 c. hot water

1 can (6 oz.) lemonade
   concentrate - frozen
1/2 c. mayonnaise or
   salad dressing

Drain fruit. Heat 1 c. syrup and dissolve red jello. Add water to remaining syrup to make 1 cup and add to jello. Pour into mold and chill. Dissolve lemon jello in 1 c. hot water; add lemonade; blend in mayonnaise and chill until partially set. Stir in fruit and pour over first layer. Other fruit may be used.

Joan Andersen
Petrified Forest NP

HALLOWEEN SALAD

2 pkg. orange jello
1 envelope Knox plain gelatine
3 c. hot cider
1 c. cold cider

1/4 c. lemon juice
1 c. seedless raisins
1 c. chopped celery
1 c. sliced apples
1 c. chopped walnuts

Dissolve jello and gelatine in 3 cups hot cider and add the raisins. Let stand until the raisins puff up. Add the cold cider. Let set a little. Add: celery, apples and walnuts. Pour into pan—when set cut in squares. Top with mayonnaise and black olives.

Chuck and Irene Adams
Regional Office

BONNIE'S COLE SLAW AND DRESSING

Put celery seed and a pinch of salt on cut cabbage. Then take 3 eggs, 1/2 c. (scant) vinegar, 1 c. sugar, pinch of salt, teaspoon prepared mustard—cook until thick, stirring so it will not scorch. Cool and then thin with milk or cream, and pour it over cut cabbage. Also great for watercress.

Louise and Lynn Herring
Regional Office

OUR BEST POTATO SALAD

6 medium Irish potatoes, boiled
  with skins (chill with skins on)
3 hard-boiled eggs (chill with
  shells on)
1/2 c. chopped celery
1/2 c. chopped dry onions
2 slices crisply fried bacon,
  crumbled
2 pinches each curry powder
  and oregano
2 t. dry parsley
1/2 t. celery salt
1/8 t. garlic salt
3 heaping T. Best Foods
  mayonnaise
1/4 t. Tabasco sauce
2 T. olive oil
1 T. vinegar
Salt and pepper to taste

Peel chilled potatoes and cut into pieces with a teaspoon. Peel chilled eggs, dice, and add to potatoes along with all other dry ingredients. Mix thoroughly. Into the center of the salad, add mayonnaise and with a table-spoon make a "cup in the center". Into this "cup" of mayonnaise, add Tabasco sauce, olive oil and vinegar. Gradually stir mayonnaise mixture thoroughly into potatoes.

Place salad into refrigerator for about 2 hours to chill. Remove and mix again. Then place salad in serving bowl, garnish with parsley, hard-boiled eggs, radishes, slices of bell peppers, or your own favorite garnish.

Notes: 1. 1 full teaspoon of dry mustard may be substituted for curry powder if desired.
2. Cutting potatoes with a teaspoon instead of a sharp knife seems make them absorb the dressing more fully.
3. I always keep a shaker filled with curry powder on hand and shake the desired amount into the salad so as to distribute it through the salad more evenly.

Lucia C. Snider
Montezuma Castle NM

PINEAPPLE/CHEESE SALAD

2 pkg. lime jello
2 c. hot water
1 c. mayonnaise
1 c. evaporated milk
1 pt. small-curd cottage cheese
1 can (No. 303) pineapple,
  crushed
1 c. chopped walnuts

Dissolve jello in hot water thoroughly. When slightly cooled off, add cottage cheese and mix well. Add milk and mayonnaise and beat with an egg beater to break up all the lumps. Add pineapple, including the juice; add nuts and pour into mold which has been rinsed in cold water. Or pour into a large oblong baking dish and chill until firm. This makes a large salad and is ideal for buffets.

Peggy Rolandson
San Francisco Office

BLUEBERRY JELLO SALAD

2 pkg. grape jello
1 (No. 303) can pineapple,
  crushed (drain juice)
1 c. hot water

1 can (No. 303) blueberries
1 pkg. (8 oz.) cream cheese
1 c. sour cream

Melt jello in 1 cup hot water. Add pineapple juice and water to make 2 cups. Add pineapple and wash blueberries. Let partially set. Mix the cheese (room temperature) and sour cream together. Add jello mixture alternately with cheese mixture in jello mold or pan and set in refrigerator.

Florence Evans
Redwood NP

AVOCADO YOKAN

1 c. mashed, strained avocado
2 T. unflavored gelatin
1/2 c. cold water
1 large pkg. (6 oz.) lime-
  flavored gelatin

2 c. boiling water
1/2 c. mayonnaise
1/2 c. undiluted evaporated
  milk
1 c. sugar

Mash avocado while unflavored gelatin is softening in cold water. Pour boiling water over lime gelatin and stir until dissolved. Beat in avocado and remaining ingredients at low speed of mixer until smooth. Pour into a 9x9x2" pan. Refrigerate until set. Serve as part of meal or as dessert.

Adele Fevella
Haleakala NP

PINEAPPLE COLE SLAW

4 c. shredded cabbage
1 c. diced, unpeeled red apples
1 c. pineapple chunks
1 c. miniature marshmallows

1/2 c. chopped celery
Mayonnaise-type salad
  dressing to moisten
Lettuce

Combine cabbage, apples, pineapple, marshmallows, celery and enough dressing to moisten and toss lightly. Chill and serve in lettuce-lined salad bowl.

Chris McKinney
Grand Canyon NP

CALIFORNIA COLE SLAW

1 envelope Lipton's onion
  soup mix
1 pt. dairy sour cream
2 qt. shredded cabbage

4 med. carrots, grated
1 med. green pepper, chopped
4 t. cider vinegar

In large bowl, blend soup mix with sour cream as for California Dip.* Add cabbage, carrots, pepper and vinegar. Mix well—cover and chill. Makes 2 quarts. *See Lipton's onion soup package.

Ruth Combs
Regional Office

FRESH SPINACH SALAD

1 bunch spinach
8 oz. fresh bean sprouts, rinsed
1 can (5 oz.) water chestnuts,
   drained and sliced thinly
4 scallions, thinly sliced
2 hard-cooked eggs, sliced

Salt and pepper
1/4 c. salad oil (not olive oil)
1/4 c. white wine vinegar
2 T. catsup
8 slices bacon, fried crisp
   and crumbled

Remove stems from spinach and discard stems. Wash leaves well; pat dry and break into bite-size pieces. Combine spinach, sprouts, chestnuts and scallions. Cover and refrigerate as long as 4 hours. Mix together oil, vinegar, and catsup, salt and pepper to taste. To serve, add bacon to spinach mixture and pour dressing over and toss gently. Garnish with egg slices. Serves 6.

Murph and Donna Kolipinski
Regional Office

MANDARIN CHICKEN SALAD

2 - 3 c. cooked chicken
1 T. minced onion
1 t. salt
2 T. lemon juice
1 c. thinly sliced celery
1 c. pineapple

1/3 c. Miracle Whip salad
   dressing (mayonnaise will not
   work)
1 can (11 oz.) Mandarin oranges,
   drained
1/2 c. toasted slivered almonds

Mix chicken, onion, salt, lemon juice and celery. Refrigerate several hours. At serving time, toss with rest of ingredients. Garnish with ripe olives and a few of the toasted almonds. Serve on lettuce leaves. Serves 6.

Silvey Cameron
Hawaii Volcanoes NP

PHILADELPHIA CREAM CHEESE SALAD

Cream together until smooth:

2 pkg. (3 oz.) Philadelphia
   cream cheese
   (room temperature)
4 level T. salad dressing
1 No. 2 can crushed pineapple
1 t. lemon juice

16 marshmallows, cut up
1/2 c. chopped nuts
1/4 c. sugar
Few maraschino cherries, diced
1/2 pt. whipping cream

Mix together all ingredients except cream and set aside. Whip cream and fold into first mixture. Place in shallow pan of ice cube tray and freeze (about 4 hours). Cut into squares and serve on lettuce leaves. This makes a nice Christmas or holiday salad.

Genevieve Dalley
Lake Mead NRA

MACARONI SALAD

2 c. macaroni
1 T. oil
1 T. vinegar or lemon juice
Chopped stuffed olives
Salad dressing or mayonnaise

1 large can crushed pineapple,
  drained
Celery seed
Parsley, salt and pepper
1 large can shrimp, drained

Cook macaroni in salted water and drain. Toss with oil and vinegar; cover and chill in refrigerator. Add shrimp, pineapple and remaining ingredients. Chill until ready to serve.

Janet Moore
Lake Mead NRA

AVOCADO SALAD

1 lg. peeled tomato, chopped
1 lg. onion, diced fine
1 small dried red pepper
  (or chili powder to taste)
6 peeled, chopped (not mashed)
  avocados

2½ t. salt
2 t. lemon juice
2 T. mayonnaise
1 t. salad oil
4 drops Tabasco sauce

Serve on lettuce. If you drop an avocado seed on top, it will help prevent salad from discoloring.

Mary and Forrest Benson
Regional Office

HOME GARDENER'S DELIGHT (Zucchini Fritata)

Large zucchini
Onions
Dozen eggs

Grated Parmesan cheese
Italian seasoning

Put raw zucchini through meat grinder; then the onions. Beat a dozen eggs and add to the ground zucchini and onions. Add cheese and seasoning. Pour into a flat baking dish and bake for an hour at 350 degrees. Serve hot or cold as a vegetable or cut into squares as an hors d'oeuvre.

Jayne Ramorino
Regional Office

BEAN SALAD

1 can kidney beans (rinsed)
1 can wax beans
1 can green beans
1 red onion, sliced thin
1 green pepper, chopped

1/2 c. celery, chopped
3/4 c. sugar
1 t. salt
1 t. pepper
1/2 c. vegetable oil
1/2 c. wine vinegar

Drain all beans. Put all ingredients into covered bowl and let set in refrigerator for 48 hours. Serves about 8 - 10. Will keep for about 1½ weeks.

Kay Marquardt
Joshua Tree NM

OLD-FASHIONED POTATO SALAD

Boil large potatoes in their jackets after thorough scrubbing. Be sure to use salt in the water. After potatoes are thoroughly cooked and cooled, peel and slice. Marinate overnight in refrigerator with Italian oil and vinegar salad dressing. Toss potatoes to insure they are coated well. In the morning, add chopped parsley, onions, black ripe olives and bell pepper. Add sliced hard-boiled eggs. Then, add mayonnaise to taste with salt and pepper. Garnish with hard-boiled egg slices and paprika. (The secret is in the marinating — be sure it is done the night before to allow the potatoes to absorb the flavor.)

Jayne Ramorino
Regional Office

CREAMED SPINACH

1 lb. frozen spinach, uncooked
1 med. onion
1 clove garlic
3 slices bacon, chopped fine
1/2 t. Lawry's salt
1/4 t. white pepper
3 T. butter
2 T. flour
1½ c. milk

Saute onion, garlic, bacon and condiments in butter. Add flour and cook until a smooth roux is created. Gradually add milk and cook for several minutes to the consistency of a medium cream sauce. Chop about 1 pound of frozen spinach (uncooked) very fine. Then squeeze all the juice from the spinach. Add spinach to sauce, bring to a slow boil and cook 5 minutes. Serves 4 to 6.

Rose Coulter
Regional Office

TACO SALAD

1 lb. ground round
1 medium onion, chopped
1 can stewed tomatoes
1 can green chili, chopped
2 t. chili powder
Salt to taste
1 large head lettuce
2 small tomatoes, chopped
1 small can chopped olives
1/2 lb. grated cheese (Longhorn)
1 small pkg. Fritos

Brown ground round and onion in large skillet. Drain. Add tomatoes, green chili and seasonings. Simmer. In large bowl, combine remaining ingredients. Add hot meat mixture and serve immediately.

Barbara Monroe
Montezuma Castle NM

COKE SALAD

1 lg. pkg. cherry jello
1 jar black cherries
1 can (No. 1½) crushed pineapple
1 c. chopped pecans
1 lg. Coke

Drain juice from pineapple and cherries; heat to boiling; mix with jello and let set until it thickens; add remaining ingredients and chill.

Cricket Carter
Petrified Forest NP

GURKENSALAT (Cucumber Salad)

3 cucumbers
Salt
1 small onion, chopped
1/2 c. cider vinegar
2 T. oil

1 T. sugar
2 T. water
2 T. caraway seeds
1/2 t. paprika
Salt and pepper

Cucumber may or may not be peeled, as you prefer. Slice thinly on the slicing side of a grater. Sprinkle with salt and let stand at room temperature for 1 hour. Drain. Combine remaining ingredients and cucumbers and mix well. Add salt and pepper to taste. Chill until ready to serve. Serves 6.

Alma Hinkley
Whiskeytown NRA

CREAMY CABBAGE AND NOODLES

8 oz. noodles
6 slices bacon, diced
1 head (med.) cabbage, shredded
1/2 med. onion, chopped
2 T. water
1 T. sugar

1/2 t. paprika
1/4 t. salt
1 c. sour cream
1 T. flour
Chopped parsley or paprika

Cook noodles in boiling salted water; drain in colander. In large frying pan, fry bacon until crisp; remove and drain. Discard all but 2 tablespoons bacon drippings. Add onions and saute until soft, then add water, sugar, paprika, salt and cabbage. Cover and cook over medium high heat until cabbage is tender, about 3 minutes. Blend sour cream with flour until smooth, and then stir into cabbage mixture. Cook, stirring until mixture boils; continue cooking 1 minute. Add bacon and noodles; mix and heat through. Serve sprinkled with parsley or paprika.

Janet Moore
Lake Mead NRA

RAW CAULIFLOWER SALAD

1 small head cauliflower
1/4 lb. Bleu cheese
2 T. lemon juice
1/2 t. salt

1/2 t. sugar
Dash of pepper
Mayonnaise to moisten

Chop raw cauliflower and cheese. Mix and blend with other ingredients. Sprinkle with paprika.

Dave and Josephine Jones
San Francisco Office

THREE-BEAN SALAD

1/2 c. oil
1/4 c. cider vinegar
2/3 c. sugar

1/2 c. chopped onion
1/2 c. chopped green pepper
Salt and pepper

Combine above ingredients and pour over:

1 can kidney beans
1 can wax beans

1 can green beans

Let marinate overnight.

Joy Gifford
Point Reyes NS

AVOCADO-PINEAPPLE SALAD

6 slices fresh pineapple
2 c. avocado slices
1/3 c. mashed avocado pulp

2/3 c. mayonnaise
2 T. lemon juice
OR 1½ T. lime juice

Place pineapple and avocado slices on lettuce leaves. Make a dressing of other ingredients; chill. Pour over salad. Serves 6.

Evelyn Ah Sing
Hawaii Volcanoes NP

CHOP CHAE (Korean Mixed Vegetables)

Bean Thread, 2 sm. pkg. (this
   can be purchased at most
   Oriental markets; they look
   like clear, thin noodles.)
Pork or beef, 1 lb. or less
Carrots, 2 or 3
Bamboo shoots, 1 sm. can
Celery, 2 or 3 stalks
Cooking oil, 4 T.

Garlic salt, pepper, Accent
   (flavor to taste) - Optional
American cabbage, 1 sm. head
Mushrooms, 1 sm. can or
   equivalent fresh
Onion, 1 large round
Soy sauce, 1/4 c. or more
   (flavor to taste)

Dice meat and vegetables; saute in skillet with a little cooking oil until half cooked; stir frequently. Place Bean Threads in boiling water and cook for 15 minutes or until soft. Rinse noodles in hot water several times and drain. Season fried vegetables and meat with an additional 1/4 cup soy sauce, or to taste, flavored with garlic salt and pepper. Add noodles and mix. Add additional soy sauce, Accent and garlic salt, again to your own taste, and mix well.

Kyung Ja and Hugo Huntzinger
Coronado NM

ZUCCHINI LOAF

For every 8 medium size zucchini (about 2 lb.):

2-3 eggs, slightly beaten
3/4 to 1 c. French bread crumbs
  (grated fine)
1/2 c. grated Parmesan cheese
1 lg. onion, coarsely chopped

1/4 t. each of thyme, marjoram,
  and sage
2 stalks sliced celery
10 sprigs parsley
Salt and pepper to taste

Clean zucchini, slice. Braise zucchini in onions and celery in small amount of beef broth or vegetable oil until slightly soft, about 5 minutes. Add rest of ingredients; mix thoroughly. Put into a lightly buttered casserole and bake in a 350 degree oven about 30-40 minutes.

Dorothy and Roland Johnson
Regional Office

OLD-FASHIONED BAKED BEANS

Wash and soak overnight: 2 cups small white navy beans, covered with cold water. Do not drain — if necessary, add more water to cover. Boil gently until tender. Pour into casserole. Add:

1 t. salt
1/4 c. brown sugar

1 t. mustard
Small cubes of bacon (as
  many as you like)

Bake, covered, all day. Add water as needed. Uncover and brown during the last half hour before serving.

Catherine Hjort
Regional Office

SOUR CABBAGE

5 c. shredded cabbage
4 slices bacon
2 T. brown sugar
2 T. flour

1/2 c. water
1/2 c. cider vinegar
Salt and pepper
Onion, sliced

Cook cabbage in boiling, salted water 7 minutes. Fry bacon; remove bacon; add sugar and flour to bacon fat and blend. Add water, vinegar, and seasonings. Cook until thick; add onion, bacon and cabbage.

Dave and Josephine Jones
San Francisco Office

CREAMED CABBAGE

1/2 c. sour cream
1/4 c. vinegar
1/4 c. sugar

1/2 head (med.) cabbage, grated
Dash of salt

Combine sour cream, vinegar, sugar and salt and pour dressing over grated cabbage. This cream dressing is also good poured over bite-sized pieces of lettuce or cucumber and onions.

Carol Reigle
Lake Mead NRA

SOUPS, SALADS, & VEGETABLES 33

CRUZAN POTATOES FROM VIRGIN ISLANDS

1 c. chopped onions
1 c. chopped sweet green
 peppers
1 c. chopped celery
1 c. raisins
2 T. thyme

1 small can tomato paste
1 T. Tabasco sauce
6 eggs
6 c. mashed potatoes (instant
 if preferred)
1/2 c. butter

For 10 minutes, saute in butter the onions, peppers, celery, raisins, and spices well mixed with the tomato paste. Beat eggs and mix well with potatoes. Add both of mixtures together and bake in 350 degree oven for 25-30 minutes until firm. Serves 8.

Chuck and Irene Adams
Regional Office

MARINATED VEGETABLES

2 lb. carrots, cooked
 (cut into strips)

2 cans green beans

Mix together:

1 can tomato soup
3/4 c. sugar
1 t. salt
1/2 t. pepper

1 c. vinegar
1 t. Worcestershire sauce
1 t. dry or prepared mustard
1 Bell pepper, chopped
1 onion, chopped

Add carrots and beans to mixture. Marinate overnight before serving. Excellent substitute for salad, especially with beef or fish.

Bobbie Davis
Redwood NP

BANANA—ORANGE YAMS

5 med. yams (OR No. 2½ can)
 (drain, if canned)
1/4 t. salt
1/8 t. pepper
1/4 t. cloves

2/3 c. brown sugar
3 T. margarine
1/3 c. orange juice
3 bananas, mashed
2 eggs

Cook and cool yams. Peel and mash. (Should have about 4½ cups.) Add seasonings, sugar and margarine. Mix well; stir in orange juice. When potatoes are cool, add bananas and the eggs. Turn into buttered 1½ quart casserole. Top with:

1 c. crushed corn flakes
1/2 c. nuts

3 T. brown sugar
1/2 stick margarine

Bake in 350 degree oven for 45 minutes. Serves 12. (This recipe was originally received from Alfa Stewart, a former NPS employee, now retired.)

Fifi and Doug Cornell
Golden Gate NRA

RICHIE'S ZUCCHINI SQUASH

1/4 c. oil
1 lb. zucchini, sliced thin
1/4 c. water

1 whole clove garlic
2 T. soy sauce

Put oil in fry pan with cover, add squash, water and garlic. Cook, stirring occasionally for 10 minutes. Remove garlic clove. Add soy sauce and cook for 5 more minutes. Probably needs no other seasoning. Sprinkle with a little salt before removing from fire, if desired.

Carla Martin
Tuzigoot NM

VEGETABLE MINGLE

1/2 lb. small white onions
1 c. water
1¾ t. salt
1¼ t. sugar

2 med. zucchini
2 T. butter
1 can (12 oz.) golden
  kernel corn
1/8 t. pepper

Forty-five minutes before serving: peel onions, cook in covered skillet with water, salt, sugar for 15 minutes. Meanwhile, wash then slice zucchini diagonally into 1/4″ slices. At the end of 15 minutes, drain water from onions. To onions, add butter, zucchini, corn, 1/2 teaspoon salt and some pepper. Simmer, covered, for 10 minutes, stirring occasionally.

Beth Leach
Redwood NP

ZUCCHINI PANCAKES

3 c. zucchini, grated coarsely
  (about 3 medium)
1/2 t. salt
2 eggs

3 T. flour
1/4 c. Parmesan cheese, grated
Freshly ground pepper (to taste)
Butter

Mix zucchini and salt; let stand about 45 minutes. Then squeeze excess moisture from zucchini. Beat eggs until thick. Add zucchini, flour, cheese and pepper; mix well. Melt butter in skillet and fry heaping tablespoonfuls of mixture until lightly browned, turning once. Keep first pancakes warm in a 250 degree oven while frying remainder of batter. Makes about 12 pancakes. Serves 2—3 people.

Mary Alice Replogle
Regional Office

BAKED TOMATOES

4 slices bacon, cut into pieces
1 onion, chopped
1 green pepper, chopped

3 slices toast, cubed
1/2 c. cheese, cubed

Saute bacon until crisp. Add onions and green pepper; cook 10 minutes. Scoop out tomatoes, chop up pulp, mix with other ingredients. Stuff tomatoes and bake 30 minutes at 350 degrees.

Helen Koch
Joshua Tree NM

HERB POTATOES

1 lb. new potatoes
1/3 c. flour
1/2 t. thyme
1/2 t. marjoram

3/4 t. salt
Few grains pepper
1 clove garlic
1 bay leaf
3 T. butter

Start oven at 450 degrees. Grease a shallow casserole with butter. Peel or scrape potatoes. Make mixture of flour, thyme, marjoram, salt and pepper. Dip potatoes into this mixture and place in baking dish. Toss in garlic clove and bay leaf; dot with bits of butter; cover tightly and bake for 40 minutes or until tender. Bake in a 350 degree oven.

Phyllis Shaw
Regional Office

ZUCCHINI PARMESAN

Set out a 2-quart casserole and a 3-quart saucepan having a tightfitting cover. Wash, trim off ends and cut crosswise into 1/8" slices 8 to 10 zucchini. Heat in the saucepan: 3 tablespoons olive oil; add zucchini with 2/3 cup of coarsely chopped onions and 1/4 pound mushrooms (sliced). Cover saucepan and cook mixture over low heat for 10-15 minutes or until tender. Grate 3 ounces Parmesan cheese (2/3 cup); remove zucchini from heat and mix in 1/2 of cheese. Pour in a mixture of 1½ cups tomato paste (two 6-oz. cans), 1 teaspoon MSG, 1/2 teaspoon garlic salt and 1/8 teaspoon pepper. Turn mixture into casserole; sprinkle with cheese and bake at 350 degrees for 20 minutes.

Avis Franklin
Lehman Caves NM

SOUFFLED ITALIAN SQUASH

3 lb. zucchini
12 crackers, rolled
1 clove garlic, crushed
Salt to taste

3 unbeaten eggs
1/3 c. cooking oil
1/2 lb. sharp Cheddar cheese,
   grated

Cook squash, drain and mash. Add all of the other ingredients and mix well. Bake until firm, about 30-45 minutes in a 350 degree oven.

Marion Chapman
Regional Office

GRITS AU GRATIN

1 c. uncooked hominy grits	2 eggs
1 stick (¼ lb.) butter	Milk
1 roll garlic cheese spread	1/2 to 1 c. grated Cheddar cheese

Cook grits according to package directions. Stir in butter and garlic cheese till melted. Beat eggs in 1 cup measure; fill with milk then add to first mixture. Bake, uncovered, at 325 degrees for 45 minutes. Cover top with grated cheese and return to oven until center is firm, about 15 minutes.

John "Pack" P. Hunter
Regional Office

ZUCCHINI EGGS

4 eggs, beaten	Cooking oil
4 zucchini, chopped	Salt and pepper
1/4 c. minced onion	

Saute zucchini and onion in oil; two or three tablespoons of oil is enough. Remove from pan and drain. Stir the zucchini and onion into the eggs. Heat 3 tablespoons oil in sloped-sided frying pan. Cook on medium heat until about half the mixture is solid. Then flip over; cook until eggs are cooked through. Slide onto a plate and slice like pie and serve. Season with salt and pepper to taste. Delicious.

Joyce Parry
Joshua Tree NM

INDEPENDENCE HALL IN PHILADELPHIA, PENNSYLVANIA HIGHLIGHTS INDEPENDENCE NATIONAL HISTORICAL PARK WHERE OUR NATION HAD ITS BEGINNINGS. (NPS photo by Richard Frear).

STUNNING NIGHTTIME VIEW OF THE JEFFERSON MEMORIAL, WASHINGTON, D.C. IS PART OF THE VAST NATIONAL CAPITOL PARKS SYSTEM. (NPS photo).

VISITORS LISTEN TO RANGER IN THE ROTUNDA OF MAMMOTH CAVE NATIONAL PARK, KENTUCKY. (NPS photo by M. Woodbridge Williams.)

Main Dishes

QUIET, RELAXED FISHING IN TRAVERTINE CREEK AT CHICKASAW NATIONAL
RECREATION AREA, OKLAHOMA. (NPS photo.)

ENCHILADAS DELICIOSAS

1 doz. corn tortillas
1/2 lb. yellow cheese, grated

1 can enchilada sauce
1 large white onion,
    finely chopped

Heat sauce in saucepan. Dip each tortilla in the sauce, then fry in cooking oil until limp. On each tortilla, place 2 tablespoons cheese, 1 teaspoon onion, roll up and place in shallow baking dish. When all tortillas have been fried and rolled, the baking dish should be full. Pour any remaining sauce over the enchiladas and sprinkle over them the remaining cheese and onion. Bake at 400 degrees about 10 minutes, or until cheese is melted. Serves four.

Margaret E. Moore
Tumacacori NM

PATIO CHICKEN

Tear off 4 pieces of 18x22" heavy aluminum foil. Onto each piece of foil put 1/4 cup cooked rice, a tablespoon of onion soup mix and a piece of raw chicken. Pour 2 tablespoons of evaporated milk, 1 tablespoon of onion soup mix and 1 teaspoon of butter on top of chicken. Fold the short ends of the foil together, and fold under twice; fold the end to seal. Bake on cookie sheet near the center of the oven at 350 degrees for 1½ hours. (This can be scaled to large gatherings.)

Marion Durham
Walnut Canyon NM

SOUR CREAM ENCHILADAS

Combine in a bowl:

3 cans cream of chicken soup

1 pt. sour cream

Put in refrigerator. Prepare and put in a bowl:

2 cans chopped green chiles

2 bunches green onion tops, diced

Mix in a bowl:

1 lb. Longhorn cheese grated

1 lb. Jack cheese, grated

Have ready: 2 dozen tortillas. Heat the shells in the skillet one at a time in cooking oil. Dip in and out to make pliable and wrap them in a towel. Now get all the other ingredients out of refrigerator. Lay out tortilla and spoon sour cream mixture on one side, then little chili mixture and a little of the cheeses. Roll up; place in pan, till all are used. Place remainder of sour cream mixture over rolls, alternating with other mixtures until all is used. Heat in oven for 20-25 minutes at 250 degrees. Serve hot.

Naidene McKay
Grand Canyon NP

AMY'S CHINESE BAKED SPARERIBS

3 lb. pork spareribs, cut in
   serving pieces
1/4 c. prepared mustard
1/4 c. light molasses

1/4 c. soy sauce
3 T. cider vinegar
2 T. Worcestershire sauce
2 t. Tabasco sauce

Place ribs in shallow baking dish. Combine remaining ingredients and pour over ribs. Chill, covered, 3 hours or longer. Bake in 350 degree oven for 1½ hours or until tender and done. Baste frequently with sauce in pan. Turn ribs once during baking. Makes 3 to 4 servings.

Mary Chilton
Montezuma Castle NM

20-MINUTE DINNER (Parisienne Bean and Mushrooms)

2 pkg. cooked frozen
   French-style green beans

1 can condensed mushroom soup
1 can French fried onions

Combine beans, soup and sprinkle with onions. Bake 20 minutes at 375 degrees.

Carla Martin
Tuzigoot NM

BOKUM BOP (Korean Fried Rice)

1 lb. beef (or less)
Ground pepper, 1 Bell pepper
1 stalk celery
Garlic salt, pepper, Accent
   (flavor to taste - optional)

2 carrots
1 large ground onion
1/2 c. soy sauce (flavor to taste)
4 T. cooking oil
3 c. cooked rice

Cut meat and vegetables into small pieces; saute in skillet with cooking oil until half cooked; stir frequently. Season fried vegetables and meat to taste with half of the soy sauce, garlic salt, pepper and Accent as you wish. Add rice and mix well. Add rest of soy sauce and garlic salt to taste. Mix again. Serves 5.

Kyung Ja and Hugo Huntzinger
Coronado NM

BAKED CHICKEN WITH MUSHROOMS

1 chicken, cut up
1 can cream of mushroom soup

1/4 c. whole milk

Place cut-up chicken in shallow baking dish. Mix soup and milk until smooth and spoon over the chicken being sure to coat each piece of chicken. Bake one hour at 350 degrees.

Polly F. Wonson
Tumacacori NM

BAKED CHILES RELLENOS

1 lb. ground beef	1½ c. milk
1/2 c. chopped onion	4 beaten eggs
2 cans (4 oz. ea.) drained green chiles	1/4 c. flour
	1/2 t. salt
6 oz. sharp Cheddar cheese, (1½ c.) shredded	Several dashes of hot pepper sauce and a dash of pepper

Brown beef in hot pan with the onion. Drain. Sprinkle meat with 1/2 teaspoon salt and 1/4 teaspoon pepper. Put half of chiles in 10x6x1½" dish; sprinkle with cheese; top with meat. Put rest of chiles over meat. Combine remaining ingredients; beat until smooth. Pour over chiles. Bake 45-50 minutes in a 350 degree oven or until a knife comes out clean. Makes 6 servings. Serve hot.

Bobbie Davis
Redwood NP

SPANISH RICE

1/2 lb. bacon or ham	1 c. uncooked rice
1 medium onion, diced	2 c. canned tomatoes
1/2 c. fresh or canned green chili, chopped	1 c. water
	Salt and pepper to taste
1 clove garlic, minced	1 c. grated cheese

Fry bacon until crisp. Remove from skillet (set aside). Saute onion, garlic and chili in bacon drippings. Add rice and fry until light brown. Add tomatoes, water, salt and pepper. Cook until rice is done. Add bacon and cheese. Serve with fried corn tortillas.

Kathleen Reid
Montezuma Castle NM

SOUR CREAM ENCHILADAS

Sauce: Combine and heat until smooth--

2 cans (10½ oz.) cream of chicken soup	1/2 c. sour cream
1/2 t. salt	1 (or ½) can diced peeled green chiles

Filling:

2 c. (8 oz.) grated Cheddar or Longhorn cheese	1/2 c. chopped green onions or chives
1 doz. corn tortillas	1 c. cooking oil

Mix cheese and green onions. Dip tortillas in hot oil for a bit to soften. Drain on mat of paper towels. Place portion of cheese filling across tortillas; add tablespoon of sauce. Roll cigarette style. Place side by side in shallow baking dish. Coat with sauce and cheese. Bake for 20 minutes at 350 degrees.

Carolyn Gunzel
Saguaro NM

MAIN DISHES 41

TATSUTA-AGE (Japanese Marinated Fried Chicken)

1½ lb. chicken, cut into 1½ inch pieces

Marinate in:

4 T. soy sauce
1 T. sugar

2 T. sake (or sherry)
3 T. vegetable oil (salad oil)

Marinate chicken in mixture for about 30 minutes. Roll in 3 tablespoons of cornstarch and let stand for 10 minutes. Deep fry at 350 degrees in hot oil about 5 cups of oil, until crisp and brown. Remove from pan and drain on paper towels. Serve with Sansho or mustard.

Heidi Kobayashi
Regional Office

BAKED NOODLES

1/4 pkg. fine noodles (2 oz.)
1/2 c. sour cream
2 T. cottage cheese
1 T. sugar

1/2 t. salt
1 T. chopped onion
1/2 t. celery salt

Cook noodles; drain; add other ingredients. Put in buttered baking dish and bake 30 minutes in a 350 degree oven or until top is brown and crusty. Serve piping hot with sour cream or tomato sauce.

Virginia Duckett
Regional Office

MUSHROOM RICE

1½ c. cooked brown rice
1 can mushrooms (buttons
   and stems) fried

1 can mushroom soup, undiluted
2 med. onions, sliced and fried
   till just tender

Mix all ingredients. Bake in 350 degree oven about 30 minutes. Excellent accompaniment for poultry or beef.

Elaine Hounsell
Lake Mead NRA

CHICKEN A LA KING

2 to 3 c. cooked chicken, boned
1/4 c. green pepper, cut fine
1/4 c. pimiento slices
1 med. onion, chopped

1 c. chicken broth with some
   fat in it
1/4 to 1/3 c. rice
1/2 t. salt

Mix all together and bake in greased casserole for 1 hour at 350 degrees.

Bettie Black
Joshua Tree NM

TACOS

Contrary to some, this is not the only food served in Mexico but it is certainly one of the best.

Use anything you like for the filling, hash, beans (refried, of course), cooked vegetables, or whatever. Here is one we like. You will need:

1/2 lb. ground beef	1/2 lb. lard
Salt	1 doz. corn tortillas
Oregano	1/2 head lettuce
Garlic powder	1/4 lb. Monterey Jack cheese
Tomato	A small onion

Lightly salt the bottom of your dry cast-iron skillet. Add the hamburger and crumble it with a spatula as the meat cooks. Add the oregano and garlic powder as if salting the mixture. Stir well. When nicely browned, turn it out onto paper towels to drain. Heat 1/2 lb. of lard (no substitutes, please) very hot but not smoking. It should cover the skillet about 3/4 inch deep. Hold a room temperature tortilla folded in half in one hand, then add the hamburger, be generous. Place folded taco on its side in the hot lard. Use tongs to keep it folded until it sets. Cook, turning once, until it is done to your liking. Only 10-20 seconds for "soft", but not until the tortilla turns dark brown or it will taste burned. Remove from lard with tongs and drain on paper towels. Serve immediately or they will get cold. Put them in a hot oven if you make a bunch at once.

TO SERVE: Chop the tomato, onion and lettuce, shred the cheese and serve in separate bowls. Let your guests add these to their tacos according to taste. Tacos should be eaten with your fingers, drench them with taco sauce, let the filling dribble onto your plate (it will anyway) or onto hot refried beans. If you must use a fork, use it to clean your plate.

Ed and Sue Jahns
Regional Office

MACARONI STROGANOFF

7 oz. pkg. macaroni	1/2 t. beau monde seasoning,
17 oz. can peas, drained	if desired
1 lb. ground beef	1/4 t. seasoned pepper
10½ oz. can condensed cream	1 t. seasoned salt
of mushroom soup	1 c. sour cream
1 c. chopped onions	2 T. cooking sherry, if desired

Cook macaroni. Combine beef, onions and seasonings (if desired), shape into meatballs. Brown beef mixture in small amount of vegetable shortening. Stir in sour cream, sherry, macaroni and peas. Pour into 2½ quart casserole. Bake at 350 degrees for 35 minutes. Serves eight.

Yvonne Razo
Tumacacori NM

MRS. ROSSI'S FAMOUS VERY SPECIAL SPAGHETTI
(San Francisco's late Mayor Rossi's wife)

Meatballs:

3/4 lb. ground beef
1/2 lb. fresh pork
1/4 lb. veal
3 slices whole wheat bread
1/2 c. milk or meat stock
1 medium onion
1 large clove garlic
1/2 green pepper
Fistful parsley sprigs
Rind of 1/2 lemon
2 eggs
1 t. salt
1 t. pepper
Pinch of cloves and nutmeg
2 bay leaves

Sauce:

1/4 lb. salt pork
1/2 lb. beef, round or pot roast
1 clove garlic
Fistful parsley sprigs
1/4 c. white wine
Salt and pepper
1/4 t. basil
1 (No. 2½) can tomatoes or
    1½ lb. fresh tomatoes
1 (4 oz.) can tomato paste
1/2 c. water
1 lb. pkg. spaghetti
1/2 c. grated Romano, Locatelli,
    or Parmesan-style cheese

First, prepare the Meatballs: Have your butcher grind the three kinds of meat together twice. Now soak the bread in milk or meat stock for about 5 minutes. While bread soaks, chop onion, garlic, green pepper, parsley, and grate lemon even some of the white pulp. Put meat in a large mixing bowl, squeeze liquid from bread, add bread, chopped vegetables, eggs, and all seasonings except bay leaves to the meat. Mix together thoroughly, cover, and let stand at least an hour for all the flavors to develop. (Mrs. Rossi makes hers the day before needed.) After the mixture has mellowed, shape 12 large meatballs about 3" (smaller ones tend to dry out during baking). Grease the bottom of a roasting pan with olive or salad oil, toss in bay leaves and carefully place meatballs in pan. Bake in a 450 degree oven for 15 minutes, then brush them with a little olive or salad oil and bake another 15 minutes.

Prepare the Sauce: Chop salt pork in little pieces, beef in good-size chunks, garlic and parsley as fine as possible (but keep them in separate piles since they are added at different times). Now, fry the salt pork and garlic until nicely browned; add the beef and brown. Pour in the wine, and let the mixture cook very gently for 10 minutes. Season with salt, pepper, parsley and basil. Stir in the tomatoes (if fresh tomatoes are used, peel them first and quarter), tomato paste and water and cook for 30 minutes. Finally, add the roasted meatballs to the sauce and cook over medium heat for 1 hour longer, stirring occasionally.

To serve: Lift meatballs from the sauce onto a hot platter and in a separate serving dish pour the sauce over cooked, well-drained spaghetti. Sprinkle with cheese. Serves 6.

Dave and Josephine Jones
San Francisco Office

CHICKEN BY CANDLELIGHT

16 pieces chicken, assorted
1/4 c. butter
1 T. lemon juice
1/2 t. salt
1/2 t. pepper

1/2 t. paprika
1/2 c. chopped green onions
1/4 c. minced parsley
1 c. dry white table wine
Grape clusters

Place chicken in baking pan, skin side down. Put all remaining ingredients over pieces. Bake in moderate oven (375 degrees) for 1 hour. Turn chicken, skin side up. Continue baking for 30 minutes. Baste and increase temperature to 400 degrees to allow browning and looseness; bake about 30 minutes more. Pour pan drippings over chicken for serving. Garnish with grape clusters. Good with rice. Yields about 4 servings.
Excellent for romantic setting and special occasions!

Lynn and Louise Herring
Regional Office

CHILI CON CARNE

No hamburger, no GRINGO chili powder, PLEASE!

3 lb. lean boned chuck
1/4 t. cumin
1 c. hot water

8 c. red chile sauce
  (see recipe below)
1 T. lard

Prepare sauce: While it cooks, remove all fat and gristle from meat and cut into 3/4" cubes. Brown meat in heavy skillet in lard. Add the hot water; cover and cook until just tender. The meat and sauce should be done about the same time. Add meat and juices to red chili sauce. Sprinkle the cumin over the surface and stir well. Cook slowly 20 minutes. This is eaten with a fork, not a spoon, and on a plate. Use a leftover piece of tortilla to clean your plate and compliment the chef.

Red Chili Sauce:

This is a basic sauce and can be used to make chili con carne, tamales, etc.

1/2 lb. lard
1¼ c. white flour
1 T. salt
8 c. water

1 c. pure red chili powder
  (no added spices, pure
  ground chiles)

Make a paste of chili powder and 1 c. water. Stir until lump-free. Add 1 cup water, stir well. In large kettle, melt lard over low heat. Add flour and salt; cook until flour is golden brown (7-10 minutes), stir constantly. Add chili-water mixture slowly, keeping stirring. Add remaining 6 cups water. You should have a smooth gravy about medium thick. Cook over low heat for 20-30 minutes. Add a little water if it gets too thick. Will keep refrigerated for about a week. Add some water when reheating. Always use fresh chili powder or a bitter taste may result.

Ed and Sue Jahns
Regional Office

BARBECUED SPARERIBS

Preheat oven to 350 degrees. Large roasting pan. Time: 1½ to 2 hours.

5 lb. spareribs	1 t. horseradish
2 T. drippings	1 c. catsup
2 large onions, finely diced	3 T. Worcestershire sauce
1 T. vinegar	2 t. dry mustard
4 T. lemon juice	1 c. water
2 T. brown sugar	1/2 c. celery or 1 T. celery salt
1/8 t. cayenne pepper	1 t. paprika
	1 c. wine

Brown meat in oven until nicely browned (about 1½ hours). Pour off all drippings. It is essential that the drippings be poured off, otherwise it will make the ribs greasy. Brown onions in drippings, then add onions to remaining ingredients and bring to boil. Pour sauce over ribs in roasting pan. Cover. Continue to bake for about an hour, basting occasionally with the sauce. Serves about 6.

Kay Marquardt
Joshua Tree NM

MAYONNAISE CHICKEN

Roll chicken pieces in mixture of following:

1 c. bread crumbs	1/2 t. pepper
1 t. onion salt	1/2 t. crushed savory
1/4 t. garlic salt	1/2 t. curry powder

Arrange on a greased cookie sheet with skin side up. Bake at 400 degrees for 15 minutes to set crumbs. Remove and brush generously with 1 cup mayonnaise. Reduce oven to 300 degrees and bake 1 hour or until done. Serves about 4 depending on size of chicken.

Marion Durham
Walnut Canyon NM

NOODLE PORK CHOPS

This dish may be prepared for two persons to two hundred! The cooking time varies also—the longer they are cooked, the more tender they become, so they can be held over to accommodate a later-than-planned dinner time. They may also be browned in an electric skillet, left there, and baked in it. The chops may also be prepared in advance and held until ready to bake—a boon if you are preparing for a large number.

Lean center cut pork chops   Chicken noodle soup (canned)

Brown chops on both sides. Arrange in baking dish. Pour undiluated soup over. Cover. Bake at 325 degrees about 1½ hours.

Pat Jones
Regional Office

LAMB SHANKS WITH LIMA BEANS

2 lb. large lima beans
6 lamb shanks
Salt, pepper and MSG
Flour
1/4 c. oil
2 garlic sausages, sliced
1/2 c. chopped onion

1 c. chopped celery
1/2 c. chopped carrot
1 No. 2 can solid pack tomatoes
1/2 t. pepper
2 t. salt
1 c. dry white wine

Soak beans overnight. Season shanks with salt, pepper and MSG and dust with flour. Heat oil in heavy skillet or Dutch oven and brown meat. Set aside. Fry garlic sausages and set aside. Saute onion, celery, and carrot until onion is limp. Add tomatoes, drained beans and pepper. Add boiling water to cover and return lamb shanks to pot. Cover and bake in pre-heated oven (325 degrees) for about an hour. Add salt and wine. Cover again and bake another 30-45 minutes, or until lamb shanks and beans are tender. If beans are soupy, remove lid and cook until liquid is sufficiently reduced. Vegetables should be completely disintegrated in the gravy. Add garlic sausages as a garnish on finished dish. Serves 6. (The original recipe calls for 1 lb. white navy beans, but we like the lima beans best. Also, I cut off every speck of fat from the shanks and trim off the skin before cooking.)

Virginia Duckett
Regional Office

CHICKEN LONG RICE

This dish is usually served at Luaus; but the cooked chicken has been hacked apart so included bones and is quite watery. My recipe is compara-tively dry and chock full of boned chicken.

1 stewing chicken (2 - 2½ lb.)
4 oz. pkg. long rice
   (Japanese name: Harusame—
   sticks of bean jelly)
2 cans (14 oz. ea.) chicken broth
2 cloves garlic
Ginger—several slices fresh,
   OR 1—2 t. powdered ginger
1 whole onion, sliced round

1 pkg. (1 oz.) dried mushrooms
   (Japanese name: Shiitake)
   sliced and soaked till soft
1 T. soy sauce
Aji — (Accent or MSG)
Salt and pepper
1 T. oyster sauce
1 bunch chopped green onions

Pressure cook or simmer the chicken till done. While chicken cooks, soak the rice in a large bowl of water. Save the chicken broth. De-bone the meat and put in the broth. Add rest of ingredients except the rice and green onions. Simmer about 20 minutes. Add strained rice and cook about another 10 minutes or more. Garnish with chopped green onions. Serves at least 6 heavy eaters! The Hawaiian word for food is "kau kau".

Emajoy Barrel
Hawaii Group

LASAGNA

2 T. salad oil
1/2 c. minced onion
1 lb. ground beef
1½ t. salt
1/4 t. pepper
1/4 t. oregano
3 T. snipped parsley

1 (8 oz.) can tomato sauce
1/2 c. Parmesan cheese
1 pkg. lasagna noodles
3/4 lb. Mozzarella cheese
1 lb. cottage cheese
1 (No. 2) can tomatoes
Garlic

Saute onions in hot oil. Add beef; cook until red color disappears. Slice garlic, mash with salt; add to meat with pepper, oregano, parsley, tomatoes, tomato sauce, 2 tablespoons Parmesan cheese. Simmer, covered, for 30 minutes. Refrigerate until ready to serve (may be made ahead of time). About 1 hour before serving, preheat oven to 350 degrees. Cook lasagna; drain; cover with cold water. Put 1/3 of meat sauce in a 12x9x2" baking dish, then a layer of noodles, grated Mozzarella cheese, a layer of cottage cheese and Parmesan cheese (2 T.). Repeat until all ingredients are used up. Bake 30 minutes. Makes 8 servings. Serve with green salad and French bread.

Clara Reid
Petrified Forest NP

MEAT LOAF

2 eggs, beaten
1½ lb. ground beef
3/4 c. minced onion

1/4 c. minced green pepper
2 c. quick cooking oats
1 can (small) tomato sauce

Add all dry ingredients together and mix. Add eggs; blend lightly with fork. Add tomato juice to meat mixture and stir. Shape into an oval loaf. Place in shallow pan. Bake 1 hour in 400 degree oven. Makes 6 servings.

Jean Begody
Regional Office

ORIENTAL CHICKEN

2 fryers, cut up
1/2 c. soy sauce
1/4 c. Worcestershire sauce
2 chopped onions (medium)
1 c. diced celery

1/4 c. cooking wine or wine vinegar
1 t. garlic powder
1/4 c. lemon juice
Salt and pepper to taste
1 t. celery salt

Combine all ingredients except chicken and simmer 30 minutes for sauce. Soak chicken in sauce overnight. Remove from sauce and bake chicken in buttered pan for 1½ hours or until tender in a 350 degree oven. Cover pan with foil. Sauce is delicious over hot rice.

Anna C. Robinson
Lehman Caves NM

SUKIYAKI

1 chicken or 1½ lb. beef
1 T. butter
1 large onion, sliced
1 (No. 2) can bamboo shoots
   OR 1 can Sukiyaki-No-Tomo
2 T. sherry

3/4 c. mushrooms, sliced
4-5 green onions, sliced
   1½" long
1/2 t. Accent
1/3 c. sugar
3/4 c. soy sauce

Cut meat into bite-sized pieces and cook in hot butter or chicken fat. Add onions, bamboo shoots, cut into strips, OR ingredients from Sukiyaki-No-Tomo, sugar, soy sauce, sherry and 1/4 to 1/2 of the liquid from the can. Fry till vegetables are partially done. Add mushrooms and green onions. Serve immediately. NOTE: Use Kikkomann Shoyu (Soy) Sauce. Suggested Menu: sukiyaki, rice, peach salad and pickled vegetables. Makes 6 servings.

Clara Shimoda
City of Refuge NHP

RICE AND BEEF PORCUPINES

1 lb. ground beef
1/2 c. well-washed uncooked
   rice
3 T. chopped onions
1 t. salt

1/4 t. poultry seasoning
1/4 t. pepper
3 T. fat
2 cans tomato sauce
1 c. water

Mix all ingredients and form into small balls. Brown in fat and drain off excess. Add tomato sauce and water. Cover and simmer 45-50 minutes or until rice is tender. Makes 12-15 meatballs.

Carla Martin
Tuzigoot NM

CRACKER ENCHILADA PIE

1½ lb. ground beef
1 chopped onion
2 cloves minced garlic
1 T. vinegar
1 c. olives, chopped
2 c. tomato sauce
3 T. chili powder

2 t. salt
1/2 t. pepper
4 2/3 c. water
1/2 c. cornstarch
2 c. grated cheese
Saltines or corn chips

Cook meat, onion and garlic. Add vinegar, olives, tomato sauce, chili powder, salt and pepper and four cups of water. Cook 20 minutes. Mix 2/3 cup water and 1/2 cup cornstarch; add to above to thicken. Layer meat with cheese and crackers in a large (or two smaller) casserole dish. Repeat layers until all meat mixture is used, finishing with cheese on top. Bake 35 minutes at 350 degrees. Serves 8.

Rachel Curran
Death Valley NM

CHICKEN TCHAKHOKHBELLI
(Armenian Style Chicken from OMAR KHAYYAM'S in San Francisco.)

2 (2 lb.) chickens (8 pieces)	1 t. paprika
1 cube butter	1/2 c. tomato juice or sauce
1 onion, sliced (large size)	1 t. salt
1/2 c. dry sherry	Pepper to taste

Melt the butter in frying pan, add chicken and braise until light brown. Remove chicken, and set in shallow pan. Fry onion in leftover butter, then pour contents of frying pan over the chicken. Add all other ingredients plus 1 cup of water. Bake in a 400 degree oven without cover. Turn over after half an hour. Cook for another half hour, then turn again and cook an additional 15 minutes. Serve with Rice Pilaff.

Rice Pilaff:

3 c. rice	6 c. broth (Spice Islands
1 cube butter	chicken stock base is excellent
Salt and pepper	for this)

Melt butter, add dry rice and braise until the butter begins to bubble. Add broth and seasonings. Mix well. Bake in oven for 30 minutes at 375-400 degrees. Cover casserole for this part of baking time. Take out of oven; mix well and bake for 15 minutes more. Serves 6 to 8, depending on appetites. Reheats well, so don't worry if you have some left over.

Dave and Josephine Jones
San Francisco Office

SCHNITZEL A LA HOLSTEIN (Breaded Veal with Fried Egg)

6 large veal scallops	2 c. crackers, crushed
Salt and pepper	OR corn flake crumbs
Flour	1/4 c. butter
1 egg, well beaten	1/4 c. oil
6 eggs	1/4 c. butter
12 flat anchovy fillets, drained	2 T. drained capers
2 T. minced parsley	Lettuce leaves, pickled beets,
	dill pickles

Pound veal until paper thin. Sprinkle both sides with salt and pepper. Dip into flour. Shake off excess. Dip into egg and place on crumbs. Coat completely, pressing crumbs firmly so they adhere. Let stand at room temperature 1 hour to dry. Heat butter and oil in large skillet and brown veal quickly on both sides. Place on a platter and keep warm. In another skillet, fry eggs in 1/4 cup butter until whites are set but yolks are still soft. Place egg on top of veal and top each with crisscrosses of 2 anchovy fillets; sprinkle with capers and parsley. Serve with a lettuce cup filled with pickled beets and dill pickles. Serves 6.

Alma Hinkley
Whiskeytown NRA

MARINATED BAKED HAM

1 bottle Rhine wine	2 bay leaves
1/2 t. tarragon	6 whole cloves
1/2 t. sage	10 peppercorns
1/2 t. marjoram	1 onion, sliced
1/4 t. ground ginger	1 ham, about 8 lb.
Peel of 1 lemon	Whole cloves for garnish
	Glaze

Reserve 1/4 cup of wine for glaze. In deep bowl, combine remaining wine and all ingredients except ham and cloves for garnish and glaze. Mix well. Place ham in bowl and marinate overnight, turning 3 or 4 times to coat with marinade. Simmer ham and marinade in deep kettle for about 2 hours. Remove ham from kettle and cut off rind. Score and stud with whole cloves, spread with glaze and bake at 350 degrees about 1 hour. Baste occasionally with glaze.

Glaze:

The reserved 1/4 c. wine	1/4 t. allspice
1/4 c. brown sugar	1 T. powdered mustard

Combine and mix well.

Mary Alice Replogle
Regional Office

ENCHILADAS

Tortillas	1/2 t. salt
1/2 c. melted shortening	1 large can chili (prepared)
1/2 t. chili powder	2/3 c. grated cheese
1 onion, chopped	

Heat tortillas in melted shortening to which chili powder has been added. Drain liquid from chili. Spread tortillas with chili; sprinkle onion and cheese and roll tortillas. Place in flat baking dish and put remainder of chili, cheese and onion on top. Place in 350 degree oven and heat. Serve at once. Serves 4.

Bobbie Brudenell
Yosemite NP

REFRIED BEANS

This is easy. Open a can of Rosarita Brand refried beans. BUT add a spoonful of the hot lard from your taco pan, 1/2 oz. of the shredded cheese and stir well over low heat. Heat only long enough for the cheese to melt and still be recognizable in the beans.

Ed and Sue Jahns
Regional Office

ORIENTAL CHICKEN WITH MUSHROOMS

This recipe is from a Hawaiian State Cooking Champion, William K. Pauole, from Kona, Hawaii. First published in the KONA TIMES, 1970 or 1971.

3 whole broiler breasts,
   boned and skinned
1/2 t. salt
1/2 t. pepper
2 T. corn oil
1/4 lb. fresh mushrooms,
   sliced

1 can (10½ oz.) chicken gravy
1 t. soy sauce
1/2 t. powdered ginger
1/4 c. water chestnuts
   (thinly sliced)
1 pkg. (9 oz.) frozen French
   style green beans, thawed

Cut each breast into 5 long strips. Sprinkle with salt and pepper. Heat corn oil in large heavy skillet, over medium heat. Add chicken strips and mushrooms and cook until brown. Mix gravy, soy sauce and ginger. Pour over chicken. Add chestnuts and beans over the top. Cover; reduce heat to low and cook gently about 10-20 minutes, or until chicken is tender and beans tender-crisp, stirring occasionally. Makes 6 servings.

Bonnie Jo Harris
Channel Islands NM

VEAL PARMIGIANA

1 lb. thin veal scallopine
2 eggs, beaten
1 c. seasoned dry bread crumbs
1/2 c. olive or salad oil

Tomato sauce (recipe below)
1 pkg. (8 oz.) Mozzarella
   cheese, sliced
1/4 c. grated Parmesan cheese

Preheat oven to 350 degrees. Wipe veal with damp paper towels. Dip into egg, then bread crumbs, coating lightly. In a large skillet, heat about 1/4 cup oil. Add veal slices a few at a time, and cook until golden brown on each side—2 to 3 minutes for each side. Add more oil as needed. Place veal in 10x6½x2″ baking dish to cover bottom in a single layer. Add half the tomato sauce and half the cheeses. Repeat layers, ending with Parmesan cheese. Cover baking dish with foil. Bake 30 minutes or until bubbly. Makes 4 to 6 servings.

Tomato Sauce:

2 T. olive oil
1/2 c. chopped onion
1 clove garlic, crushed
1 can (1 lb. 1 oz.) Italian
   tomatoes, undrained

3/4 t. salt
1/2 t. dried oregano
1/4 t. dried basil
1/4 t. pepper
2 t. sugar

In hot oil, in medium saucepan, saute onions and garlic until golden brown—about 5 minutes. Add the undrained tomatoes, and seasonings; mix well, mashing the tomatoes with a fork. Bring to boiling, reduce heat; simmer covered ten minutes.

Rose Coulter
Regional Office

MEAT LOAF

1 lb. ground beef   3/4 c. poultry stuffing
1/2 can tomato sauce

Combine ingredients and press into flat layer pan, 6x10x2". Bake 20 minutes at 375 degrees. Cut in half, place two slices of cheese between layers. Pour sauce over all and serve.

Meat Loaf Sauce:

1/2 pkg. spaghetti sauce mix   1/2 can tomato sauce
1/4 c. water

Combine and bring to a boil. Heat 2-3 minutes.

Carla Martin
Tuzigoot NM

LITTLE CRANBERRY MEAT LOAVES

1 lb. ground beef   1 T. Kitchen Bouquet
1 c. cooked rice   1½ t. salt
1/2 c. tomato juice   1 can (1 lb.) whole cranberry
1 slightly beaten egg   sauce
1/4 c. minced onion   1/3 c. brown sugar
                                     1 T. lemon juice

Combine meat with rice, tomato juice, egg, minced onion, Kitchen Bouquet, and salt; mix thoroughly. Shape meat mixture into 5 individual loaves, place in a 13x9x2" pan. For topping, combine cranberry sauce, brown sugar and lemon juice; spoon over loaves. Bake in moderate (350 degree) oven for 40 minutes. Remove meat loaves to warm serving platter. Pour cranberry sauce from pan; pass with meat loaves. Makes 5 servings.

Fifi and Doug Cornell
Golden Gate NRA

CHICKEN A LA KING

1 can mushrooms   2 c. chicken broth
1/2 c. diced green pepper   2 c. light cream
1/2 c. butter   2 c. cooked, cubed chicken
1/2 c. flour   1 jar pimientoes, chopped
1 tsp. salt   Patty shells
1/4 t. pepper

Cook and stir mushrooms and green pepper in butter for 5 minutes. Remove from heat. Blend flour, salt and pepper. Cook over low heat; stir until it bubbles. Remove from heat. Stir in broth and cream. Heat to boiling, stirring constantly. Boil 1 minute, add chicken and pimientoes; heat through. Serve hot in shells. Makes 8 servings.

Joy Gifford
Point Reyes NS

KAISER'S POT ROAST

3 lb. pot roast
1 c. dry white wine
1 large onion

1 can cream of mushroom
  soup
Flour, salt, pepper and oil

Brown seasoned and floured roast with oil. Add chopped onion; add soup, 2 cans water and wine. Simmer for 3 hours; serve with noodles or rice. Serves 6.

Lola Kaiser
Lake Mead NRA

GREEN CHILI CHICKEN

2 cans (4 oz. size) Ortega
  roasted and peeled whole
  chiles
2 t. olive oil (or more as required)
1 med. yellow onion
3 cloves, chopped garlic
1/2 t. salt

1 c. commercial sour cream
1/4 t. crushed tarragon
1 bunch green onions
1/4 t. MSG
1/2 c. chicken stock or
  strong bouillon
Wings and breasts of 2 chickens

Heat olive oil in heavy pan (some use pressure cooker). Finely chop onions including green tops. Lightly brown these in the oil and as they are starting to turn golden, add the garlic and cook slightly and remove from the pan. Add salt and MSG to the oil, then lightly brown the chicken. Add the stock, onions and garlic and chiles (chopped). Close up the pressure cooker and cook 8 to 10 minutes at 10 lb. pressure. Now add the sour cream and tarragon. Stir, reheat and serve. This recipe is supposed to serve two persons.

Dave and Josephine Jones
San Francisco Office

CHICKEN IN WINE

One fryer, cut up in serving pieces. Mix 1/4 cup white or whole wheat flour, 1 teaspoon salt, pepper. Coat chicken with this mix. Fry in 6 tablespoons oil to brown. Place in a casserole or roaster. Slice 1 large onion over chicken, add 1 can mushroom soup and 1 cup sherry. Cover and bake 1½ hours at 350 degrees.

Virginia Duckett
Regional Office

PORK CHOP AND POTATO SCALLOP

4 pork chops
1 can cream of mushroom soup
1/2 c. sour cream
1/4 c. water

2 T. chopped parsley
4 c. thinly sliced potatoes
Salt and pepper

In skillet, brown chops. Blend soup, sour cream, water and parsley. In 2-quart casserole, alternate layers of potatoes, and meat. Sprinkle with salt, pepper and sauce. Cover and bake at 350 degrees for 1¼ hours.

Faye Lukens
Chiricahua NM

KAL-BI (Korean Barbecue Spareribs)

1 pkg. spareribs (2 to 3 lb.)
1/2 to 1 c. soy sauce
1 c. chopped green onion
1 c. water
1 T. garlic powder

2 c. barbecue sauce
1 c. white wine
1 c. taco sauce (in bottle)
1/2 T. black pepper

Separate ribs and trim off fat. Then boil in water for 1/2 hour. Drain. Prepare marinade sauce: In medium size bowl, put soy sauce, wine, green onion, taco sauce, barbecue sauce, water, garlic powder and black pepper and mix well. Dip ribs well and place in big bowl; pour leftover sauce over the ribs. Then marinate for several hours. Bake in a 375 degree oven for 1/2 to 3/4 hour. (Use slot-type baking dish that will hold some of the sauce.) Pour all the sauce on the ribs in the pan. Serve hot.

Kyung Ja and Hugo Huntzinger
Coronado NM

SPANISH PORK

2 lb. pork, cubed
2 large Bell peppers, diced

2 T. cornstarch
Garlic seasoning

Place pork and Bell peppers in a 4-quart pan of boiling water and boil for 1/2 hour. Add garlic seasoning to suit your taste; cover saucepan and cook at low heat for another 45 minutes, until there is just enough juice left to thicken for gravy by adding cornstarch. Blend the cornstarch in 1/4 cup of cold water and add slowly to mixture. Stir constantly with wooden spoon for 5-10 minutes and then serve. Delicious served with flour tortillas (roll up like burritos) and refried beans and rice. Enough to serve at least 6 people.

Willa Sawyer
Yosemite NP

CHINESE SEASONING FOR TURKEY OR DUCK

1 (6 lb.) turkey or 2 (3 lb.)
   ducks
2 T. Hawaiian salt (rock)
1 T. five spice
2 T. sherry

6 or more stalks Chinese parsley
4 T. Hoisin sauce
2 T. honey
2 T. shoyu
1/3 c. green onions

Wash and clean turkey. Mix salt and five spice and sprinkle some into cavity, the rest on outside of bird, being sure to rub more on breast and drumstick part. Marinate overnight. Two hours before roasting, mix remaining ingredients. Use all but one tablespoon in the cavity. Rub remaining tablespoonful evenly over skin. Let stand 1 to 2 hours. Start roasting at 375 degrees for 30 minutes. Reduce heat to 250 degrees for 1 hour, then increase heat to 400 degrees for 30 minutes (or use rotisserie). Test whether turkey is done by taking hold of drumstick, if it feels loose, it is done. Serves 8 as main course, 12 with other main dish.

Adele Fevella
Haleakala NP

AUSTRALIAN FRIED CHICKEN

Brown 3/4 cup onion in 1/2 c. oil. Add and simmer:

3/4 c. tomato sauce
3/4 c. water
1/2 c. lemon juice
3 T. brown sugar

3 T. Worcestershire sauce
1/2 t. dry mustard
Salt and pepper

Pour over 2 cut-up fryers. Cover and roast for about 1 hour in a 400 degree oven. Makes 4-6 servings.

Karla and Peter Allen
Lake Mead NRA

STUFFED CHICKEN BREASTS DELUXE (or SUPREME)
(Or whatever you want to call it.)

The following recipe stuffs approximately 11 whole chicken breasts. They are halved, boned, and flattened slightly. Also, remove the skins.

Stuffing:

2-3 c. dry, very fine bread
    crumbs
2 T. to 1/2 c. chopped onions
1 to 1½ c. ground ham
Salt and pepper to taste

1/2 t. poultry seasoning
    (or sage, thyme and
    rosemary)
1 c. grated Swiss cheese
1/2 c. chopped parsley

Mix with 2 tablespoons melted butter and 1 cup chicken broth. Stuff, place about 1 tablespoon of stuffing on flat chicken breast; roll the chicken breasts (hold with toothpicks). Dip chicken in melted butter (or oleo); place in baking dish. If any butter remains, drizzle over top. Bake in slow oven, 325 degrees, about 45 minutes; turn and bake an additional 45 minutes, or until tender. (If it has to remain in the oven for a longer time, cook covered with foil for part of the time.) Serve with Sour Cream Mushroom Sauce.

Sour Cream Mushroom Sauce:

1 lb. fresh mushrooms, sliced
1/4 c. minced onions
3 or 4 T. butter or oleo
3 or 4 T. flour (depends on how
    thick you want your sauce)

About 2 c. chicken broth
About 2 c. dry white wine
Salt and pepper to taste
3/4 c. sour cream

Cook mushrooms and onion lightly in butter until soft—about 4-5 minutes, over low heat. Stir flour into mixture. Add broth, wine and seasonings. Heat slowly, stirring constantly, until smooth and boiling slightly. Before serving, reheat until simmering, add sour cream, and heat until almost boiling. (To cut down on calories—I have used buttermilk instead of sour cream—GOOD!)

Dorothy Johnson
Regional Office

CHILI PIE

1. Grease a 9x13" pan. Spread 2 cans Ortega diced chiles over bottom.
2. Put 1 lb. Tillamook cheese, grated, over the chiles.
3. Combine: 2½ c. milk   1 c. Bisquick
                 3 eggs   1 t. salt

4. Pour over cheese and bake for 1 hour at 350 degrees.

Shirley Rees
Cabrillo NM

COMPANY STEW

This is called Company Stew because it is a handy recipe to use when you have company visiting. You can put it in the oven while you take your visitors to points of interest in the park; come home and an excellent dinner is waiting for all of you.

1½ to 2 lb. stew meat
  (cut into bite-size pieces)
2 pkg. (1 lb. ea.) frozen
  mixed vegetables

1 can whole onions
1 or 2 cans whole potatoes
2 pkg. Lawry's stew seasoning
Salt and pepper - water

Put all ingredients into large casserole in order given. Fill casserole with water - or to 1" below rim. Cover with foil; put in oven at 250 degrees for 6 to 8 hours. You may want to add more water if you come home during day. Excellent. Serve with no beat popovers.

No Beat Popovers:

2 eggs
1 c. milk

1 c. flour
1/2 t. salt

Break eggs into bowl. Add milk, flour and salt. Mix well with spoon. (Disregard lumps.) Fill greased muffin pans 1/4 full. Put in oven; turn to 450 degrees. Do not open the oven door for 30 minutes.

Kathleen DeWitt
Death Valley NM

PORKINNI (Pork Chops and Zucchini)

8 pork chops
2 cans tomato sauce (8 oz. ea.)
1 can stewed tomatoes
2-3 cloves garlic
1 sliced onion

6 med. zucchini
1 stalk celery (optional)
Chili seeds or cayenne
Salt and pepper
White wine (optional)

Cut chops into bite-size pieces and brown well. Add stewed tomatoes (cut up), tomato sauce, crushed garlic, onion, celery, chili seeds, salt and pepper. Simmer until meat is tender, approx. 30 minutes. Add zucchini and simmer until tender. Serve over hot rice. Serves 6.

Theresa Fisher
Regional Office

SAUERKRAUT AND PORK CHOPS

All quantities based on appetites and number of eaters.

1. Fry pork chops. Cut up cooked strips of bacon with a large quantity of chopped onions and a little chopped garlic. Brown. Pepper and garlic salt to taste, saving all oils resulting from this initial step. Do this about 8 in the morning. (Other type pork can be used.)

2. In large covered pot, place sauerkraut (unwashed) and stuff in one to three bay leaves and a few whole cloves. Pour contents from frying pan on top. Spread thoroughly so oils and meat juices work through kraut. Allow to cook all day (on back of stove), very low heat, stirring from time to time. Keep covered. Stirring should be done with vigor so as to mix all ingredients together.

3. In late afternoon, you will note that some meat is falling off bones and kraut is getting dark. At this stage, the delicious aromas are becoming very noticeable. Things are progressing very well.

4. About 5 to 7 pm. The aroma is driving you mad. If you've weakened and tasted what is not necessarily a "fancy" sight—you will immediately know it is ready!

5. Dole out portions; add spuds or other foodstuffs that you have also cooked, and if you even remotely like beer, pour yourselves some suds and have a real feast.

6. If bitterness has dampened your liking for sauerkraut—this recipe is guaranteed to make you a kraut convert. It will be mellow, tasty, juicy and a sheer delight. Try it!

Francis (Jake) Jacot
Regional Office

CHICKEN MARENGO

1 broiler-fryer, cut up (about 2½ lb.)	1 t. salt
1/4 c. vegetable oil	1/8 t. pepper
1/2 c. chopped onion	1/2 c. dry white wine or chicken broth
1 clove garlic, minced	1 can (3 oz.) B&B sliced or chopped mushrooms
1/4 t. marjoram, crushed	2 tomatoes, peeled (canned, OK)
Chopped parsley	

Brown chicken slowly in hot vegetable oil. Add onion, garlic and marjoram; cook until onion is soft. Season with salt and pepper. Add wine or broth drained from mushrooms. Scrape bottom of pan to loosen browned bits. Cover and cook over low heat until chicken is tender, about 35 minutes. Skim off any fat. Cut tomatoes into quarters or eighths and add with mushrooms to chicken. Continue cooking, covered, for 5 minutes. Garnish with parsley. 4 servings.

Sarah Hurd
Regional Office

BARBECUED CHICKEN

2 lb. chicken wings
3/4 c. sugar
1/2 c. Japanese shoyu sauce*
1/2 c. catsup

2 oz. sake (Rose wine will
   do—but sake is best)
1 small joint ginger, crushed
2 small cloves garlic

Take chicken and cut all pieces at joints. Do not use the pointed tips. The rest will resemble small chicken legs. Marinate in above mixture either overnight or all day. Put in large heavy frying pan and bring to boil. Turn down immediately and simmer with cover on pot until done, about 1 hour. Serve with rice and salad.

   *Japanese shoyu is preferred because Chinese soy is too sweet.

Marcie Ladd
City of Refuge NHP

BACON STEW

1/4 lb. bacon, diced
4 potatoes, quartered

2 (1 lb.) cans green beans
   OR 2 pkg. frozen green beans

Brown bacon. Do not drain off drippings. Add canned green beans and potatoes. Simmer until potatoes are tender. If frozen green beans are used, add enough water to simmer potatoes in.

Carol Reigle
Lake Mead NRA

TAMALE PIE

2 c. cooked pinto beans
2 cans (8 oz.) tomato sauce
1 c. cheese (Longhorn or Cheddar)
1 pkg. (7 oz.) Fritos

1/2 small onion
1 t. oregano
1/2 lb. hamburger
2 T. red chili

Fry hamburger; add onions and oregano. Drain, then pour into casserole. Spread in bottom. Put cooked beans in skillet; add 2 cans tomato sauce, stir. Add red chili powder, mix, simmer for 5 minutes. Pour over hamburger. Grate cheese and crush Fritos; mix and pour over casserole. Bake in oven for 20 minutes at 375 degrees. Serves about 8.

Dan Jaramillo
Saguaro NM

CHILI CON QUESO

1 cube margarine
1 med. onion, chopped
1 small can milk

1/2 lb. Velveeta cheese
1/2 to 1 t. garlic salt
1 small can green chiles

Melt margarine. Add onion and cook until transparent (do not brown). Put margarine and onion in double boiler. Add milk, cheese, and garlic salt. Melt cheese—add chili. Keeps well. Serve hot.

Lydia S. Mason
Petrified Forest NP

CHICKEN TOSTADOS

4 full chicken breasts

Bake the chicken breasts and cut into bite-size chunks.

3 green onions, chopped
1 can celery soup
1 can mushroom soup

2 cans milk
2 cans green chili salsa with
  tomatoes

Grate 1 pound Cheddar cheese for top. Use 1 package corn chips for bottom.

Grease 9x11" baking dish. Cover bottom with corn chips. Place chicken on top, cover with sauce, sprinkle cheese over top. Refrigerate over-night. Bake for 40 minutes at 325 degrees.

Harry and Nancy Sloat
Regional Office

BROILED SPARERIBS

5 lb. BBQ spareribs, cut into
  sections

3 inches of ginger, crushed

Sauce:

1 c. white sugar
3/4 c. shoyu sauce

1 c. catsup
1/3 c. oyster sauce

Boil spareribs and ginger with just enough water to cover meat for 1½ to 2 hours. Drain water. Mix all sauce ingredients well. Pour over cooked spareribs and soak for 3 hours or more. Mix several times within the 3 hours to stir up the ingredients. Broil in 350 degree oven for 15 minutes or charcoal broil. Chicken thighs may be used instead of spareribs. Decrease boiling time 1 hour if chicken is used.

Setsuko Tanaka
City of Refuge NHP

CHILI VELVET RICE

3 c. uncooked minute rice
2 pkg. (8 oz.) Jack cheese,
  shredded
2 small cans green chiles

1 pt. sour cream
Butter and paprika
Salt to taste

Cook rice as directed on package. Wash and dice green chiles. In buttered casserole, layer the rice, cheese, chiles and sour cream until all ingredients are used. Sprinkle top with paprika and butter. Bake 30 minutes at 350 degrees or until cheese melts. Serves 10 to 12. Potatoes can be used instead. Serve with broiled steak.

Kathleen DeWitt
Death Valley NM

RICE AND GREEN CHILI

Rich tasting and very easy to make. Mildly hot. Great with everything.

1 can (4 oz.) Ortega diced
   green chiles
3 c. cooked rice

3 c. sour cream
3 c. Jack cheese, grated
Salt

Mix ingredients well in pan and cook over medium heat until hot. Stir frequently or it will stick and burn. OR, mix well and bake at 350 degrees for 30 minutes.

Ed and Sue Jahns
Regional Office

KNISHES

Dough:

2 eggs
1¼ glass water
1/2 glass oil

Pinch of salt
1 level t. baking powder
Flour, enough to make dough
   (not too hard)

Mix all well together. Let rest.

Filling:

1 lb. roasted stew meat
Small chunk of roasted
   beef liver
2 or 3 c. mashed potatoes

1 egg, mixed into potatoes
2 small onions, sliced, fried
   in chicken fat
Salt and pepper to taste

Chop meat, liver and onions. Roll out, cut dough about 4" square. Place some mashed potatoes onto dough; add meat and some chicken fat and fold over. Place in baking pan which has been oiled and bake the knishes; add some oil onto knishes so they will not dry out and bake until brown. Be careful not to bake them too long. Should be baked about 30 to 40 minutes (until golden).

Leonard Lebovitz
Regional Office

DARN GOOD

2 cans green chiles, washed,
   dried
1 lb. Monterey Jack cheese,
   grated

4 eggs, beaten
1 pt. sour cream
1/2 t. salt

Grease 9x13'. pan. Then place a layer of green chiles and a layer of cheese until all used up. Mix beaten eggs with sour cream and salt and pour over the cheese and chiles. Bake, uncovered, in 350 degree oven for 1 hour and 15 minutes. Serves 4-6.

Karen Donaldson
Lake Mead NRA

STEWED MEAT

2 c. diced celery
2 c. diced carrots
1 can Mexicorn

1 can sweet green peas
1 lb. beef stew meat
Seasonings to taste

Add all ingredients in large pan. Add water and cook for 1 hour, or until tender.

Jean Begody
Regional Office

SWEDISH MEAT BALLS

1 c. fine dry bread crumbs
1 lb. ground round steak
1/2 lb. ground pork
1/2 c. mashed potatoes
   (Instant OK)
1 egg, beaten
1 t. salt
1/2 t. MSG

1/2 t. brown sugar
1/4 t. pepper
1/4 t. nutmeg
1/4 t. allspice
1/8 t. cloves
1/8 t. ginger
3 T. butter

Combine 1/2 cup bread crumbs with meat, potatoes and egg. Mix 8 spices together and add to meat. Shape into balls about 1" in diameter. Roll balls lightly in remaining 1/2 cup crumbs. Heat butter in large, heavy skillet with a tight-fitting lid. Use low heat. Add meatballs and brown on all sides. Shake pan frequently to brown evenly and to keep round. Cover and cook about 15 minutes or until they are thoroughly cooked.

Grace H. Wilson
Lake Mead NRA

BURROS

1 doz. flour tortillas (18"
   diameter, if you can find
   them!)

Refried beans, taco filling,
   chile con carne, or other filling

Lay tortilla out flat. Fold the top third down towards the center. On this folded part, place 2 or 3 tablespoons of filling in a strip about 1½" wide but not out to the edges. Now fold the top edge toward you once more. Then fold the "ears" or sides inward. Continue to fold the top edge towards you until the burro is fully rolled. Should the tortilla tear during this you can eat it with a fork as a penance. They should be eaten by hand, starting from one end which exposes the filling and allows you to drench it with TACO SAUCE prior to each bite. Do not wear your best clothing the first time you try burros.

VARIATION: Burros can be deep-fried until crisp. This changes the flavor in some mysterious way and produces a "chimichanga". For real adventure—use favorite pie filling, deep fry, then sprinkle with powdered sugar for dessert. Good!

Ed and Sue Jahns
Regional Office

SEVEN LAYER DINNER

1 box macaroni, uncooked
   in bottom of casserole dish
1 (8 oz.) can English peas
1 (8 oz.) can whole kernel corn

1 small onion, chopped
1 small Bell pepper, chopped
1½ - 2 lb. hamburger, uncooked
1 (8 oz.) can tomato sauce

Put each ingredient in a layer at a time. Bake in preheated oven (350 degrees) 1 hour, last 30 minutes uncovered.

Patricia Myers
Montezuma Castle NM

SPANISH HAMBURGER

2½ lb. hamburger (ground chuck)
3 onions, diced
3/4 c. sweet pickle relish
1 t. dill seed

1 green pepper, chopped
1/2 bottle catsup
1/4 c. water

Fry hamburger brown; add other ingredients. Turn fire low and simmer covered, for 2½ hours.

Bettie Black
Joshua Tree NM

LAZY CHILI RELLENOS

1 large can (No. 2½) whole
   green chiles
1 lb. sharp Cheddar cheese

12 eggs, beaten with 1/2 t. salt
1½ c. milk

Remove seeds from chiles; stuff with strips of cheese. Place side by side in shallow baking dish. Add milk to beaten eggs and mix well. Pour over chiles. Bake 50-60 minutes in 350 degree oven. Holds well. Serves 8 as a main dish or 12 as a side dish.

Kathleen DeWitt
Death Valley NM

QUICK HAMBURGER PIE

1 med. onion, chopped
1 lb. ground lean beef
Salt and pepper (Accent, Lawry
   salt or other)
1/2 lb. fresh or frozen green
   beans, cooked

1 can condensed tomato soup
5 med. potatoes, pared and
   boiled in salted water
1/2 c. warm milk
Salt and pepper
1 egg, beaten

Brown onion lightly in small amount hot fat. Add meat and seasonings, brown. Add drained, cooked beans, and soup. Heat. Pour into greased casserole. Mash potatoes; add milk, egg and seasonings. Spoon over meat in mounds or use a pastry tube. Bake in moderate oven, 350 degrees, for 30 minutes. Serves 6.

Helen Goodlund
Muir Woods NM

PORK CHOPS ON RICE

6 pork chops
1 1/3 c. uncooked rice

1 c. prepared Tang
1 (10½ oz.) can condensed
   chichen with rice soup

Brown chops on both sides; season with salt and pepper. Place rice in 12x7½x2" pan; pour Tang over rice. Arrange chops on rice. Pour soup over all. Cover and bake at 350 degrees for 45 minutes. Uncover; bake 10 minutes more. Serves 6.

Georjean McKeeman
Tonto NM

CHILI POR GARDNER

(This recipe was taken from the ARIZONA REPUBLIC. It was first place winner in the "Great Arizona Magazine Chili Burn-off Contest—1972" submitted by J.I. Gardner of Lakeside.)

5 lb. beef chuck, elk or venison
1 large onion
12 to 16 red chiles (dried)
1 t. cumin
Salt to taste

2 lb. pork shoulder
6 med. cloves garlic
1 T. oregano
1 t. black pepper

Trim all fat, gristle, and bone from meat; cut into 1/2" cubes. Cut all usable fat into small cubes and render until fat is brown. Lift out rendered fat pieces and save the grease for frying cubed meat. Saute meat until it has just left the red stage. Do not over fry. Wash red chili pods and remove stems and seeds. Soak chiles in hot water for 20-30 minutes. Pour water from chiles into blender and add chiles a few at a time. Blend until a creamy consistency. Peel onion and garlic. Cut into small pieces and put into blender with enough oil to start the onions and garlic to blend. Blend until creamy. Place in fry pan and saute until lemon colored. Put all ingredients into large pot which will hold all including 6 to 8 cups of hot water. Simmer until meat is tender. Skim off excess oil and thicken with flour or cornstarch to desired consistency. To add more "bite" add a small amount of cayenne or other hot chili. Be careful as you want flavor with a little zip—not burn. This freezes well.

Chris McKinney
Grand Canyon NP

CATTLEMEN'S BARBECUED CHICKEN

Chicken, halved or cut up
Salt and pepper to taste
Season All

Liquid smoke
Cattlemen's Barbecue Sauce

Sprinkle seasoning and liquid smoke over chicken; cover and marinate for 15-25 minutes. Bake for about 30 minutes with foil over top. Pour Barbecue Sauce over chicken and cook another 30 minutes or until tender in a 350 degree oven.

Mary McAlister
Regional Office

64 MAIN DISHES

BITS OF BEEF IN WINE SAUCE

2 lb. beef stew (1" cubes)
1 can (8 oz.) tomato sauce
1½ c. water

1/2 c. sherry
1 envelope onion soup mix
2 cans sliced mushrooms
(optional)

Combine all ingredients except mushrooms in a 2-quart COVERED casserole (change container to serve). Bake 2 hours at 325 degrees (can be held at 250 degrees for an additional 2 hours—even improves). Add mushrooms, drained, during last 5 minutes. Serve over rice. Good served with green string beans as a vegetable sprinkled with almonds, and an Ambrosia for salad. (1/2 c. vinegar [wine] and 1/2 teaspoon garlic salt can be substituted for the sherry, if desired.)

Bobbi Muller
Petrified Forest NP

CHICKEN ORIENTAL

1 broiler, cut up (3 lb.)
1/2 c. flour
1 t. salt
1/4 t. pepper

8 T. butter or oleo
1/4 c. honey
1/4 c. lemon juice
1 T. soy sauce

Wash chicken; drain. Shake in mixture of flour, salt and pepper in paper bag. Melt 4 T. butter in baking dish, 9x12x2". Roll chicken pieces in melted butter. Place skin side down in single layer in dish. Bake at 350 degrees for 30 minutes. Meanwhile, melt remaining 4 T. butter in small saucepan. Stir in lemon juice, soy sauce and honey. Turn chicken. Pour honey mixture over it. Bake one hour, basting 3-4 times until richly glazed. Serve drippings and syrup over hot rice.

Nancy Smith
Petrified Forest NP

VEGETABLES ORIENTAL WITH TURKEY OR CHICKEN

1/2 c. thinly sliced onion
2 T. vegetable oil
2 c. diagonally cut celery
1 c. peas, uncooked
2 cans (3 oz. ea.) mushroom
crowns, with liquid

1 1/3 c. chicken broth
3 T. cornstarch
1 t. Kitchen Bouquet
1/2 t. ginger
1 t. salt
1/2 lb. sliced cooked turkey
or chicken

In large skillet, cook onion in oil until transparent. Stir in celery and cook one minute. Stir in peas; cover and cook about 4 minutes—vegetables should be tender-crisp. Combine broth from 1 can of mushrooms, chicken broth, cornstarch, salt, Kitchen Bouquet and ginger. Add liquid to skillet and cook, stirring constantly until sauce thickens. Stir in mushrooms. Arrange poultry slices over vegetables. Cover and cook over moderate heat until meat is hot, about 5 minutes. Serve with rice.

Geraldine Robison
Lehman Caves NM

ENCHILADAS AND SAUCE

Enchiladas:

1 lb. ground beef
1 recipe sauce
1 pkg. corn tortillas

1 lb. Longhorn cheese,
   shredded
1 large onion, chopped

Steam the ground beef. In saucepan, heat enchilada sauce. In another pan, heat 1 cup shortening. Dip tortillas in hot fat, then dip in the sauce. Put tortilla flat—on it, place beef, cheese, onion, and roll. Place in casserole dish with seam side down. Finish till all is used. Pour rest of sauce on top; cover with shredded cheese and chopped olives. Now the best part: Let them set overnight or at least 6 hours, then bake at 40-45 minutes at 350 degrees. Serve hot with shredded lettuce and ripe olives.

Sauce:

4 T. flour

2 T. lard

Lightly brown flour and lard together. Add at one time:

2 c. tomato sauce
3½ c. water
1½ t. salt
2 T. chili powder

1 t. sugar
1/2 t. garlic powder
2 t. oregano

Cook slowly for 45 minutes, if it becomes too thick, then add a small amount of water. This is the basic sauce used in almost every Mexican dish.

Kathleen DeWitt
Death Valley NM

ITALIAN SPAGHETTI AND MEAT BALLS

1½ lb. ground beef
1 slightly beaten egg
1/4 c. warm water
1/2 T. basil

1/2 c. dry bread crumbs (fine)
1/4 c. grated Parmesan cheese
1½ t. salt
1/4 t. pepper

Combine all ingredients. Form in about 36 (1 inch) balls. In large skillet, brown slowly in small amount of hot fat.

Sauce:

1 (No. 2½) can Italian tomatoes
1 can (6 oz.) Italian tomato
   paste (regular can be used,
   but not as good)
1/4 c. chopped onion

2 cloves minced garlic
2 T. chopped parsley
1 t. salt
1 t. crushed oregano
1/4 t. anise seed

Combine, add meatballs and simmer, uncovered. Do not boil. Stir occasionally; cook 1½ to 2 hours until thick. Cook 1 pkg. (8 oz.) long spaghetti in boiling, salted water (1 tablespoon salt to 3 quarts of water), till tender but still firm. Serve meatballs and sauce over spaghetti with Parmesan cheese. Serves 6. Good served with a tossed green salad, oil and vinegar dressing and garlic bread.

Alma Hinkley
Whiskeytown NRA

SOUR CREAM ENCHILADAS WITH QUICK CHILI SAUCE

12 corn tortillas
Hot oil
1 lb. shredded Jack cheese
2 cans (4 oz.) peeled green
    chiles

Salt and pepper
1½ c. white sauce
1 c. dairy sour cream
1 c. QUICK CHILI SAUCE

Dip tortillas in hot oil. On each, put 1/4 cup cheese, 1/3 of a chili (in a strip), salt and pepper and 2 tablespoons CHILI SAUCE. Roll and put into a baking dish, seam side down. Mix white sauce and sour cream; pour over all and bake at 350 degrees for 30 minutes. Makes 6 servings (4 if a favorite dish).

Quick Chili Sauce:

1/2 c. chopped onion
1 large clove garlic
1 T. lard
1 T. flour
1/4 c. chili powder

1/2 t. oregano
1 t. cumin seed
1 c. tomato puree
1 c. water
1 t. salt

Cook onion and garlic in lard until wilted. Add flour; cook 1 minute, then add other ingredients. Simmer 10 minutes before serving hot. Makes about 2 cups.

Deanna Yardic
Lassen Volcanic NP

TERIYAKI SKEWERED BEEF

1 pt. Kikkoman Shoyu sauce (soy)
1/4 pt. alcoholic beverage
1 thumb-size ginger root
    (peeled and minced)

1/4 c. Ajina-moto MSG
1 c. brown sugar
2-3 cloves garlic
1-2 drops Tabasco sauce
Steaks

Mix and blend thoroughly all ingredients except steaks. Marinate the steaks or kabobs for 24 hours in the sauce for thin pieces. For thick steaks or pieces, marinate 48 hours.

Marilyn J. Scott
Kings Canyon NP

GREEN CHILI STEW

1 c. frozen green chili (canned
    green chili can be used)
1 c. canned tomatoes

2 lb. cubed meat (beef, pork,
    venison, mutton)
Salt to taste

Chop chilies; brown cubed meat in hot fat. Add chilies, tomatoes, chopped onion (to taste), garlic and salt. Simmer from 1 to 1½ hours, until meat is tender.

Cora Thompson
Petrified Forest NP

HAWAIIAN-STYLE SPARERIBS

3 lb. country style spareribs

Sauce:

1 small (8 oz.) can crushed pineapple	1 T. soy sauce
	1 can (8 oz.) tomato sauce
3 T. brown sugar	1/4 c. vinegar
2 T. cornstarch	1 onion (medium)
1 t. salt	1 c. celery

Mix together. Heat until slightly thickened. Layer sauce and ribs and bake at 350 degrees for 2 hours, uncovered.

Kathy Dimont
Lake Mead NRA

CHINESE POT ROAST CHICKEN

3 lb. chicken thighs and drumsticks	1 T. sherry
	1 t. sugar
1/2 t. salt	1/2 c. Chinese peas (Snow peas)
1/4 c. soy sauce	2 green onions, cut in 1" pieces
2 T. salad oil	1 T. cornstarch
6 dried mushrooms, soaked	1 c. water
1 small piece ginger, crushed	1 T. soy sauce
	1 t. MSG

Rub chicken with salt and 1/4 cup soy sauce. Let stand for 15 minutes. Heat oil in skillet and brown chicken well on all sides; add quartered mushrooms. Combine ginger and sherry; pour over the chicken. Cover and simmer slowly for 30 minutes or until chicken is tender. Transfer to serving dish, leaving mushrooms in skillet. Add vegetables and combined remaining ingredients to the mushrooms; cook until sauce thickens and pour over chicken. Yields 6 servings.

Evelyn Ah Sing
Hawaii Volcanoes NP

BRAISED OXTAILS

2 lb. oxtails, cut into 2" pieces	1½ c. water
3 T. fat or salad oil	1/2 c. cooking sherry
1 c. minced onion	1 T. vinegar
2 t. salt	1/2 t. minced garlic
1/8 t. pepper	1 T. sugar
1 can mushrooms (4 oz.)	

Broil oxtails about 10 minutes, turning them frequently until browned. Meanwhile, in hot fat in Dutch oven, saute onions until tender. Add meat and rest of ingredients. Simmer, covered, 4 hours, or until very tender, adding more water if necessary. Remove meat to heated platter; keep warm. Thicken gravy and pour over, or serve with meat.

Elaine Hounsell
Lake Mead NRA

COUNTRY-STYLED BEANS WITH SAUSAGE

1 lb. dried white beans
1 c. chopped onion
1/2 c. chopped green pepper
1 can tomatoes
1½ t. salt
1/4 t. pepper
3 T. chopped parsley

2 T. pure vegetable oil (or bacon grease)
2 lb. bauernwurst, knackwurst, or kielbasa sausage (or Polish sausage which can be found in almost any supermarket)
3 T. vinegar

Soak beans in water, to cover, overnight. Drain. Cover beans with fresh water; simmer gently 1½ hours or until tender. Drain; save 1/2 cup of bean liquid. While beans cook, saute onion and green pepper in oil in large pot. Simmer sausage in skillet in small amount of water until water evaporates. Slice some sausage; leave rest whole; brown sausage on all sides. Combine onion, green pepper, tomatoes, salt, pepper, parsley and vinegar and mix thoroughly. Add beans, bean liquid, and sausage. Cover. simmer 15 minutes. Serves 6.

Dave and Josephine Jones
San Francisco Office

SOUTH-OF-THE-BORDER-STACK-UP

1 lb. ground beef
1 c. chopped onion
1 pkg. Kraft chili seasoning

2 cans (8 oz.) tomato sauce
12 tortillas
2 c. Cheddar cheese

Brown meat. Add onion; cook until tender. Stir in seasoning mix, and tomato sauce. Simmer 10 minutes. Layer tortillas, meat sauce, and shredded cheese in two stacks, using 6 tortillas in each. Place stacks in 9x13" baking dish. Cover tightly with foil. Bake at 350 degrees for 20 minutes.

Carolyn Gunzel
Saguaro NM

CHICKEN OR TURKEY TACOS

This is a great way to use up the left-over holiday bird.

Shred, tear, or otherwise reduce left-over cooked poultry into bite-size pieces. Make up a red sauce either from a can of enchilada sauce or by cooking red or green chiles; warm the chicken in the sauce. Grate a large pile of Cheddar cheese. Chop onion. Warm a dozen tortillas by dipping them in hot oil quickly so that they are flexible. Drain them on paper towels. Fill the tortillas with the chicken sauce, add cheese and onion as desired and wrap as for enchiladas or fold as for a taco. Chopped tomatoes can be added if anyone likes them—just put a bowl at the table, along with shredded lettuce and hot sauce. Warm all in the oven. Can be topped with sour cream or with guacamole. (This recipe can be scaled to large gatherings.)

Marion Durham
Walnut Canyon NM

BARBECUED SPARERIBS

4 lb. country-style ribs
2 T. butter
1/2 c. chopped onion
1 c. water
1 c. ketchup
2 T. vinegar

2 T. lemon juice
2 T. Worcestershire sauce
2 T. brown sugar
1 t. dry mustard
1 t. salt
1/2 t. pepper

Cut ribs in serving size pieces. Brown in skillet; put into a baking pan. Pour fat from skillet. Melt butter in skillet, add onions and cook until brown. Add remaining ingredients and simmer 20 minutes. Pour over ribs and cover. Bake 1½ hours at 350 degrees. Serves 6.

Chris McKinney
Grand Canyon NP

TURKEY LEGS (Good for a picnic)

2 lb. veal (shoulder or leg)
2 lb. pork
Bread crumbs
1 egg

3 celery leaves
1 sliced onion
Salt and pepper to taste

Cut veal and pork in cubes. Alternate cubes on stick. Dip covered sticks first in egg then in crumbs. Brown in oil. After well-browned, add little water, salt, pepper, onion slices, celery leaves; cover and cook for 1 hour. Remove cover last 15 minutes. Check after 1/2 hour to be sure all water has not boiled away.

Dorothy Ruse
Regional Office

TEXAS CHILI

3 lb. chili meat
1 t. black pepper
1 t. salt or salt to taste
3 cloves garlic
1 med. size onion
1½ t. cumin
2 T. chili powder (or to taste)
1 med. size bell pepper

2 T. crushed chile peppers
1 small can tomato paste
1 med. sized can whole
    tomatoes
2 T. shortening
1/2 c. flour
2½ to 3 c. water

Use a 5-quart heavy pot. Mix the following ingredients into chili meat with hands: salt, black pepper, 1/2 pkg. chili powder, 1½ t. cumin, 1/2 cup flour. Make sure flour is mixed into meat well. Melt shortening in pot over low flame; add chili meat mixture; cook and stir to keep meat from sticking; use low flame. While meat is cooking, cut up following ingredients and add to meat mixture: onion, garlic. bell pepper; mash whole tomatoes before adding to meat mixture. Add can of tomato paste. Pour 2½ to 3 cups water into pot. Continue to cook over low flame 1 hour or until chili is the desired thickness. Add crushed chili peppers while cooking. (One half pkg. makes chili mildly hot while a whole pkg. makes it medium hot.)

Rosie Jefferson
Regional Office

BEER BRISKET

Beef brisket (4-5 lb.)
1 onion
1/4 c. chili sauce (or more)

2 T. brown sugar
1 clove garlic
1 can (12 oz.) beer

Place brisket in pan and slice onion over the top. Mix together remaining ingredients and pour over meat. Cover and place in 350 degree oven. Cook about 3 hours or until meat is tender. If desired, make a flour and water gravy with the sauce, or serve sauce alone over meat.

Janet Moore
Lake Mead NRA

CHOW MEIN CASSEROLE

Fry 1 lb. ground beef until it is lightly brown; add 1½ cups sliced celery, 1 or 2 diced onions and continue cooking until vegetables are tender. Preheat oven to 350 degrees. Add:

1 t. salt
A little pepper
1 can cream of chicken
    soup

1 can cream of mushroom soup,
    plus 1½ c. water
3 T. soy sauce
1 (1 lb. 4 oz.) can pineapple chunks
1/2 c. uncooked rice

Put all this into a 2-quart baking dish. Bake, uncovered, for 1/2 hour at 350 degrees and then reduce heat to 300 degrees. Sprinkle 1 can chow mein noodles over the top and bake 1/2 hour more. Serves 6.

Marion Durham
Walnut Canyon NM

CHILES RELLENOS

12 whole green chiles
6 eggs

1 lb. Monterey Jack cheese
6 T. flour

Salsa:

16 oz. chopped tomatoes
2 c. chicken bouillon
1/2 medium onion
1 clove garlic

1/2 t. salt
1/2 t. black pepper
1 t. oregano

Stuff the chiles with cheese and dip into the batter prepared as follows: Allow one egg for each 2 chiles and allow one tablespoon flour for each egg. Separate the yolk from the white and beat the white until stiff. Then blend in yolk and flour until smooth. The coated chiles may now be fried in oil until golden brown and consumed immediately or may be refrigerated until later. Before serving, rewarm the chiles in the following sauce: Saute onion and garlic in 1 tablespoon butter. Add the tomatoes and bouillon and bring to a simmer then season with salt, pepper and oregano. Now you are ready for the chiles you have prepared and some mighty good eating is ahead of you!

Mike Sipes
Chiricahua NM

SWISS FONDUE

Shake 3 tablespoons flour and 4 cups (1 lb.) shredded Swiss cheese in a paper bag until cheese is coated with flour. Rub chafing dish with cut clove garlic. Pour in 2 cups dry white table wine and set over a slow fire. When the wine is hot (bubbles rise to surface), but not boiling, stir a handful of cheese into the wine with a fork. Each batch of cheese should be thoroughly melted and blended before more is added. Keep stirring until the mixture starts bubbling. Season with a little salt, freshly ground black pepper and a few grains of nutmeg. One jigger of brandy may be added if desired. Keep just enough heat under the fondue to keep it bubbling lightly. Give guests quartered rounds of fresh French bread (or any other type desired). Each guest dips his piece of bread into the pot. Bite-sized pieces of toast could be used with forks.

Dave and Josephine Jones
San Francisco Office

BARBECUED SPARERIBS

2 slabs spareribs (about 4 lb.)	4 T. catsup
2 T. soy sauce	1 T. wine (burgundy)
4 T. sugar	1 T. salt

Mix above ingredients together and rub over spareribs and let marinate.
Cut spareribs in 3 pieces for barbecue; and marinate again in sauce for about another half-hour. Puncture holes in between the ribs and secure with string; suspend spareribs in oven or broiler. Turn temperature to 325 degrees for 45 minutes or until thoroughly cooked. Put a shallow pan under the ribs to catch drippings.

John and Maizie Dong
Regional Office

YOSENABE

1 lb. chicken breasts	1 t. MSG
12 shrimp	1 Chikuwa**, sliced
8 stalks watercress	1 block Tofu***, cubed
4 green onions	1 can (5¾ oz.) large button
1 can (13¾ oz.) chicken broth	mushrooms
3 T. sugar	2 carrots, sliced
1/4 c. soy sauce	1/2 small head celery cabbage,
1/4 c. Mirin*	sliced and blanched
1 t. salt	

Remove bones from chicken; cut into strips. Shell and clean shrimp. Cut watercress and green onion in 1½" lengths. In an electric skillet, combine broth, sugar, soy sauce, Mirin, and seasonings. Bring to a boil; put in chicken, shrimp, watercress, Chikuwa, Tofu, mushrooms and carrots in separate sections of the skillet. Do not stir. Lower heat for 5 more minutes; serve hot. Makes 8 servings.
*Mirin - sweet rice wine; **Chikuwa - broiled fish cake;
***Tofu - soy bean curd.

Adele Fevella
Haleakala NP

SPARERIBS

1½ or 2 lb. spareribs
1 c. vinegar
1 c. water
1 t. salt

3/4 c. brown sugar
1 T. flour
1 T. soy sauce

Cut spareribs in pieces and roll in mixture made from soy sauce, flour and salt. Let stand a few minutes. Fry in hot oil until brown, drain excess oil, leaving 2 tablespoons in pan with spareribs; add vinegar and water, sugar, and cook until tender.

Evelyn Ah Sing
Hawaii Volcanoes NP

OVEN-COOKED KALUA PORK

1 pork roast, any size
Ti leaves

Liquid smoke

Gash the roast all around and rub well with liquid smoke. Remove center vein from some Ti leaves; wrap pork well in leaves; tie with string. Cover with aluminum foil and place on a rack in a shallow baking pan. Roast at 350 degrees. Allow 40-45 minutes per lb. To serve, shred the cooked pork and sprinkle with Hawaiian (rock) salt. (This is usually cooked underground in Ti leaves.)

Marcie Ladd
City of Refuge NM

ASADO (Roast)

2 lb. 2" round steak
3 T. fat or oil
1 c. flour
Salt and pepper to taste

1 small onion, sliced
4 ripe tomatoes, cubed
2 green peppers, chopped
Chili, to taste

Pound flour into steak and season. Brown on both sides in very hot fat. Add onions, chili, green peppers and tomatoes, and 2½ cups hot water. Cover and bake about 2 hours until tender. Bake in a 350 degree oven.

Alma Hinkley
Whiskeytown NRA

BEEF STROGANOFF

4 lb. round steak, sliced 1/2"
2 c. sliced onions
1/4 lb. butter
1 lb. sliced mushrooms

1 c. bouillon
3 c. sour cream
Salt, pepper and mustard
  to taste

Pound steak very thin, then cut in pieces about 3" long and 1/2" wide. Cut onion slices in halves and cook in the butter until wilted. Add mushrooms and beef; cook 5 minutes. Pour in the bouillon (half of which may be dry white table wine) and cover. Simmer until meat is tender and liquid almost evaported. Stir in sour cream; season to taste; heat gently but do not boil. Serve with rice, green beans with almonds, French bread and herb butter and an elaborate dessert. Will serve 12 people.

Dorothy Ruse
Regional Office

NAVAJO BEANS

This recipe was started in Phoenix; progressed at Wupatki; and perfected at Carlsbad and Death Valley.

Take 1 lb. pinto beans. You may or may not soak them overnight. Cook until tender in water—no salt. When tender, remove from fire and let cool while you steam 1 pound of hamburger in 2 cups water. Add 2 large onions, finely chopped. Add 1 tablespoon instant minced garlic and salt. When hamburger loses pink color, add bean mixture. Add 1 small can tomato sauce and 1 can El Paso chili sauce. Set on back of stove and let simmer at low heat for 3 hours. Add 1 cup hot water when the water level goes down. Best with lots of juice to dip Navajo Fry Bread into. (For NAVAJO FRY BREAD — see Bread Section.)

Kathleen DeWitt
Death Valley NM

TACOS

2 lb. ground beef	2 t. minced chili peppers
1/2 t. oregano	2 t. chili powder
3/4 t. ground cumin	1 c. beef stock
3/4 c. minced onion	1½ c. tomato sauce
1 t. minced garlic	18 Taco shells
2 t. salt	Grated cheese, shredded lettuce,
1/4 t. pepper	diced tomatoes

Brown meat and drain off excess fat. Stir in spices, onion, garlic, and chili peppers. Saute for 5 minutes. Add stock and tomato sauce. Simmer very slowly for at least 3/4 hour or until sauce is thick and flavored well. Heat taco shells. Let each person fix his own, taking a shell and spooning in some of the meat mixture, then topping with some cheese, lettuce and tomatoes. Have commercial taco sauce available for those who desire it.

Georjean McKeeman
Tonto NM

TAMALE PIE

1½ lb. hamburger	2 c. water
1/4 c. oil	1½ t. salt
1/3 c. dried minced onions	1/4 t. pepper
3 T. dried green pepper	2-3 t. chili powder
3/4 c. water	1-2 T. Worcestershire sauce
1 can corn (12 oz.)	1 pkg. corn muffin mix (10 oz.)
2 cans tomato sauce (small)	1 pkg. grated cheese
1 can pitted olives, sliced (4 oz.)	

While frying hamburger in a 10 inch pan, soak onions and pepper in 3/4 cup water. Add to meat and cook 5 minutes. Add everything else except corn muffin mix and cook 15 minutes. Mix muffin mix and put on top of mixture. Top with cheese; cook 10 minutes, uncovered, and then 10 minutes covered. Serves 6.

Ginny Wagoner
Petrified Forest NP

SPECIAL ENCHILADAS

Make these either with taco filling, raw chopped onions, or whatever. Several make a meal in themselves (with refried beans).

8 corn tortillas
2 c. finely grated cheese (Jack, Longhorn, or Mexican)
1 c. finely chopped onion (optional)

1/2 head shredded lettuce
4 c. red chili sauce (see recipe elsewhere)
Enough lard to fill skillet 1/4" deep

Heat lard until hot but not smoking. Place tortilla in pan until soft and pliable, only a few seconds. Remove; put on plate and spread 1 or 2 tablespoons taco filling, onions, or whatever you like down the center of the tortilla. Fold each side over the center then turn the enchilada over. Several can be lined up side by side. Spoon enough sauce on to cover well. Sprinkle cheese on top. Place under broiler (or in oven) until cheese melts. Garnish with plenty of lettuce and onion.

Ed and Sue Jahns
Regional Office

RED DEVIL FRANKS

1 lb. franks
4 T. butter
1 c. finely chopped onion
2 cloves minced garlic
1½ t. sugar

1/2 t. salt
1/8 t. pepper
1½ T. Worcestershire sauce
1½ T. prepared mustard
1/2 c. chili sauce

Cook onion and garlic in fat over low heat until onion is tender—about 10 minutes. Stir frequently so as not to brown. Add all other ingredients. Continue heating until flavors are well blended—about 5 minutes. Split franks lengthwise; arrange split-side up in shallow pan. Spoon sauce over franks and heat under broiler. Serve piping hot on buns, piling on extra sauce. Sauce may be prepared in advance and kept in refrigerator until needed.

Elaine Hounsell
Lake Mead NRA

SPANISH RICE

1 lb. ground beef OR 1 lb. diced wieners
1/2 c. chopped onions
1/3 c. chopped green pepper
1 large clove garlic, minced OR 1/2 t. garlic powder

1 can condensed tomato soup (10¾ oz.)
1 c. water
1/2 c. rice
2 t. Worcestershire sauce
Dash of black pepper
1/2 t. salt

In skillet, brown meat, onion, green pepper and garlic until vegetables are tender. Pour off fat, add remaining ingredients. Cover; bring to a boil. Cook over low heat until rice is tender and liquid is absorbed, or about 15 minutes. Serve with carrots and celery sticks, corn bread and iced tea for a complete meal.

Chris McKinney
Grand Canyon NP

CARNE ASADA (Portuguese Pot Roast)

4 lb. rolled beef (round or
   rump) in 1 piece
2 c. red wine
Juice of ½ lemon
6 T. olive oil
2 cloves garlic, chopped
1 t. salt
1/2 t. freshly ground pepper

2 bay leaves
2 cloves
1 rounded T. flour
Garnish: fried potatoes
           asparagus tips
           halved hard cooked eggs
Paprika

Marinate beef overnight in red wine, lemon juice and 2 tablespoons olive oil, flavored with garlic, salt, paprika, freshly ground black pepper, bay leaves and cloves. Drain, reserving juices; brown meat in heatproof casserole in the remaining olive oil. Add marinade juices. Cover casserole; cook in 325 degree oven for 2½ hours. Uncover; baste meat with pan juices and continue to cook until meat is tender—about 1/2 hour. To serve: Remove beef to a heated serving dish and keep warm. Thicken pan juices with flour; correct seasoning and strain. Arrange fried potatoes, asparagus tips and eggs around carved meat by color. Pour a little sauce over meat and asparagus tips; serve remaining sauce separately. Serves 6.

Virginia Duckett
Regional Office

TERIYAKI STEAK

3 lb. beef
1/2 c. soy sauce
3 T. sugar
2 T. sherry (cooking)

1 clove garlic, crushed
1 small piece of ginger-root,
   crushed OR 1/2 t. powdered
   ginger

Slice meat 3/8" thick, across the grain if possible. Combine remaining ingredients and soak meat in this sauce for 30 minutes. Drain. Place on rack, broil 2 to 3 " from heat for 5-10 minutes, or until brown. Turn and brown on other side. Serve immediately with rice and vegetables. Makes 6 servings.
NOTE: For "pupus" (Hawaiian term for cocktail appetizers), Teriyaki Steak is served as meat on stick. Slice meat in very thin 1" strips; thread on bamboo sticks or small skewers; soak in sauce, and then broil. Use Kikkomann Shoyu (Soy) Sauce!). Suggested menu: Teriyaki steak, rice, buttered mixed vegetables, salad and a light dessert.

Clara Shimoda
City of Refuge NHP

INDONESIAN PORK CHOPS

6 large loin pork chops (1")
Salt and pepper
1 can (1 lb. 13 oz.) sliced peaches
2 T. cider vinegar
1 T. brown sugar
1 T. minced onion
1 T. soy sauce

1/4 T. ground ginger
1/2 t. salt
1/8 t. dry mustard
1/4 t. ground pepper
1/8 t. garlic powder
1 large green pepper

INDONESIAN PORK CHOPS (Continued)

Trim excess fat; rub heated skillet with fat. Season chops with salt and pepper, brown in hot skillet. Drain off all but 2 tablespoons of fat. Drain peach slices, reserving all syrup. Combine syrup, vinegar, brown sugar, onion and seasonings. Pour over chops; cover; simmer 40 minutes. Cut green pepper into diamond shapes. Add pepper and peach slices to chops; cover, simmer 5 minutes. Serve at once with buttered rice. Serves 6.

Dorothy Ruse
Regional Office

STIFADO (Greek Beef Stew)

3 lb. beef stew meat, cut into 2" cubes	2 cloves garlic, minced
Salt and pepper	1 bay leaf
1/2 c. butter or margarine	1 small cinnamon stick
2 cans (1 lb. ea.) onions, drained	1/2 t. whole cloves
1 can (6 oz.) tomato paste	1/2 t. ground cumin
1/3 c. dry red wine	3 T. raisins or currants
1 T. brown sugar	3 T. red wine vinegar

Season meat with salt and pepper. Melt butter in Dutch oven, add meat and stir to coat with butter—do not brown. Add onions. Mix tomato paste, wine, vinegar, sugar and garlic; pour over meat and onions. Add remaining ingredients; cover and simmer about 3 hours, or until meat is very tender. Makes 6 servings. Delicious served with rice, crisp green salad and sourdough French bread. This stew can be made ahead—earlier in the day or day before and reheated before serving.

Mary Alice Replogle
Regional Office

CURRIED EGGS

2/3 c. chopped onion	2 t. curry powder, to taste
1/4 c. butter or margarine	1/2 t. ginger
1/4 c. flour	1/4 t. celery seed
1/2 t. salt	1/4 t. pepper
1½ c. chicken broth	1 t. grated lemon rind
1/2 c. milk	8 hard-cooked eggs (hot)
	Hot cooked rice

Cook onion in butter until tender. Add flour and salt; stir until well blended and bubbly. Add all remaining ingredients except the eggs and rice. Cook and stir until smooth and thickened. Place hot rice on serving dish. Cut eggs in halves lengthwise and arrange on rice. Pour curry sauce over all. Serve with desired accompaniments, such as chutney, pickles, nuts, coconut, sliced bananas or tomatoes, etc. Makes 4 servings. (Use for brunch or dinner.)

Mary Alice Replogle
Regional Office

TAMALES DE ELOTE (Green Corn Tamales)

Utensils:

Cutting board
Butcher knife
1 large flat pan
Large mixing bowl
Meat grinder with fine blade
Large deep Dutch oven OR
   2 gal. covered pan
Mixing spoon
Rubber scraper

Ingredients:

2 doz. ears fairly mature white-
   kernel corn and husks
1 lb. fresh pork lard
2 t. baking powder
4 T. salt
2 T. sugar
3-4 lb. cheese, grated (Jack or
   Longhorn)
2-3 doz. fresh green chili peppers
   or 4-6 cans Ortega

Cut off 2-3" of bottom of corn ears. Husk carefully; discard outer dirty husks. Use largest, most tender inner husks to wrap tamales. Soak in sink with warm water and add 1/4 cup vinegar and a handful of baking soda. Set aside the smallest clean husks to line bottom of pan. Trim husks for wrapping so that lower ends will not curl upwards. Wash husked ears; remove all silk. Cut corn and put through fine-blade of grinder (catch all the juice, you will need it) or put through the blender. The proper consistency should be like "masa Harina" (like an elastic dough with a grainy texture). To this "masa" add the 1 lb. lard, 2 teaspoons baking powder and 4 tablespoons salt, 2 tablespoons sugar and all the grated cheese. Mix thoroughly; dough must be creamy and light. Rinse and dry husks that have soaked. Spread a spoonful (large) on lower half of husk to within 1" of bottom, leaving 2" free on one side. On it place 3-6 narrow strips of chili (more if you like it hotter). Roll husk lengthwise, then fold over end. Cover the bottom of a steaming pan with small inner husks; pour 2-3 cups warm water in with them. Do not come above level of husks. Cover this layer with a few flat husks to make a level surface, or place a piece of foil over the husks. Stand tamales on folded-over end (open end up), arranging them in circles until pan is full but not tightly crowded. Cover with a damp dishtowel; put on lid. Steam for 45 minutes. Uncover and allow to cool a little before removing tamales with tongs. They may be eaten immediately or reheated by steaming. They freeze well, if you have any left! Two dozen ears will make 70 green corn tamales. You will need assistance from 4 people to do all the work, but it is worth it! These may be made "sweet" by adding fruit, such as apricots with cinnamon or canned pineapple with ginger.

Artie Julander
Estella Hernandez
Phyllis Broyles
Organ Pipe Cactus NM

TURKEY HAWAIIAN

1/2 c. chopped onion
2 T. butter or margarine
1 pkg. (10 oz.) frozen peas,
   thawed
1½ c. bias sliced celery
1 can (3 oz.) sliced mushrooms,
   drained
1 can (5 oz.) water chestnuts,
   drained and sliced

1 can condensed chicken broth
3/4 c. water
3 T. soy sauce
1 can (8¾ oz.) pineapple chunks
1/4 c. cornstarch
1/4 c. water
3 c. diced cooked turkey

In 3-quart saucepan, cook onion in butter or margarine until tender but not brown. Stir in peas, celery, mushrooms, chicken broth, the 3/4 cup water and soy sauce. Drain pineapple, reserving liquid. Add syrup to saucepan; bring to boiling; cover and simmer for 5 minutes. Stir in 1/4 cup water with cornstarch; add to saucepan. Cook and stir until thickened and bubbly. Add turkey, pineapple and chestnuts; heat through. Serve hot over cooked rice. Pass additional soy sauce. 8 servings, 352 calories per serving.

Karla and Peter Allen
Lake Mead NRA

FOLLOWING PIONEER TRAILS THE NATCHEZ TRACE NATIONAL PARKWAY RUNS DIAGONALLY ACROSS TENNESSEE, ALABAMA AND MISSISSIPPI. (NPS photo by M. Woodbridge Williams).

Casseroles

OUR GREAT PRESIDENTS IMMORTALIZED IN STONE AT MOUNT RUSHMORE NATIONAL MEMORIAL, SOUTH DAKOTA. (NPS photo by Jack Boucher)

CATHY'S LASAGNE

Prepare a meat sauce as below. Layer the meat sauce with the cooked, drained, and cooled lasagne noodles first, then meat sauce, then cottage cheese mixture, then Jack cheese; repeat. Bake at 325-350 degrees for 45 minutes. Serves 6-8.

Meat Sauce: Brown 1 pound of ground beef with 1/4 lb. ground pork (latter is optional). Chop 1 onion and press 1 clove garlic; these can be either browned before the meat or cooked with it. When all is brown, add 1 large can tomatoes, a small can of mushroom bits (this also is optional), and 1/4 tsp. to 1/2 tsp. of tarragon, basil, oregano, rosemary or mixed Italian herbs. Add salt and pepper and approximately 1 Tbsp. sugar. Simmer all this for as long as you can—1/2 hour minimum, but the longer, the better—until it is a thick consistency. Add some red wine if you have it and like it.

Cottage Cheese Mixture: Cottage cheese is easier to obtain, but if Ricotta cheese is "your thing" then use that. Mix 3 cups of cheese with 3 slightly beaten eggs; add 1/2 cup Parmesan cheese with 1/4 cup parsley, chopped and salt and pepper to taste.

Marion Durham
Walnut Canyon NM

TAMALE PIE

1½ lb. ground beef	1 pkg. (10 oz.) frozen corn
1 onion, chopped	1 c. pitted black olives
1 clove garlic, minced or mashed	1 c. yellow corn meal
1/2 c. chopped green pepper	1 t. salt
1 t. seasoned salt	2½ c. water
1 pkg. chili seasoning mix	1 jar (4 oz.) pimiento, drained
1 can (1 lb.) tomatoes	1 c. shredded Cheddar cheese

Brown beef in skillet, breaking up meat with a fork. Add onion, garlic, green pepper, seasoned salt, chili mix and undrained tomatoes; simmer about 5 minutes. Add frozen corn and olives; mix well and pour into shallow baking dish. Combine corn meal, salt and water, and cook, stirring until thick. Stir in pimiento. Spread over beef mixture, and bake in 350 degree oven about 40 minutes. Sprinkle with cheese and bake 5 minutes longer. Makes 6 servings.

(This dish can be prepared ahead and refrigerated or frozen. Bake for 30 minutes, then allow to cool before refrigerating or freezing. When serving, allow dish to warm up to room temperature, bake about 20 minutes at 350 degrees, sprinkle with cheese and bake 5 minutes longer.)

Ron and Mary Alice Replogle
Regional Office

HAMBURGER CASSEROLE

1 lb. hamburger
2 to 4 carrots (depending on
   size)
4 medium potatoes
Dash of pepper
1 medium onion

1 can cream of mushroom soup
   or cream of chicken soup
1 c. milk
1 t. salt
Dash of powdered garlic (optional)

Shred carrots and potatoes with medium shredder. Dice onion. Mix all ingredients together in large bowl, except soup and milk. Make into patties and brown on both sides in a little shortening. Place browned patties in casserole dish and cover with soup and milk mixture. Bake 45 minutes to one hour in a 350 degree oven (moderate).

Genevieve Dalley
Lake Mead NRA

PORK AND DRESSING CASSEROLE

2 lb. cubed pork shoulder
   (cut into 1" cubes and trim
   off fat)
2 T. shortening

1 c. boiling water
4 slices bacon, cut into 1" pieces
1 c. chopped onion
1 c. chopped celery

Brown pork shoulder in shortening, add water, cover and cook 45 minutes. Fry bacon until brown. Add onion and celery and cook until tender. Mix together the following:

6 c. day-old bread cubes
1 t. salt
2 or 3 t. poultry seasoning

1/2 t. baking powder
1/8 t. black pepper
8 oz. can mushrooms (drain
   and reserve liquid)

Combine pork, celery, onion and bacon and add to seasoned bread cubes and place in greased casserole, 13x9". Mix 3 cups liquid (stock from pork, mushrooms, and milk) with 2 beaten eggs. Pour over bread and meat mixture. Top with chopped parsley and paprika. Bake at 300 degrees for 1 hour and 10 minutes. Serves 8 to 10.

Al and Eleanor Lense
Regional Office

BUSY DAY CASSEROLE

Brown 1 lb. hamburger with 1 chopped onion. Add salt and pepper to taste, and 1/2 teaspoon chili. Cook well and add 1 can mushroom soup and 1 can tomato sauce. Simmer 5 minutes. Pour over cooked macaroni, sprinkle with cracker crumbs and grated cheese. Bake at 350 degrees for 10 minutes or until bubbly.

Olina Stout
Petrified Forest NP

GREEN CHILI CASEROLE

Mix together:

1 can cream of mushroom soup	1 can chopped green chili
1/2 can milk	1 can corned beef

Heat corn tortillas in hot grease and place enough to cover bottom of 8" casserole. Pour about 1/3 of the above mixture over tortillas; top with grated cheese; cover with more tortillas. Repeat layering until mixture is used. Bake about 400 degrees for 30 minutes. Usually takes about 6-9 tortillas and some tortilla chips. Grate about 1 pound of cheese.

Marquita McCollough
Chiricahua NM

MEXICAN CASSEROLE

6 tortillas	1 can Ortega chiles
1 lb. Jack cheese	1 c. (pkg.) sour cream
1 can cream of mushroom soup	

Break tortillas into small pieces and crisp fry in butter. Break cheese into small pieces. Add sour cream, chiles in pieces in layers. Pour soup over all. Bake at 350 degrees for 30 to 45 minutes.

Chuck and Irene Adams
Regional Office

HIDE-THE-LIVER CASSEROLE

I have found if you soak liver in some milk for an hour or so it will remove much of the toughness and also some of the taste most people don't like. This recipe calls for removing the membrane—presumably your butcher does it before he sells it; if not, then do as the recipe says.

Mix 1/4 cup flour, salt and pepper, and roll slices of liver in this. (I slice mine about 1/2" wide and as long as the liver is wide). Brown liver in hot shortening; put to one side and brown some chopped onions in remaining fat (amount of onions depends on your taste—I use about 1 cup). Put liver and onions in a pretty casserole—1 quart size. Add 1/4 cup diced celery, and 1 cup tomatoes (used stewed or plain); season with salt and pepper. Bake, covered, at 350 degrees for 45 minutes.

Marion Durham
Walnut Canyon NM

CHICKEN CASSEROLE

Put 1 cup raw rice in bottom of buttered casserole. Spread 1 package of dry Lipton's onion soup mix on rice. Spread 1/2 can mushroom soup and 1/2 can chicken broth over rice and soup mix. Lay pieces of chicken (preferably chicken breasts) on top and pour remaining soup and broth over top. Cook 2 hours, covered, at 325 degrees.

Bobbie Brudenell
Yosemite NP

GREEN BEAN CASSEROLE

1 can green beans
1 can mushroom soup
1 small can water chestnuts,
   sliced thin
Butter

Parmesan cheese
Chopped onion
Worcestershire sauce
Slivered almonds

Saute onions in butter until golden. Add soup and dash of Worcestershire sauce. (For each can of beans, use a can of soup, increase the recipe accordingly.) Butter a shallow baking dish and layer as follows: beans, chestnuts, sauce, Parmesan. Top with almonds. Bake 35-45 minutes in a 350 degree oven. May be made a day ahead and baked later.

Helen Robinson
Petrified Forest NP

SPINACH AND ZUCCHINI CASSEROLE

2 lb. chopped frozen spinach
   (cook separately and drain)
2 lb. zucchini (chop fine and
   cook separately and drain)
1 c. grated cheese
6 finely ground crackers or
   1 c. corn flakes, crushed

Pinch of garlic salt
1 small onion, chopped
2 cans B&B mushrooms or
   1 c. fresh mushrooms
3 beaten eggs
Dash of pepper

Fry onion in 2 tablespoons olive oil; add garlic salt, salt and pepper. Cook spinach and zucchini separately until tender, drain thoroughly. Make a layer of spinach in well-buttered casserole; sprinkle mushrooms over; a layer of zucchini next. Continue until all used. Pour eggs over gently. Top with cheese and crumbs. Cover and bake in a medium oven for 40 to 50 minutes, until eggs are set. (Insert knife, must come out clean.) Serve very hot.

Peggy Rolandson
San Francisco Office

HERBED CHICKEN CASSEROLE

3 lg. chicken breasts, cut in
   halves (or 1 whole chicken,
   cut up)

Salt and pepper
1/4 c. butter

Season chicken and brown slowly. Arrange "skin" side up in baking dish.

1 can cream of chicken soup
1 (5 oz.) can water chestnuts,
   drained and sliced

1 (3 oz.) can broiled mushrooms
3/4 c. sauterne wine

Add to chicken drippings, stir until smooth; add sauterne plus 2 tablespoons chopped green peppers and 1/4 tsp. thyme. Heat to boiling and pour over chicken; cover and bake 25 minutes in a 350 degree oven. Remove cover and bake 25 more minutes or until tender. Serve with rice.

David and Cora Hughes
Regional Office

BROCCOLI-CHEESE CASSEROLE

2 pkg. frozen chopped broccoli (prepare as directed), drained

Saute:

6 T. butter   1/4 c. chopped onion
2 T. flour   1/4 c. water

Combine:

8 oz. jar Cheese Whiz   2 eggs, beaten

Mix with broccoli and onions; place in greased casserole, cover top with buttered cracker crumbs. Bake at 325 degrees for 30 minutes, or until center is set.

Avis Franklin
Lehman Caves NM

ENCHILADA CASSEROLE

1 lb. hamburger   1 can chopped green chiles
1/2 lb. grated Longhorn cheese   1/2 c. milk
1 can cream of mushroom soup   1 pkg. corn tortillas
1 can enchilada   1 can enchilada sauce

Brown hamburger and season to taste. Grate cheese. Combine the soup, sauce, chili and milk; mix well. Fry tortillas in skillet until crisp; drain well. Alternate the soup mixture, meat, cheese, and tortillas until all are used. Bake at 350 degrees for 30 minutes or until cheese is melted.

Bertha Wharton
Saguaro NM

CHICKEN ENCHILADA CASSEROLE

1 (2-3 lb.) chicken, cooked   1 lb. grated Longhorn cheese
   and boned   1 c. chicken broth
1 med. onion, chopped   1 small can chopped green
Shortening to saute   chiles
1 can cream of chicken soup   1 pkg. corn tortillas
1 can cream of mushroom soup

Cook and bone chicken. Saute onion in shortening. Add soups, chicken broth and green chiles. Add pieces of chicken and heat well. Place a layer of broken or cut-up tortillas in a flat greased baking dish, then a layer of sauce and cheese. Repeat until all is used. A 13x9x2" pan will take 2 layers. Top with grated cheese. Bake at 350 degrees for 30 minutes. However, flavors blend better if you bake at 300 degrees for 1 hour. Substitute: 1 lb. ground beef for chicken, 1 minced garlic and 1 can celery soup for mushroom and 1/2 soup can of water for broth if desired.

Marian Evans
Petrified Forest NP

CHICKEN WITH APRICOTS AND AVOCADO

6 large whole chicken breasts,
   split, boned and skinned
Salt and pepper
1/4 t. nutmeg
4 T. butter
3 green onions, thinly sliced
   (include some of the tops)

1/4 c. dry Vermouth
1 c. whipping cream
12 ripe apricots, halved
   and pitted
2 T. minced parsley
1 large ripe avocado
1 T. lemon juice

Sprinkle chicken lightly with salt and pepper and nutmeg. Melt butter in a wide frying pan, over medium high heat, and brown chicken on all sides. As the breasts are browned, remove them from pan. While the last breasts are browning, stir the onions into the pan. Return all the chicken to the pan; pour in the Vermouth (at this point you can chill chicken in pan several hours). Cover and simmer until breasts are white in the center. The chicken will take 8 to 10 minutes to cook. (If chilled, allow 1 or 2 additional minutes to cook.) Lift chicken from pan, draining, and keep warm on a serving platter. Add cream to frying pan; cook on highest heat, stirring and scraping pan until liquid is reduced to about half and thickens. Add apricots and parsley; cook just to warm fruit, turning fruit in sauce. Spoon apricots around chicken and pour sauce over all. Peel and slice avocado, drizzling lightly with lemon juice. Arrange on platter. Serves 6-8.

Murph and Donna Kolipinski
Regional Office

DANNENFELZER POTATOES

Slice 4 white rose potatoes. Lightly grease or "Pam spray" a baking pan. Alternate layers of potatoes with salt and pepper, green onions (or instant white onions and parsley), and Parmesan cheese. On the last layer, omit the cheese. Heat 1-2 cans of beef consomme until boiling; pour over the potato layers to just cover. Top with last layer of Parmesan. Bake in 400 degree oven until consomme boils. Reduce heat to 350 degrees and continue baking for 1 hour, or until tender. Will serve 4 (but probably not much for seconds).

Marion Durham
Walnut Canyon

GREEN CHILI RICE

1 c. uncooked rice
1 c. sour cream

1/2 lb. cubed Cheddar cheese
1 small can green chili peppers,
   chopped

Cook and cool rice. Mix rice and sour cream. Spread half of mixture in buttered casserole. Spread cubed cheese and chilis on rice. Cover with remaining sour cream mixture. Bake at 350 degrees 30-40 minutes. Goes good with chicken, any barbecued meat, or just corn bread and salad.

Betty Berrett
Petrified Forest NP

CHILI RELLENO CASSEROLE

2 or 3 cans sliced, seeded
  green chiles
1 lb. Monterey Jack cheese,
  thickly sliced

4 eggs, separated
1/2 t. salt
3 T. flour
1/2 c. evaporated milk

Place alternate layers of cheese and chiles in casserole. Beat egg whites until stiff. Beat yolks and add salt, flour and milk. Fold in whites. Pour over chiles and cheese. Bake 1 hour at 325 degrees. If desired, you may use sauce of:

1 diced onion
1 clove garlic, minced

2 c. tomato sauce
2 t. oregano
Salt and pepper to taste

Half of the sauce can be poured over the Rellenos and baked a few minutes more or Rellenos may be served without sauce.

Alice Dexter
Tumacacori NM

ARTICHOKE SQUARES

2 jars marinated artichoke
  hearts (6 oz. each)
1 small onion, chopped finely
1 clove garlic, minced or mashed
4 eggs
1/4 c. fine dry bread crumbs
1/4 t. salt

1/8 t. pepper
1/8 t. oregano
1/8 t. liquid hot pepper seasoning
1/2 lb. sharp Cheddar cheese,
  shredded
2 T. minced parsley

Drain marinade from 1 jar of the artichokes into a frying pan. Drain the other jar well. Chop all the artichokes and set aside. Put onions and garlic in frying pan and saute until limp.

Beat eggs with fork. Add crumbs, salt, pepper, oregano and hot pepper seasoning. Stir in cheese, parsley, artichokes and onion mixture. Turn into a greased 7x11" pan. Bake at 325 degrees for about 30 minutes. Let cool in pan. Cut into 1" squares. Serve hot or cold. Makes about 6 or 7 dozen.

Harry and Nancy Sloat
Regional Office

SOLE — CRAB CASSEROLE

1 lb. sole, barely browned
  in toast crumbs
1 c. crabmeat

1 recipe white sauce
Dash of Parmesan cheese

Arrange crabmeat in casserole; pour sauce over. Gently place sole on top. Bake in 350 degree oven for 45 minutes. Serve with white wine. Sprinkle top with Parmesan cheese. Serves 6.

John and Janet Sage
Regional Office

SPAM AND SHRIMP CASSEROLE

1/2 c. uncooked rice
1/2 c. Spam, cubed
1/2 lb. uncooked shrimp
1 can beef consomme

1 medium clove garlic
1½ t. curry powder
1/4 c. salad oil
Chopped olives (optional)

Combine all ingredients and bake, uncovered, in 350 degree oven until moisture is absorbed—about 45 minutes to 1 hour.

Bill and Barry Fink
Tuzigoot NM

CORNED BEEF AND CAULIFLOWER CASSEROLE
(Excellent for brunch or supper — men love this!)

1 large head cauliflower,
   separated into flowerettes,
   salted slightly

1 can corned beef
1 recipe cream sauce with cheese
   (recipe below)

Mix cauliflower and corned beef. Pour cheese sauce over all, top with crumbs. Bake at 300 degrees for 1½ to 2 hours.

Cream Sauce with Cheese:

3 T. butter, melted
3 T. flour

1 c. milk
1 c. or more Cheddar cheese

Stir butter and flour into paste, blend milk in and cook until thick. Add cheese and stir until melted.

John and Janet Sage
Regional Office

SHRIMP CASSEROLE HARPIN

2 lb. large raw or 1½ lb.
   small shrimp
1 T. fresh lemon juice
3 T. salad oil
3/4 c. raw regular or processed
   rice (or 1 1/3 c. pre-cooked
   rice)
2 T. butter
1/4 c. minced green pepper
1/4 c. minced onion

1/8 t. pepper
1 t. salt
1/8 t. mace
Dash of cayenne pepper
1 can undiluted condensed
   tomato soup
1 c. heavy cream
1/2 c. sherry
1/2 c. slivered almonds
Paprika

Early in day: Shell, devein, then cook shrimp in boiling water (salted) 5 minutes; drain. Place in a 2-qt. casserole; sprinkle with lemon juice and oil. Meanwhile, cook rice; drain. Refrigerate all. One hour, 10 minutes before serving: Heat oven to 350 degrees. In butter in skillet, saute green pepper and onion for 5 minutes. Add to shrimp, along with rice, salt and rest of ingredients except 1/4 cup almonds and paprika. Top with reserved almonds; sprinkle with paprika. Bake, uncovered, 55 minutes, or until bubbly. Makes 6 to 8 servings.

John and Bobbie Davis
Redwood NP

CHICKEN ENCHILADA CASSEROLE

1 canned chicken, boned
2 cans cream of chicken soup
2 cans green chili salsa

1 pkg. medium size flour
   tortillas
2 c. grated Longhorn cheese

Bone chicken and drain well. Combine green chili salsa and cream of chicken soup and set aside. Tear tortillas into small pieces. In large baking dish, place in layers: tortillas, chicken, cheese and cover with chili soup mixture. Make about 3 layers this way, finally topping with layer of cheese. Bake at 350 degrees for 40 minutes.

Donna J. Byrne
Montezuma Castle NM

INSIDE—OUT RAVIOLI

1 lb. ground beef
1 chopped onion
1 clove garlic
1 can tomato sauce
1 can tomato paste
1 pkg. shell macaroni

1 can Chef-Boy-Ar-Dee's spaghetti
   sauce
1 pkg. frozen chopped spinach
1 c. grated cheese (Cheddar)
2 beaten eggs
2 slices soft bread (crumbs)

Cook spinach and drain WELL reserving liquid to make 1 cup. Brown meat, onion, garlic and drain fat. Add tomato sauce, paste and spaghetti sauce and spinach juice. Cover and simmer.

Cook macaroni, drain well. Mix spinach and macaroni and cheese. Toss in bread crumbs and beaten eggs. Put in greased 9x13" pan. Pour sauce over and bake at 350 degrees for 30 to 40 minutes.

Harry and Nancy Sloat
Regional Office

CHILI RELLENOS CASSEROLE

1 lb. ground beef
1/2 c. chopped onion
1/2 t. salt
1/4 t. pepper
2 (4 oz.) cans green chiles, cut
   in halves crosswise and
   seeded
1½ c. shredded sharp Cheddar cheese

1½ c. milk
1/4 c. flour
1/2 t. salt
Dash of pepper
4 beaten eggs
Several dashes bottled hot
   pepper sauce

In skillet, brown beef and onion; drain off fat. Sprinkle meat with the first 1/2 tsp. salt and the 1/4 tsp. pepper. Place half the chiles in 10x6x1½" baking dish; sprinkle with cheese; top with meat mixture. Arrange remaining chiles over meat. Combine remaining ingredients; beat until smooth. Pour over meat-chili mixture. Bake in moderate oven, 350 degrees, 45 to 50 minutes, or until knife inserted just off-center, comes out clean. Let cool 5 minutes; cut in squares to serve.

Elaine Hounsell
Lake Mead NRA

NOODLE CASSEROLE ½ the recipe is enough
~~too much liquid~~

1 pkg. (12 oz.) noodles, cooked
1 large carton cottage cheese
1 pt. sour cream
Salt and pepper
1 or 2 bunches green onions
  (use tops)

Lots of parsley
1 can bouillon
Dash Tabasco and Worcestershire
  sauces
Parmesan cheese

Combine all ingredients and sprinkle Parmesan cheese on top. Bake in a 350 degree oven for 30 to 40 minutes, until done. This casserole may be made up the day before and refrigerated.

Anne and Ron Walker
Director, NPS

COMPANY CASSEROLE

1 lb. fresh mushrooms, sliced
1 sm. onion, chopped
1/2 lb. each pork and veal
  round, sliced
4 T. butter
1/2 c. each - white and wild rice

4 T. soy sauce
2 c. celery, cut on bias
1 can mushroom soup
1/2 can water and 1/2 can milk
  (use soup can)

Saute mushrooms, onions and meat in butter until brown. Put mixture in large casserole. Wash wild rice and add both rices to mixture. Add soy sauce, celery, soup and liquids. Put in refrigerator for 24 hours. Bake at 325 degrees for 1¾ hours, covered.

Chuck and Irene Adams
Regional Office

ARROZ CON JOCOQUI (Rice and Sour Cream Casserole)

3/4 lb. Jack cheese
3 c. commercial sour cream
3 c. cooked rice, salted

8 oz. can green chiles, peeled
  and chopped
1/2 c. Cheddar cheese, grated

Cut Jack cheese into strips. Thoroughly mix sour cream with chiles. (Add 1/2 teaspoon salt if cream is not salted.) Layer rice, sour cream mixture and cheese strips in that order in a well-greased casserole, ending with rice on top. Last five minutes of baking, sprinkle with grated cheese. Bake at 350 degrees for 30 minutes. Yields 6-8 servings.

Chris McAfee
Channel Islands NM

CREAMED CARROTS CASSEROLE

1/2 stick butter
1 onion, minced
2 T. flour
1 t. salt
1/4 t. seasoned pepper

2 c. milk
5 c. sliced cooked carrots,
  drained
5 slices American cheese
1 c. bread crumbs (optional)

Melt half of butter in saucepan. Add onion and mix until tender. Mix in flour, salt and pepper. Add milk, stirring constantly until thickened, set aside. Arrange cooked carrots in layers in buttered dish alternately with cheese and carrots. Melt remaining butter and add to bread crumbs; sprinkle on top of casserole; bake about 25 minutes at 350 degrees. Serves 8.

Bernice Butler
Regional Office

WILD RICE CASSEROLE

1 c. wild rice (or white and wild mixture)

Wash thoroughly in cold water and drain. Cover with boiling water 3 times, let stand 10 minutes each time; drain. (Or use slightly pre-cooked Uncle Ben's rice.)

1/3 lb. butter or margarine	1 or more c. celery, diced fine
1 medium onion, chopped	

Saute above in butter until soft with drained mushrooms, 1 cup milk heated with 3 or 4 bouillon cubes, salt and pepper to taste. Mix all together. Pour into a casserole and bake for 1½ hours in a 325 degree oven. If it seems a little dry, add more milk (maybe cream of mushroom soup).

John and Janet Sage
Regional Office

HALLET PEAK FROM DREAM LAKE IN ROCKY MOUNTAIN NATIONAL PARK, COLORADO. (NPS photo.)

CANOEING IS BECOMING AN INCREASINGLY POPULAR SPORT ON THE OZARK NATIONAL SCENIC RIVERWAYS IN SOUTHERN MISSOURI. (NPS photo).

AERIAL VIEW OF FORTRESS OF SAN FELIPE DEL MORRO AT THE SAN JUAN NATIONAL HISTORIC SITE, PUERTO RICO. (NPS photo).

Fish and Game

THE PEACEFUL TRANQUILITY OF THE APPALACHIANS ATTRACTS MANY VISITORS TO GREAT SMOKY MOUNTAINS NATIONAL PARK, TENNESSEE. (NPS photo).

SHRIMP SCAMPI

Sauce:

1 lb. butter	6 T. Sauterne
1/2 lb. margarine	1 T. Tabasco sauce
1 oz. garlic, chopped or	6 T. lemon juice
crushed (about 15 medium	1 c. chopped chives
cloves)	1 T. dry mustard
6 medium shallots, chopped	

Melt butter and margarine. Add all other ingredients and simmer for 10-15 minutes. Use this sauce for the following ways of fixing shrimp.

Broiler-Style Shrimp Scampi:

6 large raw shrimp (prawns) per sering

Split the shrimp down the back and de-vein but do not peel off shell. Place shrimp in a shallow pan with the tails pointing up. Pour sauce over shrimp and broil 4" from heat for about 8 minutes. Shrimp should be lightly browned—shells pink or meat white.

Casserole-style Shrimp Scampi:

2 to 2½ lb. large raw shrimp (prawns) for 4 people

Shell and de-vein shrimp. Place in a casserole dish and pour sauce over all. Sprinkle with bread crumbs or tear-up chunks of French bread, and tuck into sauce. Bake in 425 degree oven approximately 25 minutes or until shrimp are done. We serve this with parsleyed rice. Pass breath mints after coffee.

P.S. Any extra sauce keeps well in the refrigerator for a long time. Delicious for making garlic bread.

Marilyn Treabess
Regional Office

BAKED ABALONE

1 large abalone	1/2 - 1 c. water
Seasoned flour	1 T. shortening
1/2 can cream of celery soup	1 T. oil
Onion to taste, chopped	1/4 c. dry white wine (sherry)

Give abalone a couple of good whacks. Roll in seasoned flour. Brown on all sides in hot shortening and oil. Put in baking dish; add soup, diluted with water; add parsley and onion. Bake at 375 degrees for 1 hour. Last half hour, add wine. Test with fork before removing to make sure it is tender.

Shirley Mae Johnson
Regional Office

SALMON MUELE (Portuguese)

1 lg. onion, sliced
1/2 c. chopped parsley
1 tall can pink salmon
1 small can tomato sauce

4 oz. water
1/4 t. garlic salt
Salt and pepper, to taste

Fry onion and parsley in lightly greased pan till onions are tender. Add all of the ingredients and let simmer for 10 minutes. Serves 4.

Stella S. Lopes
Haleakala NP

BAKED CRAB

3 medium crabs
Heavy cream

2 T. butter and 1/2 t. dry
    mustard

For every 2 handfuls shredded crabmeat, add 1 handful soft bread crumbs (fine). Add a little garlic, pepper and salt, 1 tablespoon cream for each handful of crab. Mix well. Sprinkle dry crumbs and butter over top. Bake in cleaned crab shells in pan with a little hot water in bottom of pan. Bake for 20-30 minutes at 350 degrees. Serve with salad and French bread or French fries.

Dorothea Miehle
Regional Office

SAUCY SHRIMP THERMIDOR

1/2 c. chopped onion
1/4 c. chopped green pepper
1/4 c. butter
2 cans frozen potato soup

1 large can evaporated milk
3" of a 2-pound loaf Velveeta cheese
4 t. lemon juice
1½ to 2 lb. shrimp, cooked

Saute onion and green pepper in butter. Add soup and evaporated milk. Heat slowly, stirring constantly until blended. Bring just to a boil. Cube cheese and add, stirring to melt. Add lemon juice and shrimp. Heat through. Serve in pastry shells or over rice.

Marilyn Treabess
Regional Office

Leftover Salmon
oyster in Jar

ESCALLOPED FISH FLAKES AND OYSTERS

2 c. fish flakes (tuna,
    salmon, cod, etc.)
2 c. canned or fresh oysters

2 c. white sauce
1 c. bread crumbs

Butter a shallow baking dish. Arrange all ingredients (except crumbs) in alternate layers until all is used. Top with crumbs. Bake in a 350 degree oven for 30-35 minutes. Serve hot. (Recipe from NEEDLECRAFT magazine, March 1917.)

Anonymous
Regional Office

ABALONE CABRILLO AND SECRET TARTAR SAUCE

With abalone becoming scarce to find, and the commercial cost almost prohibitive, now is the time to release a method of preparation by which even the most novice of cooks can achieve tremendous success.

PREPARATION: After removal from the shell, clean abalone by carefully cutting off all excess trimmings, leaving only "button" of firm meat. Be sure to trim off tough outside tissue between foot and stem. Remove 1/8" slice at end of foot, since being thrifty will only result in a very tough, unpalatable steak. Cut into steaks approximately 3/8" wide. To pound abalone, use only a notched wooden mallet. Begin at center of steak and work outward. Do both sides, being careful not to tear steak. Pound well.

FRYING STEAK: In order to obtain a beautiful golden tender steak, the following procedure is recommended: Using rolling pin or bottle, crush an applicable amount of Hi-Ho, Ritz, or similar crackers to crumbs. Beat one egg per abalone into dish. Dip abalone steak into egg, then crumbs, coating completely. Use large skillet; heat 1/4" shortening or oil to approx. 400 degrees. This can be checked by flicking drops of water into grease, which should cause a popping noise. When pan is ready, add steaks. The secret for tender steaks is not to overcook; 15-20 seconds on each side is all that is needed. If you are cooking a large amount, the steaks can be placed on paper towels and placed in a warm oven (use oven-proof dish) until all steaks are fried.

Tartar Sauce:

1 c. Best Foods mayonnaise	3 green onions, chopped
1/2 med. dill pickle, minced	2 T. lemon juice (1 lg. one)
1 t. dill pickle juice	Dash of Worcestershire sauce

Mix all into bowl; add or subtract ingredients for individual taste. Chill at least one hour before serving on fish.

Hoyt Rath
Petrified Forest NP

FISHERMAN STEW

2 lb. any firm fish	2 T. salt
1½ c. sliced celery	1/2 T. chili powder or a
1/2 c. chopped onion	few drops of Tabasco sauce
1 clove garlic, minced	1/4 T. pepper
1 can (1 lb. 12 oz.) tomatoes	Cubed potatoes and carrots
1/4 c. margarine	1½ c. boiling water
1 can (8 oz.) tomato sauce	

Cut fish into 1-inch chunks. Cook celery, onion and garlic in butter or margarine in a large heavy pan just until tender. Add tomatoes, potatoes, carrots, tomato sauce, seasonings and water. Bring to a boil, cover, and simmer for 40 or 50 minutes, or until vegetables start to get tender. Add fish, cover and cook slowly for 10 minutes or until fish flakes easily when tested with a fork.

Marilyn Treabess
Regional Office

FISH (FOR BOILING)

2 qt. water (cold)
2/3 c. cider vinegar
2 med. onions, minced
2 med. carrots, scraped and
  sliced
8 whole peppercorns, gently
  bruised
2½ t. salt

A herb bouquet made of:
        4 sprigs green celery tops
        6 sprigs fresh parsley
        1 large or 2 med. bay leaves
        1 sprig thyme or its
          equivalent of dry thyme
          (1/4 t.)

Bring these ingredients to a boil; then reduce flame and allow mixture to simmer 30 minutes. Salmon, trout, or any large fish can be used.

Dorothea Miehle
Regional Office

DUCKLING HAWAIIAN

2 ducklings (4-5 lb.)
1 onion, chopped
1 can (8 oz.) water chestnuts,
  chopped
3/4 c. celery
1/4 c. butter or margarine
4 c. bread cubes, toasted
1 apple, chopped
1 can (3½ oz.) flaked coconut

2 T. minced parsley
1 t. salt
1 t. poultry seasoning
1/4 c. chicken broth or water
1 T. butter
1/4 c. honey (glaze)
2 T. prepared mustard
1/2 t. salt
1/2 t. curry powder

Rinse ducks; pat dry. Saute onion, chestnuts and celery in butter; mix with bread cubes. Stir in apple and coconut, parsley, seasonings and broth. Fill cavities with stuffing mixture. Close openings with skewers; tie legs and tail together. Prick skin with a fork. Place ducks, breast down, in a shallow pan; roast at 350 degrees for 1½ hours. Combine remaining ingredients; heat, stirring constantly until well mixed. Turn ducks, brush with glaze and roast for about 30 more minutes or until tender. Makes 4 to 6 servings.

Adele Fevella
Haleakala NP

SAUTEED DOVE

6 doves
1/4 c. butter
1 c. sherry wine
1/4 c. chopped onions

2 T. minced celery leaves
1/3 t. tarragon
Salt and pepper

Salt and pepper doves. Saute doves in butter for 5 minutes, or until lightly browned. Add wine, onion, celery leaves and cover and simmer over low heat for 20 minutes. Add tarragon and simmer 15 minutes longer.

Dorothea Miehle
Regional Office

DOVE

Allow 3 to 4 birds per adult. Soak cleaned dove in salted water in refrigerator overnight. Take out of water and dry just before cooking. Put into pan with 2" deep sides, breast up, and placing birds closely together. Put teaspoon of margarine on each breast and cover with strip of bacon. Bake in 350 degree oven for an hour. Season with garlic salt and pepper; return to oven for approximately 1/2 hour, or until done. Serve with long grain brown and wild rice. (Baste occasionally while cooking.) OR: Place birds in large Brown 'n Bake bags, breast side up. Lay small pieces of bacon across each breast, a small amount of margarine and season with garlic salt. Cook in a 300 degree oven for 1 hour or until done to taste.

Tomie Patrick
Point Reyes NS

VENISON STROGANOFF
(Other meats may be used)

1 lb. venison steak, cut in
   long thin strips
3 T. flour
Salt and pepper
1 onion

1 c. tomato juice
1½ c. water
1 t. sugar
1 can mushrooms
1/2 c. sour cream

Dredge meat with flour and salt and pepper. Brown lightly in fat with the onion. Add tomato juice, water, sugar. Simmer until tender. Ten minutes before serving, add mushrooms and sour cream. Do not boil. Serves 4.

Bunny Chew
Lake Mead NRA

BREAST OF WILD GOOSE OR WILD DUCK

3 average geese
3 eggs
1 c. bread crumbs
Butter and bacon drippings
1 t. pepper
1/4 t. paprika
2 bay leaves
4 whole cloves

2 cloves garlic, chopped
1/4 c. wine vinegar
1/2 c. catsup
2 T. Worcestershire sauce
1 T. A-1 sauce
1 glass currant jelly
1 t. Kitchen Bouquet
1/2 c. burgundy wine

very good

Fillet the breast; if large, cut in 3 or 4 pieces lengthwise. Use only breasts and legs. Dip in beaten eggs then into crumbs and brown on both sides in butter and drippings. Add salt, pepper, paprika, bay leaves, cloves and garlic. Mix together in bowl, the following: wine vinegar, catsup, Worcestershire sauce and A-1 sauce, Kitchen Bouquet and pour over meat. Let simmer 1 hour or until tender. The last 10 minutes, add the currant jelly and burgundy wine. Serves 8.

Dave and Josephine Jones
San Francisco Office

DUCK

Allow one bird per adult. This is best for young ducks: soak bird(s) in water heavily salted overnight in refrigerator. Dry birds, cover with plastic wrap and refrigerate until baking time. Stuff birds with celery tops, quartered onions, and apples after rubbing cavity with salt. Place ducks in Brown 'n Bake bags and bake in 350 degree oven for 2½ hours to 3 hours. Take ducks from bags and remove stuffing and discard. Serve the ducks on bed of wild rice with mushrooms. No stuffing served with this recipe, the stuffing absorbs gamey taste and leaves meat much milder in flavor.

Tomie Patrick
Point Reyes NS

PHEASANT DELIGHT

1 pheasant, cut up
1 small can beer

1 can cream of mushroom soup
Oil, salt and pepper, and flour

Quickly brown salted, floured, and peppered bird with oil in large skillet. Add soup, 2 cans water and beer. Let simmer for 2 hours and serve with noodles or rice. Serves 4.

Lola Kaiser
Lake Mead NRA

PHEASANT

Dressing: Soak 6 slices dried French bread in water. Saute one small chopped onion in 1/2 cube butter until golden brown. Squeeze water from bread and add to onion mixture, browning slowly. Add to bread mixture, chopped liver and chopped parsley, mixing whole egg into dressing. Mix well and add salt, pepper, and a dash of nutmeg. Stuff pheasant and brown in butter, in a Dutch oven. Add water and simmer slowly for approximately 1½ hours, depending on size of bird. Add fresh mushrooms during last 15 minutes.

Dorothea Miehle
Regional Office

QUAIL

Allow 4 birds per adult. Soak cleaned quail in salted water in refrigerator overnight. Dry and refrigerate until cooking time. Put quail, breast side up, in pan with 2" sides and add one full pound of butter or margarine. Bake in moderate oven, 350 degrees, for 1 hour basting FREQUENTLY! Season with dash of garlic salt (use sparingly), salt and paprika. Return to oven for 1/2 hour or until done to personal preference, basting 3 times. Serve on bed of wild rice and mushroom caps. The large amount of butter and the frequent basting is the secret to this delicious dish, so don't skimp on either.

Tomie Patrick
Point Reyes NS

ELEPHANT STEW

1 med. sized elephant
1 ton salt
1 ton pepper
500 bushels potatoes

200 bushels of carrots
4,000 sprigs parsley
2 small rabbits (optional)

Cut elephant meat into bite-size pieces. This will take about 2 months. Cut vegetables into cubes (another 2 months). Place meat in pan and cover with 1,000 gallons of brown gravy and simmer for 4 weeks. Shovel in salt and pepper to taste. When meat is tender, add vegetables. A steam shovel is useful for this. Simmer slowly for 4 more weeks. Garnish with parsley. Will serve 3,800 people. If more are expected, add the 2 rabbits—this is not recommended as very few people like hare in their stew.

Elaine Hounsell
Lake Mead NRA

WILD DUCK TREAT

✓ *Excellent*

1 mallard, pintail or other
    duck, skinned, boned and
    cut up

1 box Rice-A-Roni
Oil
Salt, pepper and flour

Brown salted, peppered, and floured duck pieces with oil in large skillet. Add Rice-A-Roni and cook according to directions on box. Serves 4.

Lola Kaiser
Lake Mead NRA

LOLA'S VENISON SPECIAL

✓ *Excellent*

1 lb. venison tips or steak
1 large onion
1/2 lb. mushrooms (or lg. can)

1 c. Rhine wine
Flour, salt and pepper
Oil

Brown floured, salted, and peppered pieces with oil in large skillet. When about half done, add sliced onion and mushrooms and finish browning. Add 2 cups water and the wine. Simmer about 1 hour. Serve with rice. Serves 4.

Lola Kaiser
Lake Mead NRA

STATUE OF LIBERTY NATIONAL MONUMENT, NEW YORK-NEW JERSEY IS SHARED WITH VISITORS FROM ALL OVER THE WORLD. (NPS photo by Jack Boucher).

**Cakes
Cookies
Pastries
Desserts**

VIEW OF MAJESTIC MOUNT RAINIER FROM VAN TRUMP PARK IN MOUNT RAINIER
NATIONAL PARK, WASHINGTON. (NPS photo by Charles J. Gebler).

GRAPE COOLER

Wash and remove grapes (green, seedless) from stems. Add 1/2 pint "+" sour cream, brown sugar (for taste) and favorite brandy. Mix until creamy. Pour over grapes, stir, "adjust" to taste. Serve chilled. May use fresh strawberries, etc., and a "light" cookie on side of dish.

Dave & Cora Hughes
Regional Office

SHAKY CAKE

Cake Jello:

1 (No. 2) can sour cherries
1/2 c. water
1/2 c. sugar

1 large box cherry jello
1 can crushed pineapple
6 oz. bottle cola

Heat cherries, water, jello and sugar until jello dissolves. Add pineapple (not drained) and cola. Let set.

Topping:

1 box Dream Whip, whipped
2 oz. pkg. soft cream cheese

1/3 c. sugar

Mix well and spread over set jello.

Lola Knapp
Montezuma Castle NM

WHITE FRUIT CAKE

1 c. butter or oleo
3 c. sugar
1 c. milk
4 c. flour
3 t. baking powder
8 egg whites, well beaten
1 medium coconut, grated

1/2 lb. candied pineapple
1 lb. citron or drained
   watermelon rind preserves
1 lb. candied cherries
4 c. pecans
1 c. almonds, blanched

Leave pecans and cherries whole, cut candied fruits into cubes. Grate coconut and combine. Sprinkle with flour. Cream butter or margarine; add sugar gradually and beat until well blended and light. Sift flour, measure and combine with baking powder; add flour and milk alternately to the mixture; add fruits and nuts; fold in stiffly beaten egg whites.

Grease two 1-pound bread pans; line with brown paper cut to fit pan and extend one inch above pans; grease paper; pack batter firmly into pans with hands. Cover top with wax paper, and place pan of water in oven under cake. Bake in 250 degree oven about 2 hours. Remove cover from top of cake during last 15 minutes of baking.

Jewell Gordon
Petrified Forest NP

SWEDISH APPLE CAKE

4 c. diced apples (about 4
   large ones) cut up the size
   of a sugar cube
2 eggs
2 c. sugar
1/2 c. Wesson oil

2 c. flour (bread flour)
2 t. soda
2 t. cinnamon
1 t. salt
2 c. chopped nuts

Beat eggs, sugar and oil together. Sift the dry ingredients together. Add apples, flour mixture to the egg mixture. Fold in nuts last. Mixture will be thick. Pour in greased large cake pan about 9x13". Bake at 350 degrees for 1 hour. When cake is done and still warm, sprinkle 2 teaspoons sugar mixed with 1 teaspoon cinnamon on the top. This cake will stay moist for days.

Doris Starkovich
Regional Office

HELEN'S CAKE

1/2 c. butter or half butter
   and half Crisco

1 c. sugar

Cream together. Add alternately: 2 cups sifted flour in which 1 teaspoon baking powder has been sifted and 1/2 cup milk. Beat in 3 eggs, break whole into mixture one at a time, beating well after each egg. Add 1 teaspoon almond extract. Bake 40 minutes in a moderate oven, 350 degrees. Drop to table, sinkboard, or floor three times when removing from oven, dropping so pan hits flat and evenly.

Dorothea Miehle
Regional Office

EGG NOG POUND CAKE

2 T. butter
1/4 c. sliced almonds
2¾ c. sifted cake flour
1½ t. salt
1 c. shortening
1½ t. baking powder

1½ c. sugar
1 t. rum extract
1 t. vanilla
1 c. egg nog
4 eggs

Grease a 10-inch tube pan or Bundt pan generously with the butter. Sprinkle with almonds. Resift flour with salt and baking powder. Cream shortening. Gradually beat in sugar, creaming until light and fluffy. Add flavorings and egg nog, then the flour mixture. Beat at low speed on mixer until all flour is moistened, then beat for 1 minute. Add eggs, one at a time, beating 1 minute at low speed after each addition. Turn into prepared pan. Bake on lowest rack of moderately slow oven, 325 degrees, about 1 hour, 5 minutes, until cake tests done. Remove from oven and let stand 10 minutes, then turn onto wire rack to cool. Makes one large cake.
Recipe appeared in Hawaiian "Garden Island".

Mike and Ruth Yoshinaka
Regional Office

GINGERBREAD

1/2 c. shortening	2¼ c. flour
2 T. sugar	1 t. soda
1 egg	1/2 t. salt
1 c. molasses	1 t. ginger
1 c. boiling water	1 t. cinnamon

Heat oven to 325 degrees. Grease and flour 9x9" pan. Mix thoroughly, shortening, sugar and egg. Blend in molasses and water. Sift together dry ingredients and stir in. Beat until smooth. Pour into prepared pan. Bake for 45 to 50 minutes.

Mary Ellen Ackerman
Death Valley NM

ZWIEBACK CAKE

1 c. Zwieback, ground (NBC)	2 eggs (as is)
3/4 c. chopped walnuts	1 t. baking powder
1 c. sugar	

Mix together and put on waxed paper in pie pan. Bake in moderate oven, 350 degrees, about 20 minutes. Spread raspberry jam on cake, and just before serving, cover with whipped cream (one package of Zwieback makes 2 cakes.)

Dorothea Miehle
Regional Office

GERMAN BUNDT CAKE - from Betty's Friend

1 c. butter	4 egg whites
1 c. granulated sugar	3 c. cake flour (sifted 3x)
1 c. powdered sugar	2 t. baking powder
4 egg yolks	1 c. milk
1 t. vanilla	Pinch of salt
1 t. almond extract	Whole blanched almonds

Have ingredients at room temperature for 2 to 3 hours before using.
Cream butter; sift the 2 sugars together; add gradually to butter. Add unbeaten egg yolks, one at a time, beat until smooth. Add extract. Sift flour, measure, add baking powder, salt and sift 3 times. Start with flour mixture add a little at a time, then a little milk, continue on low speed with mixer, start with flour and end with flour. Fold in beaten egg whites, stiffly beaten. Grease Bundt pan well and dredge with flour. To each flute in the pan, add one whole blanched almond covered with a dab of dough, then pour remaining dough gently into pan. (Maraschino cherries with brown sugar and a dab of butter in each flute can be substituted for the almonds, if desired.) Bake 1¼ hours in a 350 degree oven. Let stand 15 minutes before turning out. Ice, if desired. Makes 24 servings.

Betty Tucker
Regional Office

APPLE FUDGE CAKE

3 sq. unsweetened chocolate
1¼ c. milk (divided)
1½ c. sugar (divided)
1 c. canned applesauce
1/2 c. shortening

1 t. vanilla
2 c. flour
1 t. soda
1 t. salt
3 eggs

Mix chocolate, 1/2 cup milk and 1/2 cup sugar in saucepan; cook and stir until thick and smooth. Stir in applesauce and vanilla; cool.

Combine and sift dry ingredients. Cream shortening with remaining 1 cup sugar; blend in eggs, one at a time. Alternately add dry ingredients and remaining 3/4 cup milk to creamed mixture, blending well after each addition. Blend in chocolate mixture. Turn batter into 2 greased and floured 8-inch layerpans. Bake in moderate oven, 350 degrees, 40 minutes, or until done. Split each cooled layer to make four layers in all. Select and spread frosting.

Apple Fluff Frosting:

2 pkg. (2 oz. ea.) dessert
  topping mix
1/2 c. cold milk

1/2 c. canned applesauce (cold)
1/2 t. vanilla

Beat topping mix with milk. When mixture begins to stiffen and form peaks, add applesauce and vanilla. Beat until firm enough to spread. Makes about 3 cups.

Lola Vukonich
Petrified Forest NP

HAWAIIAN BEEHIVE CAKE

1 c. sugar
1 envelope unflavored gelatin
2½ c. milk
1 can (13½ oz.) crushed
  pineapple
1/2 c. cornstarch
1/8 t. salt

5 egg yolks, well beaten
1 t. vanilla
1/2 pt. heavy cream, whipped
1 (9 inch) layer of yellow cake
1/3 c. shredded coconut
1/4 c. chopped macadamia nuts

Mix sugar and gelatin in the top of a double boiler. Pour in milk. Place over hot water and heat until milk is scalded. Drain syrup from pineapple and measure out 1/2 cup liquid; blend with cornstarch and salt. Add beaten yolks and hot milk mixture. Return to top of double boiler; cook over hot water, stirring, until thickened. Stir in vanilla and pineapple; cool. Fold in whipped cream.

Cut cake in half horizontally, making two layers. Spread a fourth of the cream between layers; cover top and sides of cake with remaining cream, mounding it high in a pyramid on top. With a spatula, swirl about five concentric circles to make a beehive shape. Sprinkle coconut around sides, and nuts on top. Chill until set, about 1 hour. Serves 10 to 12 people.

Dave and Josephine Jones
San Francisco Office

GRANDMA'S GINGERBREAD

1/2 c. brown sugar
1/2 c. lard and butter
1 or 2 eggs, in season
1½ c. molasses or sorghum
1½ t. soda
About 2½ c. flour

1/2 t. cinnamon
1/2 t. cloves
1/2 t. nutmeg
2 t. ginger
1 c. hot water

(This recipe dates back to 1850. Mix in a single bowl with a large spoon.)

Cream sugar, lard and butter, eggs and molasses. Mix spices in hot water. Sift together flour and soda. Add alternately with spice water and mix well. Bake in a large pan (9x13") in moderate oven, 350 degrees, until broom straw comes out clean. Serve warm with whipped cream.

Georjean McKeeman
Tonto NM

PUDDING CAKE (Bundt)

1 pkg. yellow cake mix
1/2 c. oil (Wesson)
2 T. poppy seeds

1 c. water
4 eggs
1 pkg. instant vanilla pudding

Put all ingredients in mixer and mix at medium speed for 2 minutes. Put in greased Bundt or angel food pan. Bake at 350 degrees for 1 hour. Let cake cool in pan about 10 minutes before turning onto cake dish.

If you wish, you can sprinkle greased pan with chopped nuts. No frosting is required, but use if desired (or dust with powdered sugar).

Other combinations—omit poppy seeds in these variations:

1. Chocolate Instant pudding and Devil's Food cake mix
2. Butterscotch Instant pudding and Spice Cake mix.
3. Lemon Cake and Lemon pudding.
4. Pineapple Cake and Pineapple pudding.
5. Coconut Cake and Coconut pudding.

Ruth Uzar
Regional Office

FRUIT COCKTAIL PUDDING CAKE

1 c. sugar
1 c. flour
1 t. soda
1/4 t. salt

1 egg, well beaten
1 (No. 303) can fruit cocktail
3/4 c. chopped walnuts
1/2 c. brown sugar

Combine sugar, flour, soda and salt; add egg. Drain fruit and add to mixture. Pour into 8x8" buttered pan. Combine brown sugar and nuts and sprinkle over cake. Bake 1 hour at 325 degrees. Cut into squares and serve with whipped cream or ice cream.

Harry and Nancy Sloat
Regional Office

PINEAPPLE UPSIDE DOWN CAKE

1/4 c. butter
6 slices pineapple

1/2 c. brown sugar
Nuts or cherries

Melt butter in 8x12" pan (glass). Sprinkle with brown sugar. Cut pineapple in halves and put over brown sugar, add cherries or nuts as desired.

3 eggs
1 c. sugar
1/2 c. pineapple juice
1/2 t. salt

1 t. vanilla
1 t. baking powder
1½ c. sifted flour

Beat egg whites (set aside). Beat egg yolks and cream in sugar. Add pineapple juice, salt and vanilla. Add flour and baking powder. Fold in egg whites. Pour over pineapple slices. Bake 35 minutes at 350 degrees. Turn upside down on board or platter after cutting around edges with knife.

Marge Murdock
Montezuma Castle NM

SEVEN-UP CAKE

1 pkg. Duncan Hines yellow
  cake mix
1 pkg. vanilla instant pudding

4 eggs
1/2 c. Wesson oil
1 c. Seven-Up

Mix all ingredients together and bake in a well-greased, floured oblong pan (13½x9½") for 55-60 minutes at 350 degrees.

Frosting:

1½ c. milk
1 egg yolk
3 T. cornstarch
1/4 c. sugar

1/4 t. salt
1 t. vanilla
1 t. butter

Mix first five ingredients and boil to a spreading consistency. Add vanilla and butter and blend thoroughly. Spread on cooled cake.

Evelyn Ah Sing
Hawaii Volcanoes NP

PRUNE CAKE

2 c. sugar
1 c. Crisco
1 c. buttermilk
1 t. soda
2 c. flour
1 c. nuts, chopped

1 t. cloves
1 t. allspice
1 t. ginger
1 t. cinnamon
1 t. nutmeg
1 c. pitted cooked prunes

Mix in order given. Bake in a 10-inch tube pan at 325 degrees for 1 hour.

Evelyn Guy
Petrified Forest NP

POTATO CAKE

1 c. butter or shortening	1 t. nutmeg
1 c. cold mashed potatoes	2 c. sugar
4 oz. melted chocolate	4 eggs
1 c. raisins	1 c. nuts
2 c. flour	1/2 c. milk
1 t. cloves	2 t. baking powder
1 t. cinnamon	1/2 t. salt

Be sure the butter, sugar and mashed potatoes are well-creamed and blended then add remaining ingredients. Bake in a tube pan in a 350 degree oven about 1 hour and 15 minutes. This is a cake that is better if made the day before it is to be used and is ideal for freezing.

Alva Cammack
Petrified Forest NP

CHOCOLATE LAYER CAKE

Sift enough pastry flour to have 2 cups, then sift it again into a mixing bowl with 1/2 generous teaspoon salt. In the top of a double boiler, melt 1 square bitter chocolate. Cream 1/2 cup butter until light and fluffy. Gradually add 1½ cups fine granulated sugar, creaming well after each addition. Add 2 eggs. To the butter-eggs mixture, add the flour gradually and alternately with 3/4 cup buttermilk, working quickly to blend the whole well. Begin and end with flour. Stir in the melted chocolate; add 1 tsp. soda diluted in 3/4 Tbsp. good white vinegar, and 1 tsp. vanilla extract. Mix well but do not overmix. Pour the dough into 2 buttered layer pans. Bake in a hot oven, 400 degrees, for 25-30 minutes.

Ruth Combs
Regional Office

LEMON PUDDING CAKE

1 box Betty Crocker lemon velvet cake mix	4 eggs
	2/3 c. oil
1 small box instant lemon pudding	1 1/3 c. water
	3 T. flour

Mix all together and beat 4 minutes. Bake at 350 degrees for 40 minutes. When cake is done, perforate top with holes and pour icing over and into cake.

Icing:

1 small can frozen lemonade, thawed	2 c. powdered sugar

Mix together and blend thoroughly.

Alma Hinkley
Whiskeytown NRA

CHEESE CAKE

Crust:

17 graham crackers
2/3 stick butter, melted

3 T. sugar

Crush crackers; mix with butter and sugar; pack into 9½" spring-form pan, bottom and sides. Grease sides with butter to make crumbs stick. Refrigerate.

Filling:

5 egg yolks
1 c. sugar

2 (13 oz.) pkg. cream cheese
Few drops lemon juice

Blend well with electric hand beater; beat 5 egg whites and fold in. Install in crust and bake about 1 hour or more at 350 degrees. Remove from oven and cool for 1 hour or more.

Topping:

2½ T. sugar
1/2 pt. sour cream
Few drops lemon juice

1 t. vanilla
6 drops almond extract
  and rum, if desired

Mix sugar and sour cream; add flavorings and mix well. Pour topping on cake, dust with cinnamon and bake again 20 minutes at 350 degrees. Let cool and then refrigerate.

Naidene McKay
Grand Canyon NP

COCONUT POUND CAKE

6 eggs, separated
1 c. shortening
1/2 c. margarine
3 c. sugar
1/2 t. almond extract

1 t. coconut extract
1/2 t. salt
3 c. sifted flour
1 c. milk
2 c. coconut

Separate eggs and let them warm to room temperature. Beat egg yolks with shortening and margarine. Gradually add sugar, then extracts, and salt while beating well. Mix in flour and milk alternately; add coconut and beat until well blended. Beat egg whites till stiff peaks form. Fold into coconut mixture. Bake in a greased 10" tube pan 2 hours at 300 degrees. Cool in pan for 15 minutes, then remove to finish cooling.

Chris McKinney
Grand Canyon NP

QUICK MOCHA CAKES

Use either pound cake mix or a "boughten" pound cake. Cut in squares or fingers. Make dressing using 3/4 cup melted butter, 1 cup white sugar and 5 tablespoons cream. Beat together. Roll cakes in dressing and then in chopped salted peanuts.

Alice Dexter
Tumacacori NM

ORANGE CAKE

1 c. butter
2 c. sugar
4 whole large eggs, or 5 small
  eggs

1 level t. soda in 1¼ c.
  buttermilk
4 c. sifted flour
2 t. grated orange rind

Cream butter and sugar, add eggs, one at a time, beating after each addition. Dissolve soda in buttermilk, add alternately with sifted flour; add 2 teaspoons orange rind. Bake in tube pan at 350 degrees for 1 hour or until done. While still hot, pour the following syrup over it:

1 c. orange juice
2 c. sugar

2 t. grated orange rind

Cook in saucepan over medium heat until sugar is dissolved.

Yvonne Razo
Tumacacori NM

WINE CAKE

1 pkg. yellow cake mix
4 eggs
3/4 c. cream sherry wine

3/4 c. salad oil
1 pkg. Jello instant vanilla
  pudding
1 t. nutmeg

Mix all ingredients together with electric mixer for 5 minutes. Cook in angel food cake pan for 50 minutes in a 350 degree oven.

Kathy Lucchesi
Point Reyes NS

COOKIE SHEET CAKE

Mix:

2 c. flour

2 c. sugar

Bring to a boil:

1 c. water
1/2 c. shortening

1/4 c. margarine
4 T. (heaping) cocoa

Pour over flour and sugar. Mix well. Add:

2 eggs

1 t. vanilla

Stir 1 teaspoon soda into 1/2 cup sour milk. Mix into above ingredients. Pour into large greased cookie sheet. Bake 20 minutes at 350 degrees. While cake bakes, prepare frosting:

6 T. milk
1/4 c. margarine

1 t. vanilla
1 lb. powdered sugar
2 T. cocoa

Bring milk and margarine to boiling point, add vanilla. Pour over powdered sugar and cocoa. Frost cake while hot. Sprinkle with nuts.

Olina Stout
Petrified Forest NP

BABY ORANGE BABAS

1 pkg. yellow cake mix

Follow directions. Fill well-greased hot drinking cups with batter. Place on cookie sheet and bake 25 minutes at 375 degrees.

Cook the following 5 minutes and drizzle over the cakes, turned out on a serving plate:

3/4 c. sugar
1/4 t. almond extract
3/4 c. orange juice

3/4 c. rum (ADD LATER)
3 T. orange peel, cut into
    thin slivers

Add the rum after removing glaze from stove. Pour over the babas.

John and Janet Sage
Regional Office

PEANUT BRITTLE COOKIES

1 c. flour
1/4 t. soda
1/4 t. cinnamon
1/2 c. brown sugar

1/2 c. butter
1 beaten egg
1 t. vanilla
1 c. salted peanuts, chopped

Cream butter; add sugar; cream well. Add 2 tablespoons of the beaten egg and vanilla; beat well. Blend in dry ingredients and half the peanuts. Spread dough on greased sheet to 14x10" rectangle. Brush with remaining egg and sprinkle with 1/2 cup peanuts. Bake at 325 degrees for 20-25 minutes. Break while warm (12 ounces peanuts makes a double batch). Makes 2 dozen cookies.

Cathy May
Petrified Forest NP

ALMOND BROD

Cream 30 minutes:

2/3 c. sugar

3 egg yolks
1 whole egg

Add:

1 c. flour
1/3 c. almonds, blanched,
    cut into strips and toasted

1 T. citron, finely chopped
1 T. orange peel, grated
Dash cinnamon
Dash nutmeg

Bake 20-30 minutes in a 350 degree oven in an 8x8" pan. Cut into strips, return to low oven; heat for 5 or 10 minutes, until they start to feel dry. A good Christmas cookie.

Dorothea Miehle
Regional Office

WALDORF RED VELVET CAKE

1/2 c. shortening
1½ c. sugar
2 eggs
1/4 c. red food coloring
  (two 1 oz. bottles)
2 T. cocoa
1 t. vanilla

1 t. salt
1 c. buttermilk
2¼ c. sifted flour, sifted
  2 or 3 times
1 T. vinegar
1 t. baking soda

Cream shortening and sugar until fluffy. Add eggs, one at a time, and beat one minute each. Mix coloring and cocoa in a cup to make a paste and add to the above. Add salt, put vanilla in buttermilk and slowly add to mixture alternating milk and flour. Mix vinegar and soda in a cup and add to the mixture. Bake in two 9-inch pans in a heated oven of 350 degrees for 25 to 30 minutes.

Frosting:

1 c. milk
1 c. butter
1 t. vanilla

5 T. flour
1 c. powdered sugar, sifted

Mix flour and part of milk, then add the rest of the flour to make a smooth paste. Cook until thick and allow to cool. Beat the butter, powdered sugar, and vanilla together with mixer and add flour and milk mixture a little at a time and spread on cake.

Lola Rush
Petrified Forest NP

FRESH APPLE CAKE

4 c. diced apples (not too fine)   2 c. sugar

Mix well and let stand. Mix:

1/2 c. cooking oil
1 c. nuts

2 eggs, well beaten
2 t. vanilla

Mix dry ingredients and add to above:

2 c. flour
2 t. salt

2 t. cinnamon
2 t. soda

Put in a greased pan, 9x13x2", and bake in 350 degree oven for 1 hour.

Gladys Clancy
Petrified Forest NP

SPUDNUTS

Mix like pie crust:

6 c. flour	4 T. sugar
1 t. salt	1/2 c. shortening

(This makes a soft dough.) Mix 3 yeast cakes, or pkgs. of dry yeast, in 1/2 cup warm water. Warm 2 cups milk, beat 1 egg; prepare 1/3 cup mashed potatoes. Mix all together and add to flour mixture. Let rise 1 hour. Roll out 1/2 inch thick and cut with doughnut cutter. Let stand 15 minutes and fry in deep fat (Crisco or similar shortening). Drain and roll in sugar, if desired.

Catherine Hjort
Regional Office

ORANGE COCONUT CAKE

1 box Swans Down orange coconut cake mix	1 c. Wesson oil
	3/4 c. water
	4 eggs, added one at a time

Add oil, water and eggs to cake mix. Beat well. Bake at 350 degrees for 30-35 minutes.

Topping:

Juice of 1 orange and 1 lemon	2 c. powdered sugar

Mix, do not cook, and pour over hot cake.

Dollie Cox
Petrified Forest NP

POTATO DONUTS

Heat 2 cups milk; then add:

1 c. sugar	1½ t. salt
1/2 c. shortening	1 c. mashed potatoes

Cool to lukewarm. Meanwhile, soak 1½ pkg. yeast in 1/4 cup warm water, let stand 5 minutes, then add to milk mixture with 3 slightly beaten eggs and 1 teaspoon vanilla. Add approximately 8 cups flour and work into dough with a strong spoon. Scrape into greased bowl and cover until double in bulk; then turn out onto floured board and roll out to 1/2 inch thickness. (If thicker donuts are desired leave thicker). Cut and cover. Let rise again until double. Fry in deep fat at 375 degrees until light brown on both sides. Turn only once.

Wanda Johnson
Petrified Forest NP

CHEESE CAKE

1/4 c. butter
1 c. graham cracker crumbs
  (about 16 large crackers)
1 t. cream of tartar
6 eggs, separated
Sugar

19 oz. cream cheese (2 large and
  1 small)
3 T. flour
1/2 t. salt
1 pt. dairy sour cream
1 t. vanilla

Butter generously a 9" spring form or loose bottom pan. Mix butter and cracker crumbs well; reserve ½ cup and press remainder firmly on bottom of pan. Add cream of tartar to egg whites and beat until foamy. Gradually add 3 tablespoons sugar and beat until stiff; set aside. Beat cheese until soft. Mix 1½ cups sugar, the flour and salt. Gradually beat into cheese. Add egg yolks, one at a time, beating well after each one. Add sour cream and vanilla; mix well. Fold in egg whites. Pour mixture into the pan. Bake in 325 degree oven about 1¼ hours, or until firm. Turn off oven, open door and leave cake in oven for 10 minutes. Remove from oven and let cool on cake rack. Chill. Cake will shrink away from side of pan as it cools.

Note: I find that it is a good idea to make a collar of foil to go around the top of the pan. It will keep the cake from running over the edge. Make the collar about 2½" high and be sure to grease.

Best not to make this while on a diet.

Harry and Nancy Sloat
Regional Office

APPLESAUCE CAKE

1/2 c. shortening
1 c. sugar
1 egg
1 c. raisins
1 c. chopped nuts
1½ c. sifted flour

1/4 t. salt
1 t. soda
1 t. cinnamon
1/2 t. cloves
1/2 t. allspice
1 c. hot applesauce

Cream shortening and sugar; add egg; add nuts and raisins, which have been dredged in flour. Sift dry ingredients together and add alternately with applesauce to first mixture. Bake 45 minutes at 375 degrees in loaf or tube pan.

Quick Caramel Frosting:

1 c. brown sugar
5 T. butter

1/4 t. salt

Bring to boil, stirring constantly. Add 1/2 cup milk and boil 3 minutes. Cool; stir in sifted confectioners sugar to right thickness. Add 1/4 teaspoon vanilla. Stir well and spread on cake.

Alice Dexter
Tumacacori NM

ICEBOX CAKE

Part 1:

1 pkg. raspberry jello
1 c. hot water

3/4 c. orange juice
1/4 pt. whipped cream
1 banana, diced

Dissolve jello in hot water, add orange juice and let stand in icebox until almost set. Then beat until fluffy - about 2 or 3 minutes. Fold in whipped cream and banana. Pour into spring pan, the sides and bottom of which have been lined with ladyfingers split in halves. Set in icebox until firm.

Part 2:

1 pkg. lemon jello
1¼ c. hot water

3/4 c. crushed pineapple
1 (5 cent*) pkg. marshmallows
(colored)

Dissolve lemon jello in hot water, let stand in icebox as before and when almost set, whip until fluffy. Fold in pineapple. Cut marshmallows in halves and lay in cake pan on top of first mixture when firm. Then a layer of thinly sliced bananas on top of the marshmallows. Then pour in second mixture and put in icebox until ready to serve.
*Remember those days? Five cents would buy a lot.

Part 3:

To serve: Remove sides from pan. Spread 1/4 pint whipped cream on top of cake and garnish with maraschino cherries.

Dorothea Miehle
Regional Office

UPSIDE-DOWN CAKE

2 egg whites, beaten stiff
2 egg yolks
1/2 c. sugar
1/2 c. cake flour

3/4 t. baking powder
2 T. water
1 t. vanilla

Beat egg whites stiff and add yolks, beat well. Add sugar, flour, baking powder. Mix well. Add water and vanilla, mix well.

Topping:

In heavy skillet, mix 2 Tbsp. butter or oleo and 1/2 cup brown sugar. Arrange desired fruit, well drained, on sugar and butter mixture; pour cake batter over fruit. Bake in moderate oven, 350 degrees. Cake batter will be very thin. Apricots or pineapple are good choices for this cake.

Alice Dexter
Tumacacori NM

SOURDOUGH CHOCOLATE CAKE - Sunset Magazine Nov., '65

2/3 c. shortening
3 eggs
1 c. sourdough starter
  (see BREADS)
1 t. vanilla (2)
2/3 c. sweet ground chocolate
  or cocoa (omit)

Chocolate or white frosting
1 2/3 c. sugar
1/2 t. baking powder
1 t. salt
3/4 c. water
1½ t. soda (1¼)
1 3/4 c. regular flour (2¼)

In large bowl of electric mixer, cream shortening and sugar. Add eggs, one at a time, beating well after each addition. Blend in the starter. Sift flour, measure and sift again with chocolate, baking powder, salt and soda. Add to shortening mixture alternately with vanilla and water, mixing at low speed. Pour into two greased and floured 9-inch layer pans. Bake in moderate oven, 350 degrees, for 35 minutes, or until cake tester is clean. Allow cake to cool ten minutes, then invert on cooling racks, removing pans carefully. Cool thoroughly and frost with package of frosting mix or with your own favorite frosting. Serves 12.

I sometimes add a small amount of instant coffee to the frosting mix, maybe another time, almond or pepermint. For a white sourdough cake, change the amounts to the quantities in parenthesis as indicated in recipe above.

Lester Bodine (Retired)
Lassen Volcanic NP

CHOCOLATE NUT PUDDING

1 c. flour
3/4 c. sugar
2 t. baking powder
1/4 t. salt

1/2 c. milk
1/2 sq. chocolate, melted in
  2 T. butter
1/2 c. nuts

Mix above ingredients and put in 9x13" pan. Mix together:

1 c. white sugar
1 c. brown sugar

1/4 t. salt
3 T. cocoa

Put over first mixture. Pour 1½ cups boiling water over all. Do not stir. Bake 40 minutes at 350 degrees. Serve with whipped cream.

Mary Adamson
Lake Mead NRA

FLAN (Custard)

1 can Eagle Brand milk
4 eggs

1 c. less 2 fingers, of water

Beat together and strain or blend in blender and pour into custard cups or loaf pan with caramelized sugar in bottom of cups or pan. Bake in pan of water like regular custard until knife comes out clean.

Claribell Webb
Pinnacles NM

JAPANESE FRUIT CAKE

1 c. shortening (part butter
   and margarine may be used)
2 c. sugar
4 eggs
3 c. sifted flour
1 t. soda
1 t. salt

1 c. buttermilk
1 t. vanilla
2/3 c. chopped nuts
2/3 c. chopped raisins
3/4 t. cinnamon
3/4 t. allspice
3/4 t. mace
1/2 t. cloves

Cream shortening and sugar until fluffy. Beat in 4 eggs, one at a time. Sift together flour, soda and salt. Stir into creamed mixture alternately with buttermilk and vanilla. Pour 1/3 of batter into 1 greased and floured 9" cake pan. Stir nuts, raisins and spices into remaining batter and pour into 2 more prepared 9" pans. Bake 30 to 35 minutes at 350 degrees. When cake is cool, put together and top with Japanese Fruit Cake Filling, placing the light layer in the middle. The sides may be frosted with a white icing if desired.

Filling:

2/3 c. sugar
1/4 t. salt
4 T. cornstarch
3/4 c. pineapple syrup from
   a No. 2 can crushed pineapple
1 T. butter
2 T. grated orange rind

1/4 c. orange juice (juice of
   1 orange)
2 T. lemon juice
1½ c. grated coconut
Crushed pineapple from No. 2 can
1/2 c. chopped pecans

Mix sugar, salt and cornstarch and slowly stir in pineapple juice. Cook over low heat, stirring constantly, until mixture thickens and boils. Boil 1 minute. Remove from heat. Blend in butter, orange rind, orange juice and lemon juice. Cool. Stir in coconut, crushed pineapple and pecans. Place between layers and on top of Japanese Fruit Cake.

Chris McKinney
Grand Canyon NP

RITZ CRACKER PIE

20 Ritz crackers
3 egg whites, beaten stiff
1/2 t. baking powder

1 c. sugar
1 c. chopped nuts
1 T. vanilla
Pinch of salt

Roll crackers very fine. Beat whites stiff and add 1 cup sugar. Fold in crackers with 1/2 teaspoon baking powder and a pinch of salt. Add nuts and vanilla. Pour into greased pie pan and spread. Bake 30 minutes in a 350 degree oven. Serve with whipping cream or Dream Whip.

Faye Lukens
Chiricahua NM

APRICOT NECTAR CAKE

4 eggs
3/4 c. apricot nectar
3/4 c. oil

1/2 c. sugar
1 pkg. lemon cake mix

Mix all together thoroughly. Bake in 325 degree oven about 45-60 minutes or until done. Glaze as desired.

John and Maizie Dong
Regional Office

CHERRY DELIGHT

2 c. cinnamon graham crackers

1/4 lb. oleo, melted

Crush crackers to very fine crumbs, add melted oleo. Press into 8" square pan. Set aside to chill in refrigerator.
Combine:

1 pkg. (8 oz.) cream cheese

2 T. milk

Cream cheese and milk until uniform consistency, then add:

1 c. powdered sugar

1 box Dream Whip (follow pkg. directions, may be prepared ahead)

Mix together with cream cheese mixture until very creamy and pour over chilled graham cracker base. Top with prepared cherry pie filling. Let set 2-3 hours before serving. Serves 8.

Kay Marquardt
Joshua Tree NM

PUMPKIN CHIFFON PIE

1 envelope Knox unflavored
  gelatin
3/4 c. firmly packed dark
  brown sugar
1/2 t. nutmeg
1 t. cinnamon
1/2 c. milk

1/4 c. water
3 eggs, separated
1½ c. canned pumpkin
1/4 c. sugar
1 baked pie shell (9 inch)
1/2 t. salt

Mix gelatin, sugar, salt and spices thoroughly in a saucepan. Stir in milk, water, egg yolks and pumpkin and mix well. Cook over medium heat. Stir constantly until gelatin is dissolved and mixture is heated thoroughly. Remove from heat. Chill until mixture mounds slightly when dropped from a spoon. Beat egg whites until stiff. Beat in sugar. Fold gelatin mixture into stiffly beaten egg whites. Turn into a baked pie shell and chill until firm. Decorate with cream cheese mixed with a little milk, sugar and vanilla.

Fifi and Doug Cornell
Golden Gate NRA

PECAN PIE

3 eggs
1 c. sugar
1 c. Karo syrup, Blue Label

1 t. vanilla
1/4 t. salt
1½ c. chopped pecans

Bake in unbaked pie shell about 375 degrees for 40 minutes or until knife blade inserted in filling comes out clean.

Naidene McKay
Grand Canyon NP

CARROT CAKE

2 c. flour
2 c. sugar
3 c. grated carrots
1½ c. oil

4 eggs (whole)
2 t. cinnamon
1 t. salt
2 t. baking soda

Blend ingredients. Bake approximately 1 hour or until done at 350 degrees.

Icing:

3 c. powdered sugar
1/2 c. butter or shortening

1½ t. vanilla
2 T. milk

Blend until smooth.

Theresa Fisher
Regional Office

WINE CAKE

Boil:

1 c. water
3 heaping T. shortening

1 c. raisins

Cool. Sift together:

2 c. flour
1 c. sugar
1/2 t. salt

1 t. cinnamon
1 t. nutmeg
1 t. baking soda

Add cooled mixture and 1/2 cup red wine and 1 large or 2 small red apples, grated. Add 1 cup walnuts and mix well. Bake 1 hour or until done in a 350 degree oven in a 9x9" pan.

Douglas and Gene Scovill
Arizona Archeological Center

CAKE OR DROP DO-NUT

2½ t. baking powder
1½ c. flour
1 t. salt
1/2 c. sugar

1 egg, beaten with fork
1/2 c. fresh milk
2 T. salad oil
1 t. vanilla

Sift baking powder, flour and salt. Put aside. Mix egg, milk and oil. Add flour and sugar and mix. Add vanilla. Do not over mix. Drop by teaspoonfuls and deep fry. Sprinkle sugar on do-nut if desired.

Setsuko Tanaka
City of Refuge NHP

CHEWY BAR COOKIES

1¼ c. flour
1½ t. baking powder
3/4 t. salt
3 eggs
1 c. granulated sugar
1/2 t. vanilla

1 (6 oz.) pkg. semi-sweet
   chocolate morsels
1/2 c. chopped maraschino
   cherries
1 c. coconut
1 c. chopped walnuts

Stir flour, baking powder and salt together. Beat eggs until light; add sugar gradually, beating well after each addition. Stir in vanilla, then dry ingredients. Fold in morsels, coconut, cherries and nuts. Spread dough evenly in greased oblong pan about 13x9½x2". Bake 30 minutes at 350 degrees. Cut into bars. Yields about 3 dozen bars.

Karla and Peter Allen
Lake Mead NRA

COCOA MOUNDS

Mix and boil 2 minutes:

2 c. sugar
1/3 c. cocoa

1/2 c. milk
1/4 c. butter

Remove and stir in:

3 c. oatmeal

2 t. vanilla

Drop by teaspoonfuls onto wax paper.

Betty Berrett
Petrified Forest NP

BANANA SPLIT PIE

1 baked 8" pie shell
1/2 c. butter
1½ c. confectioners sugar
2 unbeaten eggs

1 t. vanilla
1 sq. (1 oz.) grated
   unsweetened chocolate
2 bananas
Chopped walnuts

Cream butter. Gradually add 1½ cups confectioners sugar, creaming well. Add unbeaten eggs, beating for 6 minutes. With mixer, use medium speed. Blend in 1 teaspoon vanilla. Fold in 1 square (1 oz.) grated un-sweetened chocolate and 2 thinly sliced bananas. Turn into pie shell. Garnish with nuts. Chill about 3 hours. Best served same day.

Mrs. Chet Miller
Whiskeytown NRA

PEACH-APPLE CRISP

3 med. peaches, peeled and
   coarsely chopped
3 med. apples, peeled and
   coarsely chopped
3/4 c. granulated sugar
2 T. lemon juice

1½ c. rolled oats
1 c. packed brown sugar
1/2 c. butter or oleo
1/4 t. salt
1/8 t. cinnamon
1/8 t. nutmeg

Mix peaches, apples and granulated sugar and lemon juice; spread in shallow baking dish. With pastry blender or fingertips, mix rolled oats, brown sugar, butter, salt and spices until crumbly. Sprinkle over fruit mixture. Bake at 350 degrees about 1 hour. Makes 6 to 8 servings. Can be served warm or cold.

Mary Alice Replogle
Regional Office

FUDGE SQUARES

1 cube margarine

2 sq. chocolate

Melt together and cool slightly.

1 c. sugar
1/2 c. flour (not sifted)
2 eggs

Pinch of salt
1 t. vanilla
Nuts (optional)

Combine all ingredients; pour into buttered pan (9" square); bake 30 minutes at 350 degrees.

Helen Koch
Joshua Tree NM

CHOCOLATE MARBLE SQUARES

1 c. vanilla wafer crumbs
   (22 wafers)
2 T. butter, melted
1/2 c. butter
1 (4½ oz.) milk-chocolate bar
4 beaten egg yolks

1/4 c. sifted powdered sugar
1/2 c. toasted slivered almonds
4 stiffly beaten egg whites
1 pt. vanilla ice cream, softened
1/2 c. whipping cream, whipped

Combine crumbs and 2 Tbsp. butter; press in bottom of 9x9x2" pan. In pan, melt the 1/2 cup butter and candy bar over low heat; cook and stir until blended. Stir small amount of hot mixture into egg yolks; return to saucepan. Cook and stir over low heat until thickened. Remove from heat; add powdered sugar; beat smooth. Stir in 1/4 cup almonds; cool. Fold into egg whites; spoon over crust alternately with ice cream. Cut thru to marble. Freeze until firm. Cut into squares; sprinkle with remaining almonds and top with whipped cream. 9 servings.

Bobbie Davis
Redwood NP

OLD-FASHIONED CREAM PIE

1/2 c. flour
1 c. sugar
Pinch of salt

2 c. heavy cream (or enough
  to fill crust)
Nutmeg to taste
9" pie shell, unbaked

Combine flour, sugar and salt, and mix well. Add cream slowly and pour mixture into pie shell. Sprinkle top with nutmeg. Bake in 425 degree oven for 10 minutes; reduce heat to 350 degrees and bake until filling is firm, approximately 1 hour. (Recipe from FORD TIMES MAGAZINE, by John and Bess Kelland, owner-manager of Trout Lodge, 21 miles from the White Pass Ski area, State Highway 5 in Naches, Washington.)

Virginia Duckett
Regional Office

PINEAPPLE NUT BALLS

1 (9 oz.) can crushed
  pineapple, drained
1 c. heavy cream

1/2 lb. or 32 marshmallows,
  cut fine
1½ c. nuts

Mix pineapple and marshmallows. Let stand 1 hour. Fold in whipped cream. Cover and chill overnight. Shape in small balls and roll in nuts. Keep chilled. Serve 3 in a dish, with a cherry on top. Makes about 2 dozen.

De Ann Thompson
Petrified Forest NP

HEAVENLY PIE

1½ c. granulated sugar
1/4 t. cream of tartar
4 eggs, separated

3 T. lemon juice
1 T. lemon rind, grated
1 pt. whipped cream

Sift together 1 cup sugar and cream of tartar. Beat egg whites until stiff but not dry, then gradually add the sugar mixture; blend thoroughly. Use to line bottom and sides of a 9 or 10 inch pie plate, being careful not to spread too close to the rim. Bake in a slow oven at 275 degrees for 1 hour. Then cool in the oven so it won't crack.

Beat the egg yolks lightly; stir in remaining 1/2 cup sugar, then the lemon juice and rind. Cook in double boiler until very thick, 8-10 minutes. Remove and cool. Whip the cream. Combine half of it with lemon-egg mixture, and fill shell. Cover with remainder. Chill in refrigerator 24 hours. Serves 6-9.

(The meringue crust is about 1/2" thick—in fact, it can be made into two 8" pies from this recipe. Also, it doesn't have to be chilled that long— just so it is cold. Twice this recipe makes 12 individual patties.) Shape with spoon with hollow in center but be sure egg whites are whipped stiffly enough to hold shape when put onto sheet. Grease sheet or pie pan.

Al and Eleanor Lense
Regional Office

POOR MAN'S PIE

Fill a partially baked pie shell with soft bread crumbs. Scald 1 pint sweet milk. Beat 1 egg until lemon-colored then add 1 cup sugar and 1 tablespoon flour to egg and beat well. Gradually add milk and beat smooth, pour over bread crumbs and sprinkle with nutmeg and bake in a moderate oven, 350 degrees, for 30 minutes or until set.

Virginia Duckett
Regional Office

LILIKOI-LEMON MERINGUE PIE

1/3 c. cornstarch	3 T. frozen lilikoi
1 c. sugar	concentrate
1½ c. boiling water	2 T. lemon juice
3 egg yolks, slightly beaten	1 t. grated lemon rind
2 T. butter or margarine	1 pie shell, baked - 9"

Mix cornstarch and sugar in saucepan and gradually stir in the boiling water. Bring to a boil and cook 5 minutes over medium flame, stirring constantly until thick and clear. Turn off flame. Stir several spoonfuls of this hot mixture into the beaten egg yolks, mixing well. Add yolk mixture to remaining starch mixture, stirring well. Bring to a boil and cook for 2 minutes over a low flame, stirring constantly. Turn off flame; stir in butter or margarine. Cool. Add lilikoi and lemon juices and rind gradually, stirring only until blended. Cool thoroughly and pour into cooled, baked pie shell. Top with meringue. Spread over cooled pie filling, making sure it is sealed well to the edge of the crust. Bake. Temperature: 425 degrees for 6-8 minutes.

Evelyn Ah Sing
Hawaii Volcanoes NP

CHOCOLATE CHIP PUMPKIN CAKE

2 c. sifted all-purpose flour	1/2 t. cloves
2 c. sugar	1/4 t. ginger
2 t. baking powder	1/4 t. allspice
1 t. baking soda	4 eggs
3/4 t. salt	2 c. pumpkin
1½ t. cinnamon	1 c. chocolate chips (16 oz.)
1 c. cooking oil	1 c. chopped pecans or walnuts
1 c. All Bran cereal	

Sift dry ingredients and set aside. Beat eggs in large bowl until foamy. Add pumpkin, cooking oil and cereal, mix thoroughly. Add dry ingredients, stirring only until combined. Fold in chips and nuts. Spread evenly in ungreased 10x4" tube pan. Bake in moderate oven at 350 degrees about 1 hour 10 minutes or until toothpick inserted in center comes out clean. Cool completely before removing from pan. Frost with confectioners sugar glaze if desired.

Genevieve Dalley
Lake Mead NRA

CHOPPED APPLE CAKE

Mix together:

2 beaten eggs	2 c. sugar
1½ c. liquid shortening	1 t. vanilla

Add:

3 c. flour	2 t. soda
1 t. salt	

Add:

3 c. finely chopped apples	1 c. chopped nuts
(about 3 apples)	

Bake 1½ hours at 350 degrees in a tube pan. Leave a little peel on apples.

Ken Cox
Chiricahua NM

GRAHAM CRACKER CAKE

1 c. graham cracker crumbs	1 t. vanilla
1/2 c. shredded coconut	1 c. sugar
1/2 c. walnuts, chopped fine	1/4 t. salt
4 egg whites	

Beat egg whites with vanilla and salt until foamy, add sugar a little at a time and beat until stiff peaks form. Fold egg whites into cracker crumbs which have been mixed with nuts and the coconut. Bake in WELL GREASED pie pan or 8x8" square pan for 30 minutes at 350 degrees.

Harry and Nancy Sloat
Regional Office

YELLOW SOUR CREAM CAKE

1 pkg. Duncan Hines butter recipe (yellow) cake mix

Add:

1/2 c. water	1/4 c. sugar
4 whole eggs	8 oz. sour cream

Beat until smooth. Bake in angel food tin at 350 degrees for approximately 45-50 minutes. Be sure to grease and flour cake tin generously. This cake will keep good and moist for several days. Resembles a pound cake.

Lucile H. Lovelady
(Retired) from the
Old Western Service Center

FRESH STRAWBERRY PIE

1 baked pie shell
2 pt. fresh strawberries (boxes)
1 c. sugar
3 T. cornstarch

1/2 c. water
1 T. lemon juice
Whipped cream

Wash berries thoroughly; remove stems. Mash 2 cups berries; reserve 2-3 berries for garnish; slice remaining berries and arrange in bottom of pie shell. In a saucepan, blend sugar and cornstarch; add water, lemon juice and mashed strawberries. Cook over a medium heat until thickened, stirring constantly. Pour glaze over berries in pie shell. Chill. Top with sweetened whipped cream and garnish with reserved berries. Serves 6-8.

Karen Donaldson
Lake Mead NRA

GRASSHOPPER PIE

2 c. Oreo cookie crumbs
1/3 c. margarine, melted
1/4 c. green creme de menthe

2 c. (7 oz. jar) marshmallow
  creme
2 c. heavy cream, whipped

Combine crumbs and margarine, reserve 1/2 cup for topping. Press remaining crumb mixture onto bottom and sides of 9-inch pie pan. Gradually add creme de menthe to marshmallow creme, mixing until well blended. Fold in whipped cream. Pour into crust, sprinkle with remaining crumbs. Freeze.

Mary Chilton
Montezuma Castle NM

MAC NUT ANGELS

1¼ c. flour
1/2 c. brown sugar

1/2 c. nuts, chopped fine
1 block butter

Make pastry. Pat into 9x13" pan. Bake for 15 minutes in a 350 degree oven.

3 egg whites

1/2 c. sugar

Beat whites stiff. Gradually add sugar and beat stiff.

3/4 c. cake flour
1½ t. baking powder

1/4 t. salt
1/3 c. sugar

Sift all together and make a well.

1/4 c. Wesson oil
1/3 c. milk
1/2 c. Macadamia nuts

2 egg yolks
1 t. vanilla

Combine liquids; blend into flour. Pour into stiffly beaten whites; fold gently. Fold in nuts. Pour over baked crust. Bake 30-35 minutes. Cool. Sift powdered sugar and sprinkle on top. Cut with bread knife.
This recipe came from Maui, Hawaii.

Bonnie Jo Harris
Channel Islands NM

MEXICAN CANDY CAKE

1 pkg. (10 oz.) pie crust mix
1/4 c. granulated sugar
1/2 c. dry cocoa (not instant)
1/4 c. cold water
3 oz. sweet cooking chocolate
2 T. butter or margarine
1 c. confectioners sugar, sifted

1 t. cinnamon
1/4 t. salt
1 egg
1 t. vanilla
1 c. whipping cream
1 pkg. (6 oz.) semi-sweet
   chocolate pieces
2 t. vegetable shortening

Combine first 3 ingredients; blend well. Stir in cold water, a little at a time, with a fork, until dough clings together and leaves sides of bowl clean. Divide into 4 portions. Roll each portion 1/4 inch thick and press on bottom of inverted 8-inch square pan to within 1/4-inch of edge. (If you do not have 4 pans, let remaining pastry stand at room temperature while first layers bake.) Bake at 425 degrees for 6 to 8 minutes, until almost firm. Loosen while warm with wide spatula. Remove to cake racks to cool. Melt sweet cooking chocolate with butter over simmering (not boiling) water. Without removing from hot water, beat in confectioners sugar, cinnamon, salt and egg. Continue beating 1 minute longer. Remove from heat. Fill bottom of double boiler with ice and water; set top in place. Beat 1 minute or until slightly cool. Beat in vanilla. Add cream very slowly, a little at a time, while beating. Continue beating until mixture is fluffy and spreadable (at least 5 minutes). A portable electric mixer makes this easier and faster. Spread each pastry layer with 1/4 of the filling. Stack evenly on serving plate. Chill overnight.

Melt semi-sweet chocolate pieces and shortening over hot (not boiling) water; blend well. Spread evenly in a paper thin layer on baking sheet. Chill until firm. Break into large chips; heap on top pastry layer. Cut in 2-inch squares to serve. Makes 16 squares.

FROM PARADE'S TEST KITCHEN, 1968

Dave and Josephine Jones
San Francisco Office

CURRIED FRUIT

1/3 c. butter or margarine
3/4 c. brown sugar
2 t. curry powder
1 (No. 1) can pear halves
Few maraschino cherries

1 (No. 1) can cling peach halves
1 (No. 1) can apricot halves
1 (No. 2) can pineapple slices
   or chunks

Day before: Start oven 325 degrees. Melt butter; add sugar and curry. Drain fruit and dry well with paper towels. Place fruit in a 1½ quart casserole. Pour curry mixture over it and bake 1 hour. Cool and refrigerate. Thirty minutes before serving, reheat in 350 degree oven. May be prepared ahead of time and frozen until needed. Delicious served with baked ham.

Catherine Hjort
Regional Office

FRENCH CHOCOLATE SILK PIE

1/2 c. butter or margarine
3/4 c. sugar
2 sq. unsweetened chocolate,
   melted

1 t. vanilla
2 eggs
1 baked pastry shell

Cream butter and sugar. Add melted chocolate and vanilla. Add 1 egg; beat 5 minutes at high speed. Add second egg; beat another 5 minutes. Pour into a baked pie shell and refrigerate. When ready to serve, top with whipped cream.

Ellen P. Croll
Grand Canyon NP

FRUIT SALAD

Tangerine oranges
Sliced peaches
Grapefruit sections

Cubed pineapple
Pkg. of frozen strawberries
Bananas

Put all in jar. Add 1/2 cup white wine. Marinate overnight. Add maraschino cherries.

Ruth Uzar
Regional Office

GONE WITH THE WIND DESSERT

1 pkg. lime jello
12 marshmallows
1 small can crushed pineapple
1/2 c. sugar

1 c. boiling water
1 pkg. crushed vanilla wafers
1 c. chopped pecans
2 c. whipped cream

Cut marshmallows; combine with dry jello and pour in boiling water and stir well. Add drained pineapple and nuts. Whip cream; add sugar, then add to jello mixture. Line dish with half of the wafers; pour in fruit mixture and top with remaining wafers.

Yvonne Razo
Tumacacori NM

STRAWBERRY SURPRISE

1 small pkg. strawberry jello
3/4 c. boiling water
1 pkg. frozen strawberries
1/2 pt. sour cream

1 (8 oz.) can crushed pineapple
   and juice
1 mashed banana

Mix jello and boiling water. Add frozen strawberries and stir well. Add pineapple, juice and banana. Pour part of mixture into mold. Cover with sour cream; add remaining jello mixture on top of the sour cream layer. Mixture should be thick from the frozen strawberries; if not, let bottom half set before adding sour cream, etc.

Kathy Lucchesi
Point Reyes NS

TARTE AUX POMMES (French Apple Tart)

1 (8") partially baked pie shell
  set on a buttered baking
  sheet
3 to 4 c. thick unflavored
  applesauce
1/2 to 2/3 c. granulated sugar
3 T. apple brandy, cognac, rum
  OR 1 T. vanilla

1 T. lemon rind, grated
2 T. butter
2-3 apples, peeled and cut
  1/8" lengthwise
1/2 c. apricot jam, strained
  and boiled to 228 degrees
  with 2 T. sugar

Preheat oven to 375 degrees. Stir 1/2 - 2/3 cup sugar into applesauce. Add the liqueur or vanilla and the lemon rind. Boil down, stirring frequently, until sauce is thick enough to hold in spoon. Stir in butter and turn sauce into pie shell, filling almost to the brim. Arrange, closely overlapping, apple slices in concentric circles. Bake for 30 minutes. Unmold the tart onto a serving plate. Paint top and sides with warm apricot jam. Serve hot, warm or cold accompanied with lightly whipped cream, if desired. Serves 6.

Alma Hinkley
Whiskeytown NRA

CREME de MENTHE DESSERT

20 marshmallows
1/4 c. milk
1/2 pt. (1 c.) whipping cream

2 T. sugar
1 t. vanilla
1/3 c. creme de menthe
6 Oreo or Hydrox cookies

Melt marshmallows in milk in double boiler. Cool. Add whipping cream, whipped with sugar and vanilla and creme de menthe. Crush cookies. Spread in bottom of loaf or freezer pan. Add above mixture. Cover with 6 more crushed cookies. Freeze. Eat!

Elaine Hounsell
Lake Mead NRA

STRAW-PRETZEL BALLS

1 pkg. (10 oz.) frozen strawberries
14 large marshmallows
1 c. heavy whipping cream

1/3 c. finely crushed pretzels
2 T. butter, melted slightly
1 c. sugar

Cook strawberries and marshmallows in a double boiler until blended. Stir now and then to blend. Put into a bowl to cool to room temperature. Whip cream and fold into mixture. Mix pretzels, butter and sugar together. Using either paper or aluminum cupcake liners, put a small amount of this mixture in the bottom of each. Fill the liner with cooked mixture and sprinkle extra crumbs on top. Freeze until ready to serve—at least 3 hours. Will keep a long time adequately covered in freezer.

Grace H. Wilson
Lake Mead NRA

FRESH APPLE CAKE

4 c. apples, cut up and peeled
2 c. sugar
2 c. sifted flour
1 t. salt
2 t. soda

2 t. cinnamon
2 t. vanilla
1/2 c. oil
2 eggs, beaten
1 c. chopped nuts
1 pkg. (6 oz.) chocolate chips

Sprinkle sugar over apples. Sift dry ingredients, mix well with apples. Stir in oil, eggs and vanilla. Add nuts and chips. Pour into oiled-floured oblong pan. Bake 40 minutes or until done, in a 375 degree oven.

Wanda Curbow
Joshua Tree NM

NEIGHBORHOOD LEMON CAKE

1 lemon or yellow cake mix
1 pkg. instant lemon pudding
4 eggs
1 c. water

1/3 c. cooking oil
juice of 1 lemon or
   2 or 3 T. lemon juice
2 T. grated lemon rind

Combine ingredients and beat 4 minutes. Bake in a well-greased and floured tube pan for 55-60 minutes at 350 degrees. Cool 10 minutes, immediately prick with a long-tined fork or steel knitting needles. Turn out on rack. Spread with lemon glaze. Will serve 24.

Lemon Glaze:

2¼ c. confectioners sugar

1/4 c. lemon juice

Betty Tucker
Regional Office

STRAWBERRY ICE CREAM CAKE

1/2 c. butter
2 c. strawberry ice cream
2 eggs
2½ c. all-purpose flour
1 T. baking powder

1/2 t. salt
1/2 c. milk
2/3 c. strawberry preserves
1/4 c. sour cream
1 c. sugar

Preheat oven to 350 degrees. Set ice cream at room temperature until very soft, but not melted. Melt butter in a large saucepan over slow heat. Remove from heat; add ice cream, eggs, flour, sugar, baking powder, salt and milk. Beat until smooth. Pour into 13x9" pan, greased and floured. Bake 30-35 minutes until top springs back when lightly touched. Combine sour cream and strawberry preserves. Spread over warm cake.

Instead of strawberry ice cream: vanilla ice cream plus 2 teaspoons strawberry flavoring and several drops of red food coloring can be substituted.

Elaine Hounsell
Lake Mead NRA

CHOCOLATE MINT PIE

2 cubes (1/2 lb.) butter
1 c. powdered sugar
2 sq. baking chocolate

2 eggs
1/2 t. peppermint extract
Whipped cream
Shaved chocolate for topping

Beat butter and sugar together. Add chocolate (melted). Add unbeaten eggs, one at a time, then beat all together for 5 minutes. Add peppermint. Pour into prepared graham cracker crust; top with whipped cream; garnish with shaved chocolate.

Kathy Dimont
Lake Mead NRA

CRAZY CAKE

3 c. flour
1½ c. sugar
1/2 c. cocoa
2 t. soda
1 t. salt

3/4 c. salad oil
2 T. vinegar
2 c. lukewarm water
1 t. vanilla

Mix all ingredients together in a 9x13x2" cake pan and stir with fork until smooth and creamy. Bake at 350 degrees for 35 to 40 minutes.

NPS Frosting:

1 c. vegetable shortening
1 c. granulated sugar
1 egg

1/2 c. warm milk
1 t. vanilla

Cream shortening, sugar and egg in small bowl. Add milk gradually in small amount. Continue beating until thick and creamy. Add vanilla. (This is a great frosting—especially when you have no powdered sugar. It keeps very well in the refrigerator for a couple of days.)

Georjean McKeeman
Tonto NM

EASY DESSERT

1 box white or yellow
  cake mix

1 stick melted butter

Mix well until all moist and crumbly. Sprinkle above mixture with a can of Lucky Leaf Instant cherry pie filling which has been spread evenly in a baking pan. Bake at 350 degrees for 40-50 minutes until done. Serve with Dream Whip. You can substitute other fruit for the cherry, if desired. For instance: Use regular canned peaches with brown sugar and cinnamon, or those pie-sliced apples with brown sugar and apple pie spice.

Kay Nelson
Redwood NP

HAUPIA (Coconut Pudding)

1¼ c. coconut milk	4 T. sugar
3/4 c. water	4 T. cornstarch

Combine. Stir and cook over low heat until thickened. Pour into a small square cake pan and allow to cool. Cut into 2" pieces and serve after being thoroughly chilled. Should be at least 1" thick. Use medium heat to cook pudding.

Marcie Ladd
City of Refuge NHP

GOLDEN NUGGETS

1/2 c. butter	4 c. flour, sifted
1/2 c. lard or shortening	1 t. baking powder
1/2 c. white sugar	1 t. soda
1/2 c. brown sugar	1 t. vanilla
2 eggs, beaten	1 c. chopped nuts
1 c. crushed pineapple, drained	

Combine butter, lard or shortening and sugars. Add remaining ingredients. Beat well. Drop onto greased cookie sheets. Bake at 350 degrees about 15 minutes or until golden brown. Remove at once onto cooling rack. Yields 50 servings.

Lois Craig
Petrified Forest NP

SPRINGERLI

4 eggs	4½ c. sifted cake flour
2½ c. fine granulated sugar	1 t. carbonate ammonium
4 drops anise oil	Anise seed for pan

Beat whole eggs until thick. Add sugar gradually, beating well between each addition until all is combined and then beat about 15 minutes. This makes the finished cookies fine-grained and light. Add anise oil and blend. Fold in the flour, lightly. Roll out dough about 1/2" thick. Flour springerli mold carefully and press firmly into dough. Remove mold and cut cookies along line of imprint. Place on greased cookie sheets. Flour the mold each time it is used. Sprinkle anise seed, if desired, on the greased cookie sheets before placing the cookies on them. Let cookies stand overnight in a cool place to dry. In the morning, place in a 350 degree oven to set the shape but reduce the heat immediately to 275 degrees. When baked (about 15 minutes) the cookies should be light in color with the appearance of having been iced. These Christmas cookies may be baked in November and stored in tins to "age". If they get hard, let stand overnight on a plate, or place a piece of apple in the tin. Carbonate ammonium may be purchased at a pharmacy.

Dorothea Miehle
Regional Office

MISSOURI COOKIES

2 c. sugar
1 cube margarine
Pinch of salt
1/2 c. crunch peanut butter

3 T. cocoa
1/2 c. milk
3 c. quick oats
1 t. vanilla

Combine milk, margarine, sugar and cocoa; bring to rolling boil for one minute. Remove from flame; add salt, vanilla and peanut butter and oatmeal. Mix well, off flame. Drop by teaspoonfuls onto waxed paper to cool. Makes 4 dozen.

Vera Boutwell
Petrified Forest NP

SNICKERDOODLES

1 c. shortening (part butter)
1½ c. sugar
2 eggs
2¾ c. flour

2 t. cream of tartar
1 t. soda
1/2 t. salt

Heat oven to 400 degrees. Mix shortening, sugar and eggs thoroughly. Sift dry ingredients. Blend dry ingredients into first mixture. Roll into balls the size of small walnuts. Roll in mixture of 2 tablespoons sugar and 2 teaspoons cinnamon. Place 2 inches apart on ungreased baking sheet. Bake 8 - 10 minutes. These puff up and then flatten out. Makes 5 dozen 2-inch cookies.

Louise Clark
Petrified Forest NP

PINEAPPLE DESSERT

1/2 c. sugar
1/2 c. milk

2 egg yolks

Cook together, remove from heat then stir in 1 Tbsp. gelatin which has been dissolved in 1/2 cup cold water. Cool mixture to lukewarm. Stir in 2 well-beaten egg whites. Add 1 cup whipped cream and 1 cup crushed pineapple. Pour into pan lined with 20 crushed graham crackers and 3-4 Tbsp. melted butter, combined. Save some crushed crackers for sprinkling on top. Refrigerate until serving time.

Marilyn J. Scott
Kings Canyon NP

CHERRY CRUNCH

2 cans pitted cherries
1 c. sugar
1 pkg. white cake mix

1 stick butter/oleo
1/2 c. chopped pecans
1/2 c. brown sugar

In a 9x12x1½" pan, put cherries and granulated sugar. Spread dry cake mix evenly over the cherries. Sprinkle nuts and brown sugar over this. Dot with butter. Bake 1 hour at 300 degrees.

Polly F. Wonson
Tumacacori NM

CAKES, COOKIES, PIES, & DESSERTS **131**

APRICOT BUTTONS

1/2 c. cooked dried apricots,
   sieved
1/3 c. sugar
1/2 c. butter
1/3 c. sugar

1/4 t. vanilla
1 c. sifted flour
1/2 t. salt
1 egg white, slightly beaten
3/4 c. chopped nuts

Combine apricots and 1/3 cup sugar, cook until thickened. Cool. Cream butter and remaining 1/3 cup sugar until light and fluffy. Beat in egg yolk and vanilla. Mix in sifted dry ingredients. Chill dough slightly. Form into balls, dip in egg white then nuts. Place on greased cookie sheet. With thumb, make indentation in center of each. Bake in 350 degree oven for 20 minutes. While still warm, fill centers with apricot mixture. Makes 2 dozen.

Marlene Yazzie
Petrified Forest NP

RUM CAKE

2 c. sugar
1 c. Crisco
1/2 t. salt
3 c. flour
1/2 t. soda

1/2 t. baking powder
4 eggs, added one at a time
1 T. rum flavoring
1 t. vanilla
1 c. buttermilk

Have ingredients at room temperature. Cream sugar and shortening. Add other ingredients gradually. Bake in tube pan at 350 degrees for 1 hour.

Glaze:

1 c. water
2 c. sugar

1 t. rum flavoring

Bring to a boil, pour gradually over hot cake by tablespoonful.

Cricket Carter
Petrified Forest NP

SHERRIED PEANUT RAISIN COOKIES

2/3 c. sherry or muscatel wine
 3/4 c. raisins
1 c. chunky peanut butter
1/2 c. sugar

1/2 c. brown sugar
Few grains salt
2 c. biscuit mix

Pour wine over raisins and allow to stand an hour or so. Heat to boiling point. Meanwhile, mix peanut butter, sugars and salt. Pour warm wine into peanut butter mixture and stir until smooth. Stir in biscuit mix. Drop by teaspoonfuls and roll in marble-sized balls. Flatten with a fork on a cookie sheet. Bake at 400 degrees for 8 - 10 minutes. Yields about 75 cookies.

Rachel Curran
Death Valley NM

RANGER COOKIES

1. Cream:

1 c. brown sugar	1/2 t. vanilla
1 c. margarine, butter	1 c. white sugar
or shortening	2 eggs

2. Sift and add to creamed mixture:

1 t. salt	1 t. soda
1/2 t. baking powder	2 c. flour

3. Add by hand and drop by teaspoonfuls onto greased cookie sheet:

1 c. quick oats	2 c. Rice Krispies
1 c. coconut	1 c. chopped nuts

4. Bake for 12 - 15 minutes at 350 degrees.

Marion Chapman
Regional Office

AMBROSIA FRUIT SALAD

1 c. (11 oz.) Mandarin oranges, drained	1 c. (13 oz.) pineapple chunks, drained
1 c. flaked coconut	1 c. cut-up or miniature marshmallows
1 c. commercial sour cream or 1/2 c. whipping cream	

Mix all ingredients. Chill several hours or overnight.

Lynn Loetterle
Joshua Tree NM

AUNT LOU'S CHOCOLATE CAKE

Cream together:

1 c. sugar	1/8 lb. butter

Add and mix lightly:

1 egg yolk	3/4 c. milk

Then add:

1 c. flour	2 sq. melted chocolate
1 t. baking powder	1 egg white, beaten stiff
1/8 t. salt	1 t. vanilla

Place in a medium rectangular baking pan and bake at 325 degrees for 25 minutes. Cool and frost with bittersweet frosting.

Bill and Barry Fink
Tuzigoot NM

COCOA CRINKLES

1¼ c. shortening
3 1/3 c. sugar
4 t. vanilla
4 eggs
3/4 c. cocoa
4 c. sifted flour

4 t. baking powder
1 t. salt
2/3 c. milk
1 c. chopped walnuts
Powdered sugar

Cream shortening, sugar, vanilla. Beat in eggs. Sift all dry ingredients, except powdered sugar. Blend in alternately to first mixture with milk. Add nuts. Chill 3 hours. Form into 1" balls; roll in powdered sugar. Place on greased cookie sheet and bake in 350 degree oven for 15 minutes. Makes 7 - 8 dozen.

Jan Shaver
Lake Mead NRA

TOASTED COCONUT PIE

3 beaten eggs
1½ c. sugar
1/2 c. butter

4 t. lemon juice
1 t. vanilla
1½ c. flaked coconut
1 unbaked pie shell

Combine eggs, sugar, butter, lemon juice and vanilla. Mix well. Add coconut and stir. Pour filling into pie shell. Bake at 350 degrees for 40-45 minutes or until knife inserted in center comes out clean.

Cricket Carter
Petrified Forest NP

PRUNE CAKE OR FRUIT CAKE

1 stick butter
1½ c. sugar
2 eggs
1/2 c. cold coffee
1 t. salt
2 t. baking powder
1/2 t. baking soda
1 t. cinnamon

1 t. nutmeg
1/2 t. cloves
2 c. flour
1/2 c. nuts
1 c. cooked prunes or
    substitute fruit cocktail,
    raisins, or any dried fruits,
    cooked and drained

Mix all ingredients thoroughly. Bake at 375 degrees until done.

Ivah Belford
Petrified Forest NP

DATE PIES

4 eggs
2 c. sugar
1 c. butter

1 c. pecans
1/2 lb. dates

Mix together; bring to a boil and cook until dates are dissolved. Pour into unbaked shells and bake in moderate oven, 350 degrees, for 20-30 minutes. This recipe will make 3 small pies or 2 large ones.

Clara Furnish
Petrified Forest NP

CARROT COOKIES

2 sticks margarine
3/4 c. sugar
1 t. lemon juice
1/2 t. vanilla
1/4 t. salt
1/4 t. soda

1 egg
2 c. finely shredded raw
  carrots
2 c. flour
2 t. baking powder

Beat together margarine and sugar until creamy. Beat in lemon juice and vanilla, egg and carrots. Stir together flour, baking powder, salt and soda. Stir flour mixture into wet mixture. Drop by level teaspoonfuls onto greased cookie sheet. Bake in 375 degree oven for 12 minutes. Makes 6 dozen cookies.

Kathleen DeWitt
Death Valley NM

PERSIMMON PUDDING

3 to 4 ripe persimmons
1 egg, very lightly beaten
1 c. sugar
2/3 c. sifted flour
1½ t. baking powder

1/2 t. cinnamon
1/2 c. sweet milk
1/2 c. buttermilk
2 T. butter, melted

Rub fruit through a colander to remove seeds. You need 1 cup of pulp. Beat in remaining ingredients. Pour into a greased 8x12" baking dish. Bake at 325 degrees about 1 hour or until done. Serve hot or cold with whipped cream or a vanilla or lemon sauce for topping. Cut into squares. Yield: 10 to 12 portions.

Polly Hayes
John Muir NHS

NO-BAKE BROWNIES

2 (6 oz.) pkg. semi-sweet
  chocolate chips
1 c. evaporated milk
3 c. vanilla wafer crumbs (fine)
2 c. miniature marshmallows

1 c. broken nuts
1 c. confectioners sugar,
  sifted
1/2 t. salt
2 t. evaporated milk

Put chocolate chips and 1 cup milk into heavy 1 quart pan. Stir over low heat until chocolate melts and mixture is smooth. Remove from heat. Into a 3-quart bowl, place crumbs, marshmallows, nuts, sugar and salt. Mix well. Reserve 1/2 cup chocolate mixture for Glaze. Stir the remainder into crumb mixture and blend well. Press evenly into a well-greased 9" pan. Stir 2 teaspoons milk into reserved 1/2 cup chocolate mixture until smooth. Spread evenly over mixture in pan. Chill until Glaze is set. Cut into squares.

Ruth Uzar
Regional Office

QUICK COOKIES

1 stick butter	1/2 c. milk (canned or reg.)
2 tea cups sugar	Light dash salt
1/4 c. peanut butter	3 c. quick cooked oats

Bring butter, peanut butter, milk, salt, sugar to hard boil. Cook for 5 or 7 minutes, stirring at all times. Remove from heat. Add the 3 cups oats, also add 1/2 cup coconut and 1/2 cup nuts if desired. Mix well. Drop on wax paper and let stand until firm. Makes 28 cookies.

Ivah Belford
Petrified Forest NP

OATMEAL SQUARES

1 c. brown sugar	1/4 lb. butter**

Mix and add:

1 t. salt	1 c. flour
1/2 t. vanilla	1 to 1½ c. oatmeal

Press into 8x8" pan. Cook approximately 10 minutes at 350 degrees. When brown on top, remove from oven. Cut in squares while still hot.
**At high altitude, add Mazola, about 1/4 cup or more to right consistency for pressing into pan. All right to add more after mixing in oatmeal if necessary.

Eleanor Wing
Petrified Forest NP

BUTTERFINGERS

1 c. sugar	1 c. shredded coconut
1 c. white Karo syrup	6 c. corn flakes (not crushed)
1 c. chunky peanut butter	1 (12 oz.) pkg. chocolate chips

Bring sugar and syrup to a rolling boil. Add peanut butter. Combine coconut and corn flakes; pour hot mixture over; mix well. Pat firmly into a cookie sheet. Sprinkle with chocolate chips. Put in 350 degree oven just long enough to melt chocolate. Spread over top. Cool and cut into bars or slices.

Helen Cropper
Petrified Forest NP

BRANDY BALLS

1 (12 oz.) pkg. vanilla wafers (crushed)	1/4 c. brandy
	1/2 c. honey
1/4 c. rum	1 lb. ground walnuts

Mix ingredients together well; roll into small balls and gently roll in powdered sugar. Store in tight container in refrigerator. Will keep for five weeks. (Perfect for the Holidays).

Cecilia Martin
Petrified Forest NP

136 CAKES, COOKIES, PIES, & DESSERTS

RANGER COOKIES

1 c. shortening (margarine)	1 t. baking soda
1 c. brown sugar	1/4 t. salt
1 c. white sugar	2 c. uncooked oats
2 eggs, well beaten	2 c. corn flakes
1 t. vanilla	1 c. coconut
2 c. sifted flour	1 c. chopped nuts
1/2 t. baking powder	

Mix all together well. Drop by teaspoonful on cookie sheet and flatten with fork. Bake in a 375 degree oven 10-12 minutes.

Mary Patterson
Pinnacles NM

CHIPERO BARS

2/3 c. shortening	3 eggs
4 c. brown sugar	1 (6 oz.) pkg. chocolate chips
2½ t. baking powder	1 c. chopped nuts
1/2 t. salt	2¾ c. flour

Melt shortening; stir in sugar; mix well. Cool. Sift flour with baking powder and salt. Add eggs, one at a time, to shortening mixture and mix well. Blend in dry ingredients; stir in chocolate pieces and nuts. Spread in greased 15x10x1" pan. Bake at 350 degrees for 25-30 minutes. Cut into squares.

Helen Crosland
Petrified Forest NP

CHOCOLATE DREAM BARS

1/2 c. soft butter	1/2 t. salt
1/2 c. granulated sugar	2 eggs
1/2 t. vanilla	1 t. vanilla
1/4 t. salt	1 c. brown sugar, packed
1 c. sifted flour	1 T. flour
1 c. (6 oz.) chocolate chips	1/4 t. baking powder
	1 c. (6 oz.) chocolate chips

Heat oven to 350 degrees. Mix sugar, butter and 1/2 teaspoon vanilla and 1/4 teaspoon salt until very light and fluffy. Mix in 1 cup sifted flour. Spread in unbuttered 13x9x2" pan. Bake 15 minutes. Remove from oven and sprinkle with 1 cup chocolate chips; let stand until melted then spread evenly over top. Combine eggs, 1 teaspoon vanilla and 1/2 teaspoon salt and beat with mixer at high speed until very thick and light. Gradually beat in brown sugar. Mix in 1 tablespoon flour and baking powder. Fold in 1 cup chocolate chips. Spread over melted chocolate layer. Bake 30 minutes. Cool and cut into bars.

Sandy Neprash
Petrified Forest NP

GUMDROP COOKIES

1 c. margarine	1/2 t. salt
1 c. white sugar	2 eggs, beaten
1 c. brown sugar	1 c. coconut
2 c. flour	1 c. gumdrops, cut into
1 t. soda	small pieces
1 t. baking powder	2 c. oatmeal

Cream margarine; add sugars. Sift flour, soda, baking powder and salt. Add dry ingredients alternately with egg to creamed mixture. Add gumdrops and oatmeal. Shape into small balls and flatten with fork. Bake in a 350 degree oven. Omit the black gumdrops. Makes 5 dozen cookies.

Dorothea Miehle
Regional Office

SOCK IT TO ME CAKE

1 pkg. Duncan Hines yellow cake mix	1/2 c. sugar
	1/4 c. water
1 c. (8 oz.) sour cream	4 eggs
1/2 c. Crisco oil	

Filling:

1 c. chopped nuts	2 T. cinnamon or nutmeg
4 T. brown sugar	

Topping:

1 c. powdered sugar	2 T. milk

Pour half of batter in pan; add filling then remainder of batter. Bake as directed on package. Make topping and drizzle over cake after removing from oven.

Bernice Lewis
Regional Office

PUMPKIN DROP COOKIES

2¼ c. flour	1/2 c. raisins
1 t. baking powder	1 c. sugar
1/4 t. soda	1/2 c. shortening
1/2 t. salt	1 egg
2½ t. pumpkin pie spice	1 c. pumpkin
1/2 c. chopped walnuts	1/4 c. milk

Mix dry ingredients, walnuts and raisins. Cream sugar and shortening. Add egg and beat. Blend in pumpkin and milk alternately with dry ingredients. Drop by teaspoon onto greased cookie sheet. Bake at 400 degrees for 12 minutes. Makes 5 dozen.

Anonymous
Southern Arizona Group

DOUBLE FUDGE BALLS

1/2 c. semi-sweet chocolate chips

Place over boiling water with heat turned off. Stir until melted; remove from heat. Stir in:

1½ T. corn syrup   1/2 t. vanilla
1/4 c. Sego milk

Add:

1/4 c. powdered sugar   1/2 c. nuts
1¼ c. crushed vanilla wafers

Fold in vanilla wafers 1/4 cup at a time. Let stand 1/2 hour. Roll in balls and roll in crushed nuts. Let stand two days before using.

Irene Thorne
Petrified Forest NP

PFEFFERNUSSE

4 c. sugar   4 eggs

Cream for 30 minutes. Add:

2/3 c. blanched almonds,   1/4 lb. citron, chopped fine
   chopped fine

Sift together and add:

4½ c. cake flour   1 t. cinnamon
1 t. nutmeg   1/2 t. cloves
1 t. ammonium carbonate

Before baking, brush balls with thin confectioners icing made by stirring confectioners sugar with milk. Place on ungreased baking sheet. Bake 15 minutes at 325 degrees. Chill. If the dough is allowed to ripen for a couple of days, the flavor and texture improves. These cookies may be baked in November and stored in airtight tins until Christmas.

Dorothea Miehle
Regional Office

DOT'S SWEDISH BUTTER COOKIES

1/4 c. milk   1 t. vanilla
1½ c. flour   1/2 c. butter
1½ t. baking powder   Pinch of salt
1/2 c. sugar

Mix dry ingredients. Cut in butter as for pie crust. Add liquid. Roll on well-floured board, very thin and cut into desired shapes. Bake 8-10 minutes at 350 degrees.

Carla Martin
Tuzigoot NM

CHEWY WHEAT GERM BROWNIES

4 sq. unsweetened chocolate
3/4 c. margarine
1¼ c. flour
2 t. baking powder
1 t. salt

1 c. wheat germ
2 c. sugar
3 eggs, beaten
1 t. vanilla
1 c. chopped nuts

In a small saucepan, melt chocolate, margarine and set aside. In large bowl, combine next five ingredients and mix well. Stir in melted chocolate mixture, eggs and vanilla. Mix well. Fold in nuts. Spread in greased 13x9x2" pan. Bake in 350 degree oven (preheated) for 30 minutes. Cool and cut. Store in airtight container.

Kathy Berg
Death Valley NM

FRUIT CAKE SQUARES

6 T. butter or margarine
1½ c. graham cracker crumbs
1 c. shredded coconut
2 c. cut-up mixed candied fruit
1 c. dates

2 T. flour
1 c. nuts, coarsely chopped
1 (15 oz.) can sweetened
  condensed milk (do not
  substitute)

Melt butter in 15½x10½x1" jelly-roll pan. Sprinkle on crumbs (tap sides of the pan to distribute crumbs evenly). Sprinkle on coconut. Cut dates into flour so they won't stick together. Distribute dates over coconut. Distribute candied fruit as evenly as possible over dates. Sprinkle on nuts. Press mixture lightly with hands to level it in pan. Pour sweetened condensed milk evenly over top. Bake in moderate oven, 350 degrees, for 25 to 30 minutes. Cool completely before cutting. Remove from pan. Makes about 54 - 1½" squares.

Adele Fevella
Haleakala NP

SEED CAKES

3/4 c. margarine
1 c. sugar
3 eggs, unbeaten

1/3 c. brandy
2½ c. sifted flour
Caraway or poppy seed

Cream margarine and slowly add sugar until light and fluffy. Beat in eggs, one at a time. Stir in brandy. Add flour and stir until blended. Divide dough into 6 parts. Cover with plastic wrap and freeze until needed. When ready to bake, remove one package of dough at a time, quickly roll out to 1/8" thickness on lightly floured board or pastry cloth. Cut with 2" cookie cutters. Place on ungreased baking sheet and sprinkle with seed. Bake at 350 degrees for 10-12 minutes. Transfer to racks to cool. This recipe makes about 14 dozen.

Peggy Rolandson
San Francisco Office

BRAUNE LEBKUCHEN

2/3 c. honey	1/3 c. butter
1 c. sugar	

Boil together for 5 minutes. Cool.

1 egg	1/3 c. water

Beat egg and add to water.

4 c. sifted cake flour	1 t. cinnamon
1/2 t. salt	1 t. cloves
1 t. baking soda	

Add sifted dry ingredients alternately with liquid ingredients to honey mixture.

2/3 c. chopped almonds, blanched	1/3 c. chopped citron

Add nuts and citron last. Chill. If the dough is allowed to ripen for several days before rolling out, the flavor and texture of the cookies are improved.

Roll about 1/4 inch thick and cut with fancy cookie cutters. Bake at 350 degrees for 15-30 minutes. Ice with sugar glace: Confectioners sugar diluted with cream or milk to make it the consistency of thin cream.

Dorothea Miehle
Regional Office

OATMEAL SESAME COOKIES

1/2 c. oil	3/4 c. sesame seeds
1 c. dark brown sugar	1/2 t. soda
1 egg, beaten well	1/4 t. salt
2 T. milk	1/2 t. nutmeg
1¼ c. rolled oats	1 t. cinnamon
1¼ c. whole wheat flour	

Mix the oil, brown sugar, egg and milk together. Add and mix the oats, flour, sesame seeds, soda, salt, nutmeg and cinnamon. Bake at 375 degrees for 15 minutes. Makes about 2½ dozen cookies.

Mary Dodd
Chiricahua NM

SUGAR AND SPICE COOKIES

3/4 c. butter	2 t. soda
1 c. sugar	1/4 t. salt
1/4 c. molasses	1 t. cinnamon
2 c. flour	3/4 t. ginger

Mix all together and form into balls. Bake 10-12 minutes in a 375 degree oven. Roll in powdered sugar.

Chuck and Irene Adams
Regional Office

WALNUT MAPLE CAKE

1/2 c. butter
1 c. brown sugar, packed
2 eggs
1/2 c. sweet milk
1½ c. flour, sifted

2 t. baking powder
1/2 t. salt
1 T. vanilla
1 c. chopped walnuts

Cream the butter, sugar and eggs until creamy. Set aside. Combine flour, salt and baking powder together. Add milk and vanilla and flour mixture to the egg mixture alternately. Stir until well blended. Bake in 400 degree oven about 17 minutes or until done. Serve with whipped cream or frost with plain white or maple frosting.

Marjorie Nichols
Montezuma Castle NM

NECTAR PIE

1 can apricot nectar
1/2 c. sugar
1/4 t. salt
3 T. cornstarch

2 T. butter
2 egg yolks, beaten
8" baked pastry shell
Meringue

Combine nectar, sugar, salt, cornstarch and butter in saucepan and stir to blend. Cook and stir until mixture boils and thickens. Remove from heat. Add beaten egg yolks. Cook and stir 2 minutes. Cool. Pour into pie shell. Cover with meringue and bake in slow oven (325 degrees) 12 to 15 minutes or until golden brown.

Chuck and Irene Adams
Regional Office

SPECIAL DATE-NUT CAKE

California has many walnut orchards, and only by getting out and picking up and shelling my nuts (or having Grandpa do it) can I afford to make much of this excellent treat.

2 lb. shelled walnuts
2 lb. dates
2 c. sugar
2 c. flour

2 t. vanilla
1/2 t. salt
3 t. baking powder
8 eggs

Separate eggs; beat whites very stiff; beat yolks well in separate bowl. Add yolks to whites and mix well. Sift flour with sugar and baking powder; add nuts and dates that have been cut coarsely. Add eggs and mix well. Bake in slow oven, 325 degrees, about an hour. Loaf pans or tube pan can be used. Line pans with brown paper and grease before putting mixture into pan.

This cake is basically nuts and dates—with a very small flour-egg mixture to hold it together.

Rachel Curran
Death Valley NM

CRUMB CAKE

2 sticks butter	2 c. flour
1½ c. brown sugar	1½ t. cinnamon

Crumb above with hands. Reserve 1/2 cup for topping. Add:

1 c. buttermilk or sour milk	1 t. baking soda

Beat in:

1 egg	1 t. vanilla

Pour into 9x9" pan and sprinkle with topping. Bake at 350 degrees for 30-35 minutes or until done.

Pat Flanagan
Joshua Tree NM

BUTTER DIPS

Melt in a 9x13" shallow pan: 1/3 c. butter. Sift together:

2¼ c. flour	3½ t. baking powder
1 T. sugar	1½ t. salt

Add 1 cup of milk to above. Stir until dough clings together. Knead 10 times on floured board. Roll out 1/2" thick. Cut into strips about 3/4" by 2". Dip each strip into butter and lay on pan. Bake at 450 degrees for 15-20 minutes.

FOR VARIATION: Add garlic powder in butter or add 1/2 cup grated sharp cheese to dry ingredients. Yummy with spaghetti.

Rachel Curran
Death Valley NM

APPLESAUCE CAKE

3/4 c. shortening	2 eggs
3/4 t. salt	1½ t. baking soda
3/4 t. cinnamon	2½ c. flour
1/2 t. nutmeg	3/4 c. chopped dates
1/2 t. allspice	1 c. raisins
2 T. cocoa	3/4 c. chopped nuts
1½ c. sugar	1½ c. unsweetened applesauce
1/2 t. baking powder	

Sift flour and add salt, cinnamon, nutmeg, allspice, cocoa, sugar, baking powder and soda. Add shortening and applesauce and beat two minutes on medium speed. Add eggs and beat 2 more minutes. Stir in nuts, raisins and dates. Pour into greased and floured 8x11" oblong pan. Bake 55-60 minutes at 350 degrees.

Sherry Collins
Petrified Forest NP

CHOCOLATE CHIP MARBLE CAKE

1 pkg. yellow cake mix
1 sm. pkg. instant vanilla
  pudding
2/3 c. oil
1 c. boiling water

1 sm. bag chocolate chips
1 (5 oz.) can Hershey's chocolate
  syrup
4 eggs

Beat above 4 minutes; pour 3/4's of the batter into greased and floured Bundt or tube pan. Mix the remaining 1/4 batter with the syrup (2/3's cup). Pour this mixture on top of the yellow batter; sprinkle chocolate chips evenly over the top. Bake 50 to 60 minutes at 350 degrees. Cool for 20 minutes in the pan, then invert. The chocolate chips and chocolate batter will work their way through the cake as it bakes. No icing.

JoAnne Hasty
Regional Office

SPICED APPLE CAKE

1 c. butter
2 c. sugar
3 eggs
2 t. vanilla
3 c. regular all-purpose flour
  (unsifted)

1½ t. soda
1/2 t. salt
1 t. cinnamon
1/4 t. mace or allspice
3 c. finely chopped apples that
  are UNPEELED (I use Pippen)
2 c. chopped walnuts

Beat butter and sugar to creamy. Add eggs, one at a time, beat well after each addition. Sift flour with soda, salt, cinnamon and mace or allspice. Add flour to creamed mixture. Add nuts and apples. Bake in well greased and floured 10" tube pan. Bake at 325 degrees for 1½ hours. (Check with toothpick after 1¼ hours.) Cool in pan for 10 minutes. Turn onto rack and let cool completely. Before serving, shake powdered sugar over top.

Harry and Nancy Sloat
Regional Office

ALL AROUND FAMILY CAKE

3 sticks butter (3/4 lb.)
1 carton powdered sugar
6 eggs
1 box (powdered sugar box) sifted flour

1 t. lemon juice
1 T. vanilla
1/2 c. pineapple juice

Have butter and eggs at room temperature. Cream butter; add sugar. Beat with electric mixer until fluffy; add eggs, one at a time. Beat well after each addition. Sift flour 3 times and add gradually to batter; add flavoring and mix well. Bake in greased and floured tube pan at 325 degrees for 1½ hours. Cool 4 minutes and invert pan. Sprinkle powdered sugar on top.

Yvonne Razo
Tumacacori NM

CHEWY MAPLE WALNUT BARS

1 egg
1/2 c. flour, sifted before
   measuring
1/3 c. Wesson oil
1/4 t. salt

1/4 t. baking powder
1/2 c. seedless raisins
1 c. walnuts, chopped
1 t. Mapleine

Beat egg, then add the sugar gradually, then the oil, flour, salt, baking powder, Mapleine, raisins and nuts. Put in 9x9x2" pan; grease well; bake about 1/2 hour or until done, in a moderate oven.

Betty Miller
Petrified Forest NP

ANISE COOKIES

4 eggs, beat 10 minutes
2 c. sugar
2 c. flour

1½ T. anise seed (rolled fine)
1/2 t. ammonium carbonate
   (moistened with drop of water)

Add sugar to eggs and beat 30 minutes longer. Add flour, anise seed and carbonate ammonium and beat 5 minutes longer. Drop by teaspoon on well-greased floured pans, one inch apart. Let stand overnight at room temperature to dry. Bake in a slow oven, 300 degrees, about 10 minutes, or until very light yellow in color. These Christmas cookies may be baked in November and stored in tins to "age". Ammonium carbonate may be purchased at a pharmacy.

Dorothea Miehle
Regional Office

JELLO CREAM CRUST

1½ blocks butter
1/3 c. powdered brown sugar

1/2 c. chopped nuts
1½ c. flour

Cream butter and sugar. Mix in nuts then flour and bake at 375 degrees for 10 minutes in a 9x13" pan.

1st Layer:

1 box lemon jello
1 c. hot water
1 (8 oz.) pkg. cream cheese

3/4 c. powdered sugar
2 small boxes Dream Whip
   (directions on box)

Dissolve jello in hot water; cool. Blend cream cheese and sugar. Add jello to cream cheese mix, then fold in Dream Whip.

2nd Layer:

2 boxes lemon jello
1/2 pkg. gelatin, any flavor

3 c. hot water

Pour first layer on crust and refrigerate until half firm; then pour second layer of jello on first layer using waxed paper for pouring to prevent holes.

Adele Fevella
Haleakala NP

RICH MAN'S RUMPOT

1 - 5th of rum or bourbon	Peel from 1 orange and
1 T. whole cloves	1 lemon, spiraled
1 t. allspice	1 stick cinnamon
8 c. sugar	FRESH FRUITS

In the order listed below, add one fruit and 1 cup sugar each week. Stir carefully (with hand is best) and cover after each addition:

1st week: Pitted cherries; 2nd - chunks of peaches; 3rd - apricots chunks; 4th - plums, chunks; 5th - strawberries; 6th - raspberries; 7th - pineapple chunks; 8th - seedless grapes. (Don't forget to add 1 cup of sugar each time!)

Scald a 7-quart stone crock with boiling water and dry it. Pour in liquor, peels and spices. Add fruits in order listed above. Cover crock with foil, place a plate on top and weigh it down to surmerge the fruit. Repeat each week until one week after the last fruit has been added before using. It can be replenished as desired if it is not used all at one time. Use as a dessert alone or as a fruit sauce over ice cream, pound cake or pudding. Very potent! Makes enough for about 30 adults.

POOR MAN'S RUMPOT

All No. 2½ cans fruit with the juices. Each week, add one fruit as listed in order and 1 cup sugar. Follow procedures as above in RICH MAN'S RUMPOT:

1st week - peach chunks; 2nd - apricots; 3rd - plums; 4th - pineapple chunks; 5th - pears, chunks; 6th - cherries (Queen Anne, pitted) and 7th - maraschino cherries BUT OMIT THE SUGAR ON THIS FRUIT. More for looks.

A one-gallon size mayonnaise jar will hold the fruit if used occasionally. This can be left uncovered at room temperature to ferment. When desired fermentation has been reached, place, covered, in refrigerator to halt fermentation. Use as desired. An 8 oz. cup of this preparation can be used as a "mother" for another potful of goodies for your friends.

Peggy Rolandson
San Francisco Office

SOUR CREAM CAKE

1 c. sugar	1½ t. baking powder
1/4 c. butter	1/2 t. salt
2 eggs	1 t. vanilla
1 c. sour cream	Grated rind of 1 orange
1 t. soda	1½ t. lemon juice
1 2/3 c. flour	2 T. sugar
1 T. cinnamon	1/2 c. chopped nuts

Cream sugar and butter. Beat in eggs one at a time. Blend sour cream and soda. Sift flour, baking powder and salt; add to first mixture alternately with sour cream. Add remaining ingredients. Pour into 8" greased square pan and sprinkle with: 2 tablespoons sugar, cinnamon and chopped nuts (mixed). Bake in a 350 degree oven for 30 minutes, or until center is firm. You may dust cake lightly with powdered sugar when cool, if desired.

Ruth Uzar
Regional Office

BUTTERSCOTCH CASHEW CLUSTERS

1/2 c. butter
1/3 c. firmly packed brown
  sugar
1 c. all purpose flour

2 (6 oz.) pkg. (2 cups) Nestle's
  butterscotch morsels
1 c. seedless raisins
1 c. cashews (or other salted nuts)

Cream butter; add sugar. Stir in flour. Mix until a dough forms. Stir in nuts. Crumble mixture onto a cookie sheet. Bake at 375 degrees for 12-15 minutes until golden brown, turning mixture occasionally to brown evenly. Cool. Melt morsels over hot water. Combine cookie-nut mixture broken in small pieces; add raisins into a large bowl. Add melted morsels; stir to coat mixture. Drop by teaspoonfuls onto waxed paper. Chill until set, about 15 minutes.

Elaine Hounsell
Lake Mead NRA

PECAN PIE SURPRISE BARS

1 pkg. yellow cake mix
1 egg
1 c. chopped pecans

1/2 c. butter or margarine,
  melted

Generously grease bottom and sides of a 13x9" baking pan. Reserve 2/3 cup dry cake mix for filling. In a large bowl, combine remaining cake mix with the butter and egg; mix until crumbly. Press into prepared pan and bake at 350 degrees for 15-20 minutes, until light golden brown. Pour filling over partially baked crust, sprinkle with pecans. Return to oven 30-35 minutes, until filling is set. Cool; cut into bars. Yields 3 dozen bars.

Filling:

2/3 c. reserved cake mix
1/2 c. brown sugar, firmly
  packed

1 t. vanilla
1½ c. corn syrup
3 eggs

Combine all ingredients and beat at medium speed 1 to 2 minutes.

Mrs. Leonard A. Frank
Muir Woods NM

APPLESAUCE COOKIES

Cream:

3/4 c. soft shortening   1 c. brown sugar
1 egg

Add 1/2 cup applesauce. Sift together, then add to the above mixture:

2½ c. flour	3/4 t. cinnamon
1/2 t. soda	1/4 t. cloves
1/2 t. salt	

Stir in:

1/2 c. chopped nuts   1 c. raisins

Drop by teaspoon onto greased baking sheet. Bake 10-12 minutes at 325 degrees. Yields 45 to 50 cookies.

Mollie Mason
Petrified Forest NP

CINNAMON DROPS

3½ c. sifted flour	1 c. molasses
1/2 t. soda	1 egg
3/4 t. salt	1/4 c. boiling water
1/2 c. shortening	1/4 c. cinnamon sugar
1/2 c. sugar	

Sift together flour, soda and salt. Cream together shortening and sugar until light and fluffy. Add molasses and egg. Beat thoroughly. Add boiling water. Add flour mixture to creamed mixture gradually, mixing well after each addition. Drop teaspoonful into cinnamon sugar. Bake on greased baking sheets in 350 degree oven about 12-15 minutes. Makes about 15 dozen.

Marlene Yazzie
Petrified Forest NP

RAISIN BAR COOKIES

1 egg	1/2 t. baking powder
2/3 c. firmly packed brown sugar	1/8 t. salt
1/3 c. melted butter	1 c. raisins
1 t. vanilla	2 T. granulated sugar mixed with 1/4 t. each cinnamon
1 c. all purpose flour	and nutmeg

Beat egg; gradually beat in brown sugar. Stir in melted butter and vanilla. Sift together flour, baking powder and salt; add to first mixture and mix well. Stir in raisins. Spread dough in greased 9" square pan and sprinkle with sugar-cinnamon/nutmeg mixture. Bake at 350 degrees about 20 minutes or until very lightly browned. Makes 24 bar cookies.

Mary Alice Replogle
Regional Office

CHOCOLATE KRINKLES

1/2 c. shortening
1 2/3 c. granulated sugar
2 t. vanilla
2 eggs
2 (1 oz.) squares unsweetened
   chocolate, melted

2 c. sifted flour
2 t. salt
2 t. baking powder
1/2 c. milk
1/2 c. walnuts
   (about 1½ cups powdered
   sugar)

Cream together shortening, sugar, vanilla, eggs and chocolate. Blend in dry ingredients alternately with milk. Add nuts and chill for 3 hours. Roll into balls about the size of large walnuts, then roll in confectioners sugar. Place on UNGREASED baking sheet about 3 inches apart. Bake in 350 degree oven for 15 minutes. Cool slightly and remove from baking sheet. Yields about 4 dozen.

Kay Marquardt
Joshua Tree NM

ORANGE KISS-ME CAKE

1 large orange with rind
1 c. raisins

1/3 c. (or more) walnuts

Grind together (coarse grind). Grind nuts first and save some for topping. Sift together:

2 c. flour
1 t. soda

1 t. salt

Cream together well:

1 c. sugar

1/3 c. shortening (or margarine)

Add 2 eggs and beat for 2 minutes. Add 1 cup milk alternately with flour mixture. (Add flour first and last). Beat well after each addition. Fold in orange mixture. Bake in 13x9x2" pan at 350 degrees for 40-50 minutes. When cool, spread on topping.

Topping:

1/3 c. orange juice
1/3 c. granulated sugar

1 t. cinnamon
A few ground nuts

Ruth Uzar
Regional Office

SPEEDY COFFEE CAKE

1½ c. self-rising flour
3/4 c. sugar
1/4 c. oil
Topping (below)

3/4 c. milk
1 egg
6 t. favorite jelly or jam

Heat oven to 375 degrees. In large bowl, blend flour, sugar, oil, milk, and egg with fork. Beat well for 60 seconds and pour into greased pan (8x8x2"). Drop the jelly or jam into the batter by tablespoons and swirl with a knife giving a marbled effect. Sprinkle the topping and bake 25 to 30 minutes, or until toothpick comes out free of batter. Serve warm.

Topping:

1/3 c. brown sugar
1/4 c. flour

1 t. cinnamon
3 t. soft margarine

Mix until lumpy and blended.
Note: If regular flour is used, add 3/4 tsp. salt and 2½ tsp. baking powder to the flour.

Tomie Patrick
Point Reyes NS

JAM-FLAVORED COOKIES

1 c. sugar
3/4 c. butter or margarine,
    softened
1 egg

1/4 c. pineapple or red raspberry
    preserves
2¼ c. sifted flour
1 t. soda
1/2 t. salt

Gradually add sugar to soft butter or margarine until light and fluffy. Beat in egg and preserves. Sift together dry ingredients; add to creamed mixture, mixing thoroughly. Drop from teaspoon, 2 inches apart on an ungreased cookie sheet. Bake in moderate oven, 375 degrees, about 10 minutes or until cookies are delicately browned. Let cool 1 or 2 minutes, remove from pan. If desired, top each cookie with a bit of preserves and a walnut half just before serving. Makes 3½ dozen.

Anne Lewis
Sequoia NP

AVOCADO CHIFFON PIE

1 baked pie crust (9")
1 c. strained avocado pulp
3 eggs, separated
1½ T. soft butter or margarine
1/2 t. nutmeg
1 t. cinnamon

Juice from 1/2 lemon
1/2 c. sugar
1/4 c. sugar
1 pkg. plain gelatin
1/4 c. water
Whipped cream

Heat avocado, yolks, butter, spices, 1/2 cup sugar and lemon juice until sugar dissolves. Dissolve gelatin in water and add to hot mixture. Cool and fold in 3 stiffly beaten egg whites, with 1/4 cup sugar. Pour into prepared pie shell. Chill in refrigerator until set. Top with whipped cream.

Marcie Ladd
City of Refuge NHP

HARVEST LOAF CAKE

1¾ c. flour
1 t. soda
1 t. cinnamon
1/2 t. salt
1/2 t. nutmeg
1/4 t. ginger
1/4 t. cloves

1/2 c. butter
1 c. sugar
2 eggs
3/4 c. canned pumpkin
3/4 c. chocolate chips
3/4 c. chopped nuts

Grease bottom of loaf pan. Combine flour with soda, salt and spices. Cream butter, gradually add sugar, cream well. Blend in eggs, beat well. At low speed, add dry ingredients alternately with pumpkin, beginning and ending with the dry ingredients. Stir in chips and half the nuts. Turn into prepared pan. Sprinkle with remaining nuts. Bake at 350 degrees for 65 to 75 minutes. Cool. Drizzle with glaze. Let stand at least 6 hours before slicing.

Edna Caresia
Petrified Forest NP

YUM YUM CAKE

1 c. sugar
1/2 c. butter and shortening
   (mixed)
2 eggs
2 c. sifted flour
1 t. baking powder
1 t. soda

1/2 t. salt
1 t. each of: vanilla, almond,
   pineapple and lemon flavorings
1 pt. sour cream
1 small can crushed pineapple
1/2 c. milk

Mix all ingredients thoroughly.

Crumb Mixture:

1/3 c. brown sugar
1/4 c. sugar

1 t. cinnamon
1/2 c. crushed walnuts

Mix well. Mix sugar, shortening and eggs. Beat well. Put flour, salt, baking powder and soda mixture into eggs. Alternate with sour cream; add flavorings and milk. Place half of the mixture into a greased, lightly floured pan. Place some crumb mixture on top, then add more of the dough mixture, top again with crumbs until all mixture is used. Bake in 325 degree oven about 40 minutes or until done.

Leonard Lebovitz
Regional Office

MOTHER'S CREAM PIE

1 unbaked pie shell (8")
1 c. granulated sugar
  (can use ½ brown and ½ white)
Nutmeg

2 T. flour (not instant)
2 c. cream (mother used
  fresh cream skimmed
  from top of fresh milk)

Combine sugar, flour and mix well. Put in pie shell and pour cream over. Sprinkle with nutmeg and bake in a 400 degree oven until silver knife inserted halfway between center and edge comes out clean, about 20-30 minutes. Cool on rack and refrigerate until served. (This pie should be baked in either a glass pan or pie pan to allow the crust to bake well. Variations can be made, such as: mixing sugar and flour and stirring in cream, then pouring in pie shell; use vanilla as flavoring in lieu of nutmeg. Do your own thing! The ingredients can be enlarged to make more pies, larger pies, or whatever, as long as the basic proportions are kept.

Virginia Duckett
Regional Office

CHOCOLATE KRAUT CAKE

2/3 c. butter or margarine
1½ c. sugar
3 eggs
1 t. vanilla
1/2 c. unsweetened cocoa
2¼ c. sifted all-purpose flour

1 t. baking soda
1 t. baking powder
1/4 t. salt
1 c. water
2/3 c. sauerkraut

Cream well the butter with the sugar. Add eggs, one at a time, beating well after each addition. Add vanilla. Sift together dry ingredients and add alternately with water to egg mixture. Stir in sauerkraut, which has been rinsed in hot water, drained and chopped. Turn into two greased and floured 8" square or round baking pans. Bake in a 350 degree oven 30 minutes or until cake tests done. Fill and frost with chocolate or Mocha Frosting.

This recipe appeared in the NATIONAL OBSERVER, February 1970.

Lester Bodine (Retired)
Lassen Volcanic NP

CORN FLAKE COOKIES

1 c. sifted flour
1 t. soda
1/2 t. baking powder
1 t. salt
1 c. vegetable shortening

1 c. white sugar
1 c. brown sugar
2 well-beaten eggs
1 t. vanilla
2 c. corn flakes

Sift dry ingredients together. Cream shortening, gradually add sugars. Beat until light; add eggs, vanilla and then dry ingredients, and corn flakes. Drop by teaspoonfuls onto greased sheet, 1½" apart. Bake at 350 degrees for 8 to 10 minutes.

Carla Martin
Tuzigoot NM

DRAMATIZATION OF AMERICAN REVOLUTION BATTLE AT GUILFORD COURTHOUSE NATIONAL MILITARY PARK, NORTH CAROLINA. (NPS photo by Richard Frear).

VIEW FROM POINT PARK ON LOOKOUT MOUNTAIN AT CHICKAMAUGA AND CHATTANOOGA NATIONAL MILITARY PARK IN TENNESSEE. (NPS photo by Jack E. Boucher).

Breads

WELCOMING VISITORS TO THE WEST" IS THE IMPRESSIVE 630-FOOT HIGH GATEWAY ARCH, PART OF THE JEFFERSON NATIONAL EXPANSION MEMORIAL, ST. LOUIS, MISSOURI. (NPS photo).

WHITE BREAD

1 c. milk
2 T. sugar
2 t. salt
2 T. cooking oil

1 c. cold water
1 envelope active dry yeast
　or 1 yeast cake
1 c. lukewarm water
6 c. pre-sifted flour

Scald milk. Remove from heat and add sugar, salt and oil. Stir until sugar is dissolved. Add cold water. Soften yeast in lukewarm water. Add to milk mixture. Gradually add flour, mixing to a smooth dough. Turn onto lightly floured board and knead 10 minutes. Place dough in greased bowl, cover, let rise 1 hour. Punch down. Let rise 1 more hour or until doubled in bulk. Knead dough down; divide in half; mold each half into a loaf. Place in 2 greased loaf pans. Cover and let rise 45 minutes. Bake at 400 degrees for 15 minutes. Reduce heat to 350 degrees and bake 30 minutes more.

Mary Chilton
Montezuma Castle NM

CALEXICO CORN BREAD

1 c. yellow corn meal
1½ t. salt
1 (11 oz.) can cream style corn
1/3 c. melted bacon fat (or 1/3
　c. Crisco oil)

1/4 c. milk
1/4 lb. cheese - or 4 slices
1 can green chili peppers

Mix first 5 ingredients; spread half in greased pan, 8x8x2"; cover with strips of chili (or use the diced chili) and cheese. Spread rest of batter on top; bake 35 to 40 minutes in a 375 degree oven.

Mary and Forrest Benson
Regional Office

ZUCCHINI BREAD

Beat 3 eggs and 2 cups sugar until light and fluffy (2-3 minutes). Add:

2 c. grated and peeled
　zucchini

1 c. oil
2 t. vanilla

Mix together and add to above:

3 c. flour
1 t. soda
1/4 t. baking powder

1 t. salt
3 t. cinnamon

Add 3/4 cup chopped nuts. Grease and flour pans, 4x8". Bake at 325 degrees for 1 hour. (Prunes, dates, raisins may be added if desired.)

Avis Franklin
Lehman Caves NM

EGG BREAD

2 cakes yeast
1/4 c. lukewarm water
1/4 c. shortening
1/2 c. sugar
1 t. salt

2 eggs, well beaten
1 c. milk, scalded
1 t. grated lemon rind
5 c. sifted flour (about)

Soften yeast in lukewarm water. Add shortening, sugar and salt to scalded milk. Cool to lukewarm. Add softened yeast, eggs, lemon rind and enough flour to make a stiff dough. Beat well. Add enough more flour to make a soft dough. Turn out on lightly floured board and knead until satiny. Place in greased bowl, cover, and let rise until doubled in bulk. When light, punch down.

When dough is light, divide into halves and cut half of dough into 6 pieces. Roll each piece until about 8 inches long. Cross 3 of the rolls in the center, braid to each end and fasten. Place on greased baking sheet. Braid remaining 3 rolls. Place on top of first braid. Cover and let rise until doubled in bulk. Brush with beaten egg yolk. Bake in hot oven, 400 degrees, for 30 minutes or until done. Makes 2 braids.

Karen Fox
Muir Woods NM

TWO LOAVES WHOLE WHEAT BREAD

1 cake compressed yeast
2 c. lukewarm water
2 T. sugar
2 t. salt
4 c. enriched white flour

1/2 c. hot water
1/2 c. brown sugar
3 T. shortening (lard or
   butter)
4 c. whole wheat flour

Soften yeast in 2 cups warm water. Add sugar, salt and white flour. Beat until smooth. Keep in warm place (82 degrees) until light and bubbly, takes about an hour.

Combine hot water, brown sugar and shortening. Stir; cool to lukewarm and add to the yeast mixture.

Now add whole wheat flour. Mix until smooth. Turn dough onto lightly floured surface. Knead smooth, about 10 minutes. Place in greased bowl. Turn over to grease surface, cover; let rise in warm place until double.

Knead down dough, cut in half with knife. Shape each half to form a ball, cover; let dough rest about 10 minutes, roll the dough into 10x14", in shape of rectangle. Break bubbles in surface. Roll dough toward you. Seal after each roll with heel of hand. Seal ends with the side of your hand. This leaves thin sealed strips to make a smooth uniform crust on both ends of loaf. Fold the strips under loaf. Place in lightly greased 9½x5¼x2¾ inch loaf pans. Cover; let double in bulk. Bake in moderate oven, 375 degrees, about 50 minutes.

Virginia Duckett
Regional Office

NAVAJO FRIED BREAD

3 c. flour
1¼ t. baking powder

1 1/3 c. warm water
3/4 c. shortening

Mix the flour, salt and baking powder. Add water. Knead dough until soft—tossing from one hand to another, shaping and thinning to a flat pancake about 5″ in diameter. Heat shortening until very hot. Spread dough in hot fat. It should rise and be turned to brown on both sides. Serve hot with honey, etc.

Marion Durham
Walnut Canyon NM

NAVAJO FRY BREAD

2 c. flour
1/4 c. salad oil

1/3 c. sugar
Enough milk or water to
  make a biscuit dough

Mix all ingredients well. Roll dough to 1/2-inch thickness. Fry in deep fat about 375 degrees temperature. Drain on paper towels.
To be authentic: You should pat the dough with your hands instead of rolling it. This bread is good for a camp trip if used along with the recipe for beans. (See section on Outdoor Cooking.)

Kathleen DeWitt
Death Valley NM

EASY BANANA BREAD

1 egg
1 c. sugar
1/4 c. butter, melted
3 bananas, mashed

1½ c. flour
1 t. soda
1 t. salt

Beat egg; add sugar and butter then the bananas. Add sifted dry ingredients. Pour into a greased and floured loaf pan. Bake at 350 degrees about 45 to 55 minutes.

Elaine Hounsell
Lake Mead NRA

BANANA BREAD

1/3 c. Crisco
2/3 c. sugar
1 egg, beaten
2 or 3 bananas, mashed

1¾ c. flour
2 t. Royal baking powder
1/4 t. soda

Cream Crisco and sugar, add egg. Sift flour, baking powder and soda. Resift and add creamed ingredients and bananas alternately. If desired, add 1 cup crushed nuts. Bake in moderate oven, 350 degrees, about an hour.

Ginny Rousseau
Joshua Tree NM

FRENCH BREAKFAST PUFFS

1/2 c. sugar	1/4 t. nutmeg
1/3 c. shortening	1/2 c. milk
1 egg	1/2 c. sugar
1½ c. sifted all-purpose flour	1 t. cinnamon
1½ t. baking powder	6 T. melted margarine
1/2 t. salt	

In mixer bowl, cream the first 1/2 cup of sugar, shortening and egg. Sift together flour, baking powder, salt and nutmeg; add to creamed mixture alternately with milk, beating well after each addition. Fill 12 greased muffin pans 2/3's full. Bake at 350 degrees 20 to 25 minutes. Combine remaining sugar and cinnamon. Remove muffins from oven. Immediately dip muffins in 6 tablespoons melted margarine and then in cinnamon/sugar mixture until well coated. Serve warm.

C. Abbett
Point Reyes NS

CANNON BALLS   (Sufficient for 22 men)

6 lb. flour	3 pt. molasses
1½ lb. suet	1 pt. water

Chop up the suet; mix with the flour. Mix the molasses with water; put the flour into a bowl and pour the molasses gradually upon it; mixing it with the flour; when the whole is well mixed, not too soft, form it into any size balls required, flour some cloths, tie up each ball separate in cloth, not too tight, and boil from one hour and upwards, according to size.

NOTE: These, with lime-juice sauce, are an excellent anti-scorbutic and will keep good for twelve months, and longer. They could be made before going on any long voyage and given out as rations. (Excerpt from Manual for Army Cooks - 1883.)

Charles Hawkins
Fort Point NHS

HOLIDAY BREAD - LDB (Christmas 1965)

4 c. sourdough starter (medium thick)	1 c. each: nuts, raisins, candied fruit; candied orange or
2/3 c. shortening	grapefruit peel and
1 T. salt	chopped nuts
1/2 c. sugar	
2 t. soda	

Flour to right consistency. Bake in a loaf or tube pan at 350 degrees until done. Test for doneness.

Lester Bodine (Retired)
Lassen Volcanic NP

POPPY SEED - CHEESE BREAD STICKS

24 (5/8") slices bread
1/4 c. melted butter

6 T. finely grated Parmesan
3 T. poppy seeds

Brush bread with butter. Roll in cheese and poppy seed mixture. Toast 20 minutes at 375 degrees or until crisp.

Carla Martin
Tuzigoot NM

PUMPKIN BREAD

3½ c. flour
2 t. baking powder
1½ t. salt
3 c. sugar
1 t. cinnamon
1/2 t. cloves

3 eggs
1 c. oil
1/2 c. water
2 c. pumpkin
2 c. dates, chopped
2 c. nuts (walnut/pecans)

Mix dry ingredients well; add eggs, oil, water and pumpkin. Mix well. Add dates and nuts. Bake in a 350 degree oven for 1 hour, 15 minutes. This recipe is enough for 2 tube pans or 3 one-pound coffee cans.

Lois Henderson
Petrified Forest NP

JIM'S POPOVERS

1 c. all-purpose flour
1/2 t. salt
1 T. white sugar

3 eggs
1 c. milk
1 T. melted shortening

Grease muffin tins and place tins in hot oven, 450 degrees. Place eggs in bowl and whip about 1 minute or until frothy. Add dry ingredients and 1/2 of the milk. Beat until combined, about 15 seconds. Scrape bowl thoroughly, add remaining milk and shortening while blending. Blend until smooth, do not overbeat, batter should be thin. Pour batter into hot tins, about 1/3 full. Bake at 450 degrees about 15-20 minutes, watching closely. Reduce heat to 350 degrees about 15 minutes, again watch closely and remove when done.

James J. Early
Montezuma Castle NM

ONE DOZEN FLOUR TORTILLAS

2 c. flour
1 t. salt

1/4 c. shortening
3/4 c. warm water

Mix flour, salt and shortening. Add warm water. Knead dough several minutes until smooth. Make into 12 balls. Grease each ball thoroughly in oil and let rest about 1/2 hour. Roll balls out in flour and fry in hot pan until lightly browned.

Karen Donaldson
Lake Mead NRA

BREADS 157

PUMPKIN MUFFINS

1½ c. flour
1/2 c. sugar
2 t. baking powder
1/2 t. salt
1/2 t. cinnamon

1/2 t. nutmeg
1/2 c. milk
1/2 c. pumpkin
1/4 c. melted oleo
1 egg

Heat oven to 400 degrees. Grease 12 muffin cups. Mix all ingredients just until flour is moistened. Batter should be lumpy. Fill muffin cups 2/3 full. Bake 18 to 20 minutes. Immediately, remove from pan. Makes 12 muffins.

Karen Donaldson
Lake Mead NRA

BRANANA NUT BREAD*

1/2 c. sugar
1/4 c. shortening
1 c. Kellogg's All Bran
1½ c. mashed bananas
1 t. vanilla

1½ c. sifted flour
2 t. baking powder
1/2 t. soda
1/2 t. salt
1/2 c. chopped nuts

Blend shortening and sugar thoroughly; add egg and beat well. Stir in All Bran, bananas and vanilla. Sift together flour, baking powder, soda and salt; add to first mixture; add nuts, stirring only until combined. Spread in well-greased loaf pan. Bake at 350 degrees about an hour. Makes 1 loaf, 9½x4¼".

*The word "branana" is not misspelled. It's called that because it has bran and bananas in it.

Helen Cropper
Petrified Forest NP

MEXICAN SPOON BREAD

1 can (1 lb.) cream style corn
3/4 c. milk
1/3 c. melted shortening
2 eggs, slightly beaten
1 c. yellow corn meal

1/2 t. soda
1 t. salt
1 can (4 oz.) green chiles, chopped
1½ c. shredded Cheddar cheese

Mix all ingredients together except chiles and cheese in order given (wet ingredients first, then dry ones). Pour 1/2 batter into a 9x9x2" square pan. Spread with chiles and 1/2 cheese. Spread remaining batter on top and sprinkle with remaining cheese. Bake 45 minutes in hot oven, 400 degrees. Remove from oven and let cool just enough to set before cutting. Serves 8 to 10.

Chuck and Irene Adams
Regional Office

SOPAPILLAS

4 c. flour	1 T. baking powder
1 T. salt	1/4 c. shortening

Mix all dry ingredients together, cut in shortening and add water to make a soft dough just firm enough to roll. Roll 1/4" thick. Cut into small pieces. Heat about 1 inch of oil in a pan to about 380 degrees. Add a few pieces of dough at a time. Drain on paper toweling. Makes about 3 to 4 dozen.

Dan Jaramillo
Saguaro NM

VERY EASY REFRIGERATOR ROLLS

2 pkg. active dry yeast	1/4 c. oil or shortening
2 c. warm water (110 degrees)	1 egg
1/2 c. sugar	2 t. salt
	6½ c. flour

Dissolve yeast in warm water in large bowl. Add sugar, oil, egg, salt and half of the flour. Beat until smooth. Mix in remaining flour with spoon or hand until easy to handle. Place in greased bowl turning once to grease top of dough. Cover loosely with plastic wrap and refrigerate for at least 6 hours (24 hours is best). When dough rises, punch it down occasionally. When fresh rolls are desired, remove dough from the refrigerator and cut off the amount needed. Return the rest to the refrigerator. (Dough can be kept well for 4 days.)

About 2 hours before baking, shape dough into desired roll (cloverleaf, butterhorns and picnic rolls are best). Cover and let rise until double (about 2 hours). Heat oven to 400 degrees and bake for 15 minutes or until golden brown. Makes 4 dozen rolls.

Tomie Patrick
Point Reyes NS

HOPI FRIED BREAD

indian bread

2 c. flour, sifted	1/2 c. non-fat dry milk (or
2 t. baking powder	sour milk*)
3/4 t. salt	1/2 t. baking soda*
	Warm water

Combine sifted flour with baking powder, salt and dry milk. (If sour milk is used instead of dry milk, add 1/2 t. baking soda.) Add enough warm water to make a dough softer than biscuit dough. In heavy skillet, put 1 cup shortening and heat to high temperature. Divide dough; roll half to 1/4-inch thickness. Use sharp knife to cut into 3-inch squares. Drop into hot oil and turn once when brown. Repeat with other half of dough, or may be used later in the day. (Use at room temperature.) Serve hot with honey, butter or powdered sugar or jam.

Marion Durham
Walnut Canyon NM

OLD TIME SOURDOUGH

Starter can be made by combining two cups water, two cups flour and one package of yeast. The old-timers made their starter by placing one cup of water and one cup of flour in a warm place to ferment, however, this is a haphazard method and you may have to try several times to get a batch that tastes right.

USE OF STARTER: Each time you use the starter, pour off 1/2 cup or more to use for your next baking effort.

Do not keep starter in a metal container. A glass or pottery container works best.

Starter will usually keep for several months in the refrigerator but frequent use will renew the starter and keep it fresh.

For camping trips, take 1/2 cup of starter and add flour until you have a pliable lump of dough then sprinkle generously with flour and seal in a plastic bag. It will keep for two weeks.

Never add anything to your starter except plain flour and warm water.

Set the starter the night before use by adding flour and water (2 cups each). Remove your fresh cup of starter and use the bubbly batter in the following recipes.

Sourdough Flapjacks:

To batter or sponge, add:

2 eggs	1 T. sugar
1 T. salt	1 t. soda

Blend, adding a couple of spoonfuls of bacon grease or fresh berries and fry. MMMmmmmmmmmm.

Sourdough Bread:

To sponge, add:

4 c. flour	2 T. sugar
1 t. salt	2 T. grease

Sift dry ingredients into a bowl. Pour in sponge and mix (also grease). Knead the dough for ten minutes, then allow to rise for 3 or 4 hours. Dissolve 1/4 teaspoon soda in 1 T. water then knead into dough. Allow to rise again. Shape into loaves and bake at 375 degrees 45 minutes.

Sourdough Muffins:

Set starter as usual and add starter sponge to the following:

1½ c. whole wheat flour	2 eggs
1/4 c. non-fat dry milk	1 c. raisins
1/2 c. sugar	1/2 c. melted fat
1 t. salt	1 t. soda

Mix fat and eggs with the sponge, then add sponge to dry ingredients. Stir to moisten flour then pour batter into greased muffin tin; bake 35 min. at 375 degrees.

Mike Sipes
Chiricahua NM

POOR MAN'S PIZZA

1 c. mayonnaise
2/3 c. Parmesan cheese
1/4 c. green onions

French bread, sliced 1-inch thick
Mild or hot Portuguese sausage

Blend mayonnaise, cheese and green onion. Spread on bread slices and top with chopped sausage. EXTRA: Add chopped Mozzarella cheese. Bake at 350 degrees for 15 minutes. Serve hot.

Adele Fevella
Haleakala NP

APPLESAUCE DATE-NUT BREAD

3/4 c. chopped walnuts
1 c. dates
1½ t. baking soda
1/2 t. salt
3 T. shortening

1 c. hot applesauce
2 eggs
1 t. vanilla
1 c. sugar
1½ c. flour

Mix dates, soda and salt. Add shortening and sauce. Let stand 20 minutes. Beat eggs and combine all ingredients. Bake 1 hour and 5 minutes at 350 degrees. The sugar may be decreased to 1/4 cup to make a tasty and less caloric bread.

Grandma Baker
Petrified Forest NP

OATMEAL CRACKERS

2½ c. oatmeal
2 c. flour
1 c. milk

6 T. shortening
2 t. baking powder
1 t. salt

Combine all ingredients. Roll dough fairly thin; cut with cookie cutter and bake in moderate oven, 350 degrees, until lightly browned, about 10 to 12 minutes. Serve warm with butter.

Peggy Rolandson
San Francisco Office

QUICK BREAD

1 pkg. refrigerator butter
   flake rolls
1 T. dried onion flakes
1 t. dried parsley flakes

1 t. sesame seeds or poppy seeds
About 1 T. melted butter or oleo
Grated Parmesan cheese to taste

Separate the butter flake rolls into 12 separate rolls. Lay two rows of 6 rolls each, overlapping each roll, in a small loaf pan. Brush on melted butter lightly. Sprinkle with seeds, parsley and cheese. Bake in moderate oven, 375 degrees, about 15 minutes, or until golden brown. Makes one loaf. (Will serve 6 to 8 people.

Dorothy Johnson
Regional Office

BANANA LOAF

Mix together:

2/3 c. sugar	2 eggs
1/3 c. soft shortening	

Stir in:

3 T. milk	1 c. mashed bananas
1 T. lemon juice	

Sift together and add:

2 c. sifted flour	1/2 t. soda
1 t. baking powder	1/2 t. salt

Blend in: 1/2 cup chopped nuts.

Pour into well-greased 9x5x3" loaf pan. Bake at 350 degrees for 50 to 60 minutes (lower temperature for Pyrex and glass pans).

Peter and Karla Allen
Lake Mead NRA

COUNTRY BISCUITS

2 c. self-rising flour	1/4 c. bacon drippings
3/4 to 1 c. buttermilk	Pinch of soda

Mix all ingredients together until dough holds together. Fold out onto well-floured breadboard and knead until easy to handle (dough should feel tender). Cut with cutter and place in lightly-greased pan, then lightly grease the tops of biscuits with the fresh bacon grease. Bake in preheated 475 degree oven approximately 12 minutes.

Ken Patrick
Point Reyes NS

APPLESAUCE DATE NUT BREAD

3/4 c. chopped walnuts	1 c. hot applesauce
1 c. cut-up pitted dates	2 eggs
1½ t. baking soda	1 t. vanilla
1/2 t. salt	1 c. sugar
3 T. shortening (use oleo)	1½ c. sifted flour

Mix walnuts, dates, soda and salt with a fork. Add shortening and applesauce, let stand 20 minutes. Heat oven to 350 degrees. Grease a 9x5" loaf pan. Beat eggs with a fork, beat in vanilla, sugar and flour. Mix in date mixture just until blended; turn into pan. Bake an hour and 5 minutes or until cake tester inserted in center comes out clean. Cool in pan 10 minutes. Remove to wire rack to finish cooling, then wrap in foil. Store overnight before slicing. This loaf freezes well. Good for picnics.

Dorothy Ruse
Regional Office

FRY BREAD

2 c. flour
2 t. baking powder
1 t. salt

1½ T. shortening
Water, enough to hold dough
    together

Knead dough at least 5 minutes. Let stand overnight. Melt lard in skillet one inch deep. Pat and shape a piece of dough into a circle 6 to 8 inches in diameter and 1/4-inch thick. Drop into hot fat, turning only once so that each side is a rich golden brown. May be served with stew or chili and beans, or with butter and honey. Serve warm.

Myrna Keeling
Chiricahua NM

FRENCH BREAD

Dissolve in a large bowl:

1 envelope dry yeast (1 t.)
1 T. sugar

2 c. lukewarm water

Add 4 cups flour and mix in gradually. Knead 3 to 4 minutes. Let rise for 1 hour. Butter a cookie sheet. Sprinkle with corn meal. Divide dough into 2 parts; shape into long narrow loaves. Mark a row of diagonal slits across top. Let rise 45 minutes. Brush with melted butter. Preheat oven to 450 degrees for 5 minutes, then turn oven to 375 degrees and bake bread 35 minutes. Place a pan of water on lower rack while bread is baking.

Chuck and Irene Adams
Regional Office

PUMPKIN LOAF

Cream together:

1½ c. sugar
1/2 c. oil

2 eggs

Stir in:

1/3 c. water

1 c. pumpkin

Stir in:

1/2 t. salt
1 t. cinnamon
1 t. soda

1/2 t. baking powder
1 2/3 c. flour

Pour into greased and floured loaf pan. Bake at 350 degrees for 1½ hours. Last hour, place foil over pan.

Harry and Nancy Sloat
Regional Office

FLOUR TORTILLAS

2 c. flour
1/2 t. baking powder
1 t. salt

2 T. shortening
1/2 c. water (or more if
needed)

Make dough, pinch into small balls. Grease them and let stand about 15 minutes. Flour them and roll out round on board. Cook on hot griddle. Makes about 16.

Marquita McCollough
Chiricahua NM

EASY-DO WHEAT BREAD

3 c. 100% whole wheat
flour, unsifted
3½ to 4 c. all-purpose flour,
sifted
1 c. milk, scalded

1 T. salt
1/4 c. honey
1/4 c. shortening
1 c. lukewarm water
2 pkg. yeast, dry or compressed

Combine scalded milk, salt, honey and shortening. Stir smooth; add water and stir to lukewarm. Add yeast, granulated or crumbled. Add whole wheat flour and stir smooth. Beat 2 minutes. Beat in enough all-purpose flour to make a stiff dough. Knead until dough springs back at finger-tip touch (about 10 minutes). Place dough in lightly greased bowl; cover and let rise in warm place (85 degrees) until double in bulk (about one hour). Punch down and divide dough into two equal portions. Shape as desired. Place in well-greased pans. Cover and let rise until almost double in bulk (about 40 minutes). Bake at 375 degrees for 5 minutes; decrease temperature to 350 degrees and bake 35-40 minutes more or until done.

Helen Goodlund
Muir Woods NM

AN EARLY MORNING SCENE FROM THE GREAT OUTER BEACH AT CAPE COD NATIONAL SEASHORE, MASSACHUSETTS. (NPS photo by M. Woodbridge Williams).

ANTIQUE CANNON OVERLOOKING GETTYSBURG NATIONAL MILITARY PARK, PENNSYLVANIA. (NPS photo by Jack E. Boucher).

Outdoor Cooking

THE BREATHTAKING SPIRES OF THE GRAND TETONS ARE A MAJOR ATTRACTION IN GRAND TETON NATIONAL PARK, WYOMING. (NPS photo by George A. Grant).

JERKY (Hiker's Trail Food or Snacks at Home)

Use any lean meat except pig or bear. Remove all fat and cut into strips approximately 1/2" wide, 1/4" thick and 3-5" long. Marinate overnight in following mixture - enough for 2 pounds meat:

1 T. salt	1/3 c. Worcestershire sauce
1 t. onion powder	1/4 c. soy sauce
1 t. garlic powder	Liquid smoke (can be used
1/2 t. black pepper	instead of some of the sauces
	or in addition)

When using a smoke house, cut soy sauce in half. A second seasoning method which is not so spicy. Prepare meat as above. Pound in salt and pepper with a tenderizing hammer. Be generous with the salt and pepper. Smoke for 1 day. Drying for both methods: Place on a rack (criss-cross), log-cabin style and place in oven with pilot light on near oven at lowest temperature so meat will dry, not cook. Leave 2-4 days. Restacking pieces of meat will speed drying time. If sun drying is possible, hang on a rack; cover with cheese-cloth and place in the sun for 7 to 10 days. Be sure to bring meat in at night or it will pick up moisture. Keeps indefinitely if dried hard.

Susie Cahill
Haleakala NP

CAMPER TIP

If you own a camper with an oven and if you have a freezer you have a care-free vacation guarantee. Whenever in the course of your daily cooking routines, you prepare one-dish meals, like stew, meat balls, etc., always double the recipe. Take one-half of the finished dish and put it in an aluminum casserole and freeze it. On your next outing, put it in your camper and all you have to do for dinner is put one of your casseroles in the oven; serve with French bread and a green salad. No muss.

Jayne Ramorino
Regional Office

CAMPER'S CASSEROLE

1 pkg. chicken dinner (rice, vermicelli in cheese sauce)	1 can boned chicken
	1 can mushroom soup
2 T. oil	1 T. parsley flakes

In large skillet, brown rice mixture in oil. Slowly pour 3½ cups boiling water into skillet. Stir; add contents of sauce envelope and boned chicken (break up the meat) and add soup. Stir; cover and simmer until liquid is absorbed and rice is tender. About 15 minutes. Serves 5. (Double recipe if wanderers from next campsite invade your island at chow time!)

Peggy Rolandson
San Francisco Office

WESTERN STEW

1 or 2 cans corned beef   1 can kidney beans
1 can stewed tomatoes

    Break beef up with spoon. Add other ingredients and heat thoroughly.

Shirley Rees
Cabrillo NM

ROUGH REUBEN'S

8 slices dark brown bread   1 can (303) sauerkraut, drained
1 can corned beef, sliced thin   Russian dressing: 1/4 c. mayonnaise
8 slices Swiss cheese   and 1 T. chili sauce

    Spread one side of bread with dressing. Place corned beef, cheese and 2 T. sauerkraut on 4 slices of bread. Cover with remaining slices. Spread top slice with butter and place buttered side down on hot griddle or skillet. When cheese is melted, remove to hot plate and cut into 3 pieces. Makes 4 hearty sandwiches.

Peggy Rolandson
San Francisco Office

COWBOY BEANS

2 lb. pink beans   1 medium onion, chopped
2½ to 3 lb. pork roast   Salt and pepper to taste

    Wash beans thoroughly. Cover beans with water, add chopped onion, pork roast and seasoning. Bring to a full boil. Make sure there is always sufficient water covering beans and boil about 2 hours. Reduce heat until they just simmer and continue cooking for 4 to 5 hours. The longer they simmer, the better they taste. They even taste better after they have been warmed up two or three times.

Donna J. Byrne
Montezuma Castle NM

CORNED BEEF STEW WITH DUMPLINGS

1 can (No. 303) potatoes,   1 can (12 oz.) corned beef,
  cubed (save liquid)   cubed
1 large onion or 1 T. onion   1 c. prepared biscuit mix
  flakes   1 egg
2 beef bouillon cubes   Milk

    Dissolve bouillon cubes in potato liquid and water to make 2½ cups. Combine all ingredients except biscuit mix, egg and milk, in a large Dutch oven or heavy frying pan with a cover. Cook about 8-10 minutes, until very hot. Mix last 3 ingredients to make dough and drop by spoonfuls into boiling stew; cover tightly and simmer about 30 minutes. Salt and pepper to taste. Will serve 4.

Peggy Rolandson
San Francisco Office

JUNGLE STEW

3 lb. hamburger
3 onions
1/4 c. plus 2 T. fat
3 cans tomatoes (1 lb. 3 oz.) (7½ cups)

1½ c. macaroni (uncooked)
4½ cans cooked kidney beans
(15 oz.)

Brown onions and meat in fat in skillet. Boil macaroni until tender and drain. Combine all ingredients and simmer for 20 minutes. Serve hot.

Anne Lewis
Sequoia NP

CITADEL SPREAD

1 jar (18 oz.) peanut butter
2-4 oz. bacon grease
1/2 c. honey
Nuts, raisins

2-4 c. granular powdered
milk (the more milk,
the less gooier)

Mix together all ingredients. Add nuts, raisins, etc. as desired. The spread will keep indefinitely in the refrigerator and last about 3 weeks unrefrigerated.

Bill and Barry Fink
Tuzigoot NM

BACKPACK JERKY

5 lb. flank steak, brisket,
rump, or bottom round
3/4 c. soy sauce
1/4 c. Worcestershire sauce
1/2 t. pepper

1 t. seasoned salt
1 t. onion powder
2 t. garlic powder
1 t. garlic salt

1. Slice meat along grain, not more than 1/4" thick. Cut to size you want; meat will shrink.
2. Heat soy sauce and Worcestershire sauce and then add all other ingredients.
3. Cool and add to meat.
4. Marinate overnight.
5. (Next day) Put meat directly over oven rack.
6. Put oven on lowest heat setting and leave door open. Time: approximately 4-6 hours.

Murph and Donna Kolipinski
Regional Office

BEER BISCUITS

Substitute beer for liquid in regular Bisquick biscuits. This is super for campfire biscuits. Put a small amount of oil in a pan on top of coals; drop in dough and cover pan with foil. Place hot coals on top of foil and bake until fluffy and brown.

Bobbie Brudenell
Yosemite NP

HIKER'S AND/OR CAMPER'S DELIGHT (Prepare at home)

2 pkg. (12 oz. each) semi-
   sweet chocolate pieces
1 pkg. (1 lb.) dried apricots
1 pkg. (1 lb.) dried, pitted prunes
4 c. miniature marshmallows

3 c. golden seedless raisins
3 c. dark seedless raisins
3 c. walnut meats, shelled
3 c. whole almonds, shelled
3 c. filberts, shelled

Wipe cots and prunes and place on a cookie sheet in a preheated (400 degree) oven. Turn off oven when placing the apricots into oven for thorough drying. Do this step far in advance. Combine all ingredients and dole out into "baggies"; place baggies into a large airtight container and tote to your place in the woods. Individual packets can be taken out when needed. Be sure prunes and cots are dry before combining with other ingredients. Other nuts can be used or quantities changed to suit individual preferences.

Peggy Rolandson
San Francisco Office

SWISS-TYPE CEREAL

Trail snack for hikers or use with milk as a high-energy breakfast.

2 c. nuts, walnuts, almonds,
   etc.
2/3 c. dried apples

2/3 c. dried apricots
1 c. currants or raisins (or
   prunes)

If nuts are used with skins on them, a bitter taste will result. Remove skins, especially on filberts. (Skins can be removed by heating briefly, 5 minutes, then rub skins off.) Grind all together except currants with coarse meat grinder alternating nuts and fruit to combat stickiness, or chop if you prefer. Mix well:

3 c. rolled oats
3/4 c. packed brown sugar

3/4 c. wheat germ (toasted or
   raw, sweetened or not, to
   your taste)

Store in a tight container at room temperature. If your fruits appear to be quite moist, spread them out to dry for a day or so. This will improve the keeping quality of the cereal.

Susie Cahill
Haleakala NP

CLAMDIGGER SANDWICHES

1 c. mayonnaise
1 c. clams, drained
10-12 chopped green onions

1/2 lb. sharp Tillamook
   cheese, grated
1 T. Worcestershire sauce

Spread on sliced French bread. Bake 15 minutes in a 400 degree oven.

Murph and Donna Kolipinski
Regional Office

CANNED CORNED BEEF AND EGGS

Brown one can corned beef using low heat. Break 6 eggs into bowl. Add eggs to browned corned beef and stir until firm. Remove from heat and serve. Throw in a little pepper, chili, garlic, onions or whatever is handy.

Irvin Duncan
Yosemite NP

MODERN BEEF JERKY

This recipe comes from Neil Hulbert, member of the Board of Directors of the California Beef Council. He lives at Oak Farms, Auburn, California and raises Luing cattle.

1 beef flank steak, well trimmed   Garlic salt
1/2 c. soy sauce   Lemon pepper

Cut steak lengthwise with grain into long strips, no more than 1/4" thick. Toss with soy sauce. Arrange beef strips in single layer on wire rack placed on a baking sheet. Sprinkle with garlic salt and lemon pepper. Place a second rack over beef and flip over. Remove top rack. Sprinkle again with seasonings. Bake at 150 to 175 degrees overnight, about 10 to 12 hours. Store in covered container.

NOTE: Beef jerky should not be crisp. If it is, oven temperature is too high.

Pat Jones
Regional Office

BEEF OR VENISON JERKY

Cut boned meat into thin strips. Heat to boiling, large container of salted water. Blanch meat (a little at a time) using a wire basket if available, until meat loses red color. Drain over water, then season, using salt, pepper (some people like a little garlic salt). Hang strips on drying rack and leave until quite dry and brittle. Hanging time depends on weather conditions. The dryer the weather is, the less time needed and the better the jerky is.

Drying rack consists of wire, either smooth wire or chicken mesh, strung in an out of the way area.

Barbara Monroe
Montezuma Castle NM

ST. MARY'S LAKE SURROUNDED BY TOWERING PEAKS IN GLACIER NATIONAL PARK, MONTANA. (NPS photo by Jack E. Boucher).

Cooking for
Singles and Crowds

MABRY'S MILL ON THE BLUE RIDGE NATIONAL PARKWAY IN VIRGINIA. (NPS photo).

MIXES

Pancake Mix:

10 c. flour	3 t. salt
5 rounded t. baking powder	3 c. crushed corn flakes
3 t. baking soda	2 c. quick oats, uncooked
1/3 c. sugar	3 c. whole wheat flour

Mix all ingredients well and store in airtight container. To use: Mix an egg with 1½ cups of milk and add enough mix for proper consistency.

Biscuit Mix:

8 c. sifted enriched flour	1 c. lard for soft wheat flour
1/4 c. baking powder	OR 1½ c. lard for hard wheat
4 t. salt	flour

Sift flour with baking powder and salt. Cut in lard until mixture has a fine even crumb. Cover closely and store in refrigerator until needed. This mixture will keep at least a month in refrigerator.

To use: 1/2 cup milk to 2 cups mix - makes 12 biscuits.

Pastry Mix:

7 c. flour	1¾ c. lard for soft wheat flour
4 t. salt	OR 2 c. for hard wheat flour

Mix flour and salt. Cut lard into flour until fine crumb stage. Cover, store in refrigerator until needed. Will keep for about a month. Makes 8 single pie crusts.

To use: Single crust — 1 to 1¼ cups mix and 2 to 4 Tbsp. water.
Double crust — 2¼ to 2½ cups mix and 4 to 6 Tbsp. water.

Ginger Pie Pastry:

2½ lb. gingersnaps	1 lb. butter, melted
(2½ qt.) fine	(2 1/3 cups)
1 lb. sugar (2 cups)	

Mix ingredients together. Divide into nine equal portions; press one-ninth of mixture into each of eight 9" pans. Save remaining mixture for sprinkling over top of open-faced pies.

Peggy Rolandson
San Francisco Office

INSTANT HOT CHOCOLATE FOR A CROWD

8 c. powdered milk	1/2 c. powdered sugar
2 c. cream substitute	1 lb. can Quik (Nestle's)

Mix together all ingredients and store in airtight container. Use as needed. Mix with hot water. Yield: 12½ cups.

Karla and Peter Allen
Lake Mead NRA

FARM APPLE PAN PIE (A Big Pie that Serves a Crowd)

1 recipe Egg Yolk Pastry
   (recipe follows)
5 lb. tart apples, pared, cored,
   sliced
4 t. lemon juice

3/4 c. sugar
3/4 c. brown sugar
1 t. cinnamon
1/4 t. salt
1/2 t. nutmeg

Roll out half the pastry and use to line 15½x10½-inch jelly roll pan. Sprinkle lemon juice on apples. Place half the apples in bottom of pastry-lined pan, spreading evenly. Combine remaining ingredients, except apples. Sprinkle half the mixture over apples in pan. Spread remaining apples on top; sprinkle with remaining sugar-spice mixture. Top with remaining pastry, rolled out; seal and crimp edges. Brush with milk, sprinkle with a little sugar, and cut vents. Bake at 400 degrees for 30 minutes, then at 375 degrees for 20 minutes. When cool, drizzle with 1 cup powdered sugar mixed with 2 tablespoons milk. Cut in squares to serve. 24 servings.

Egg Yolk Pastry:

5 c. sifted flour
4 t. sugar
1/2 t. salt
Cold water

1/2 t. baking powder
1½ c. lard
2 egg yolks

Combine dry ingredients; cut in lard. Place egg yolks in measuring cup and stir with fork until smooth. Blend in enough cold water to make a scant cupful. Sprinkle gradually over dry ingredients; toss with fork to make a soft dough. (This makes pastry for one Farm Apple Pan Pie or three 9-inch 2-crust pies. The dough will keep in the refrigerator about two weeks.)

Georjean McKeeman
Tonto NM

HOT SEASONED BISCUITS

8 c. flour
1½ T. seasoned salt
1½ c. shortening
2 2/3 c. milk

4 T. baking powder
1 T. rosemary, dill weed,
   oregano, or parsley

Sift flour, measure, and sift with the baking powder, salt and herbs; sift together several times. Cut in the shortening with a pastry blender. Add milk; mix to moderately stiff dough. Turn out onto a slightly floured board and knead gently to round up and smooth out dough. Roll out to 3/8 to 1/2-inch thickness. Cut with a 1½" biscuit cutter. Bake on ungreased cookie sheet in a hot oven, 450 degrees, for 10 minutes, or until crusty and brown. Serve hot. Makes about 100 small biscuits.

Peggy Rolandson
San Francisco Office

OVERNIGHT SALAD

Dressing:

4 eggs
Juice of 1 lemon

1/4 t. dry mustard
1/2 c. warm milk

Mix eggs, lemon juice and dry mustard and beat well all together. Add milk and cook in double boiler until thick. (Thickens quickly and will curdle if over cooked.) Cool.

Salad:

1 lb. small marshmallows or
large ones cut into quarters
1/4 c. nuts (almonds,
pecans or walnuts)

1 can Royal Anne cherries, seeded
(No. 2½ can)
1 (No. 2) can sliced pineapple
chunks

Whip 1 pint heavy cream. Add cooled dressing. Stir in marshmallows and nuts and last the fruit (well drained). Let set overnight in refrigerator. This is a good salad for the Holidays or special occasions. Serves 20.

Mary and Forrest Benson
Regional Office

FANCY ENGLISH MUFFINS

4 English muffins, split
8 slices bacon, fried to
medium stage

Butter or margarine
8 slices sharp Cheddar cheese
(2x2")

Toast muffins and spread with butter or margarine. Break each slice of bacon in half so as to fit the muffin halves. Place cheese on top of bacon and place under hot broiler until cheese melts. Serve hot. (Great for a fast breakfast!)

Karla and Peter Allen
Lake Mead NRA

CROWD PLEASERS BARBECUES

These are called "taverns" in the Upper Great Plains where I was raised. This recipe was used at Church gatherings and will serve a large crowd.

4 lb. hamburger
2 large onions, minced
1 (10½ oz.) can chicken
gumbo soup
1 (10½ oz.) can tomato soup

2 T. catsup
1 T. mustard
1 T. brown sugar
Salt, pepper and chili powder
to taste

Brown meat and onions lightly. Add remaining ingredients and simmer at least one hour. Fills 2 to 3 dozen hamburger buns.

Georjean McKeeman
Tonto NM

BACHELOR'S APPLE CAKE

2 c. sugar
2 eggs, well beaten
1/2 c. Wesson oil
2 c. flour
2 t. baking soda

1 t. salt
2 t. cinnamon
4 c. diced raw apples
1 c. chopped walnuts
1 t. vanilla

Mix all together well. Bake at 350 degrees for 30 minutes or until done in an 8x12" loaf pan.

Mary Adamson
Lake Mead NRA

BEANS AND BEEF

1/2 lb. ground beef
1/3 c. chopped onion
1/2 t. salt

1 can (20 oz.) pork and beans, or baked beans
1/2 c. to 2/3 c. barbecue sauce

Brown beef and onion; drain off excess fat. Add salt, pork and beans and barbecue sauce. Heat to boiling, then reduce heat to low. Top with several slices American processed or Cheddar cheese. Simmer mixture until cheese melts. Serve hot. Makes 2 servings. (Other spices may be added.)

Georjean McKeeman
Tonto NM

BEEF WITH BROCCOLI

1/2 lb. beef (tender)
1 lb. broccoli
1 small round onion, sliced
1/4 lb. fresh mushrooms, sliced
  (canned can be used)
1 piece fresh ginger, crushed
  OR 1/2 t. powdered ginger
1 clove garlic, crushed
1/2 c. water or stock or 1/4 c.
  soy sauce

1/4 c. water with 2 T. sugar
Seasoning-mixed in bowl:
  2 t. soy sauce
  Dash of pepper
  1 T. cornstarch
  1 T. sherry, cooking type
  1/4 t. sugar
  1 t. salt
  1/4 t. Accent (MSG)

Slice beef very thin and soak in seasoning for 10 minutes or more. Cut broccoli into thin diagonal slices. Slice onions and mushrooms. Heat a pan with oil and brown ginger and garlic slightly. Add beef and fry until medium rare. Add broccoli and onion. Fry for 2 minutes. Add mushrooms and water (or mixture of soy, water and sugar). Stir fry until vegetables are barely done. Suggested menu: beef with broccoli, rice, peach salad, and pickled vegetables. This is good "bachelor" fare. Makes 2 to 3 servings.

Clara Shimoda
City of Refuge NHP

LAZY MAN'S LASAGNE

1/2 lb. ground beef
1/4 c. chopped onion
1 can (8 oz.) tomato sauce
1/2 t. sugar
1/2 t. salt
Dash of garlic salt
Dash of pepper

1 c. uncooked fine noodles
1 c. Ricotta cheese
  OR 1/2 c. cottage cheese
  (cream style) and 1/2 c.
  cream cheese
1/4 c. chopped green pepper
2 T. Parmesan cheese

Cook meat and onion until lightly browned and tender. Stir in sauce, sugar, salts and pepper. Remove from heat. Meanwhile, cook noodles, drain. Combine Ricotta cheese and green pepper. Spread half of noodles on bottom of a 1 quart baking dish; top with half of meat mixture. Cover with cheese mixture. Add remaining noodles and meat sauce. Sprinkle top with Parmesan cheese. Bake at 350 degrees for 30 minutes. Makes 2 hearty servings. (This has basically the same ingredients as lasagne and is much simpler to make.) Oregano, basil and cumin may be added to the meat sauce if a more "Italian" flavor is desired.

Georjean McKeeman
Tonto NM

BISCUITS AND GRAVY

Biscuits:

2 c. flour
1 t. salt
2 T. sugar

2 heaping t. baking powder
1/4 c. lard
1 c. milk

Roll the dough out to about 1/2" thickness. Cut the dough with a water glass. Place the dough in a greased pan about 1/4" apart. Bake at 370 degrees until brown.

Gravy:

Use 3/4 cup flour. Have enough grease in a skillet to make a flour paste. Take the skillet off the fire to cool a little, then add 3 cups milk. Let the gravy simmer until the gravy reaches the desired thickness.

Kenneth C. Garvin
Tonto NM

BACHELOR DAYS MACARONI

1 c. sea shell macaroni
2 or 3 c. water

1/4 to 1/2 c. Velveeta cheese
Salt to taste

Heat water to boiling. Add macaroni and Velveeta and salt to taste. Cook until cheese melts and macaroni is tender, stirring enough to prevent sticking. Eat as you would soup. Good with fried fish, cole slaw, and hush puppies. (Concocted during bachelor days.)

Zeb McKinney
Grand Canyon NP

BEEF AND RICE SKILLET FIESTA

1/2 lb. ground beef	Dash of pepper
2 T. diced onion	1 can (8 oz.) tomato sauce
1 t. salt	1 can (8 oz.) corn
1/2 t. chili powder	3/4 c. hot water
1/4 c. diced green pepper	1 medium tomato, chopped
3/4 c. minute rice	

Brown meat; add onion and cook over medium heat until onion is tender. Drain. Add seasonings, sauce, corn and water. Bring to boil. Stir in green pepper and tomato; bring to a boil again. Stir in rice; cover and simmer 5 minutes. Fluff with fork and serve. Makes 2 servings.

Georjean McKeeman
Tonto NM

TODAY AND TOMORROW'S UPSIDE DOWN BREAD

4 T. butter	1 pkg. honey-bran muffin mix
1/2 c. brown sugar, packed firm	4 oven/freezer type casseroles, or metal or Pyrex pans - 1
1 can (No. 303) pear halves	serving size

Butter each container with 1 tablespoon butter and leave excess in pan. Sprinkle sugar evenly between them. Divide pears evenly. Prepare muffin mix according to directions and spoon into dishes. Bake in a preheated oven, 350 degrees, for 15-20 minutes until done. Serve warm with whipped cream. Cool unused ones and wrap in foil and freeze for another day.

To use: Defrost overnight at room temperature and heat for 7-10 minutes in hot oven and serve with whipped cream. A good dish for the single person who wants something "homemade".

Peggy Rolandson
San Francisco Office

SCALLOPED POTATOES (50 portions)

1 c. butter	3/4 c. flour, sifted
4 T. salt	3/4 t. pepper
3 qt. milk, heated	1 onion, thinly sliced
1½ pecks potatoes, peeled and sliced	1 can pimientos, cut into strips

Make a thin white sauce by melting butter in large skillet; add flour, salt and pepper and stir until smooth. Then add, slowly, the heated milk, stirring constantly until thickened. Place thinly sliced onion in bottom of greased pans and add half of the potatoes; add white sauce, more potatoes and dots of butter in the layers, and more white sauce. Put pimientos over the top; cover with heavy foil and bake until tender. Remove foil covering last 20 minutes if you want to brown the top. Serve hot. This dish is excellent to serve for a brunch with baked ham.

Peggy Rolandson
San Francisco Office

GLUMPH

1 c. macaroni, cooked and
   drained
1/2 lb. hamburger

1 can (10 oz.) vegetables
   (any kind, or mixed)
Salt and pepper

Saute hamburger and drain off excess fat. Add macaroni and drained vegetables. Season to taste. Heat thoroughly and serve. (My husband Bruce invented this dish during his bachelor days.)

Georjean McKeeman
Tonto NM

BACHELOR DAYS BAKED BEANS

No. 2 can pork and beans
Molasses to taste (about 2 T.)
Bacon strips

Brown sugar to taste
   (about 2 T.)

Pour beans into baking dish; stir in molasses and brown sugar. Cover with bacon strips. Bake at 350 degrees until hot and bubbly and bacon is brown.

Zeb McKinney
Grand Canyon NP

SOUTHERN PORK BAR-B-QUE
(Recipe from a small restaurant in Virginia about 20 years ago.)

6 pork butts
1 T. red pepper
1 to 2 c. vinegar

1 gallon ketchup
1 T. chili powder
Salt and pepper to taste

Cook butts in a slow oven all day (300 degrees or less). Meat will fall apart. Mix sauce (makes just over 1 gallon). Pour over pork and simmer.

Betty Berett
Petrified Forest NP

SCRAMBLED EGGS A LA KITTLE

Prepare egg mixture in usual manner and set aside. (Keep close at hand to add to hot pan as described below.) Lightly grease frying pan with fresh bacon grease and when thoroughly coated, sprinkle sesame seeds over entire surface. Brown seeds, but do not burn them. When hot and browned sufficiently, quickly pour the egg mixture into pan and stir well. When eggs are cooked to desired consistency, serve on hot plate with buttered toast.

Otis A. Kittle
Regional Office

The following group of quantity recipes was submitted by Betty Tucker, Regional Office. Betty's mother, Fern Stange, Fargo, North Dakota, graciously shared them with us for this section. Mrs. Stange was camp cook for the Boy Scout's CAMP WILDERNESS near Park Rapids, Minnesota, for over five years. We think that these recipes will offer some selection to those of you who find it necessary and expedient to prepare large quantities of food either for church gatherings, socials, or your own freezer needs and desires.

BATTER FOR FRENCH TOAST

To each 12 eggs, beaten with wire whip, add 1 quart of milk, a dash of salt, a little sugar, and a dash of cinnamon. Blend thoroughly. (Toast can be prepared as usual; wrapped in freezer wrap; frozen and used at a later date. Good item to keep in the freezer for quick morning breakfasts; also, better than that purchased in the freezer sections at the supermarkets.)

PANCAKES - for 200

3 (10 lb.) bags white flour
2 (3 lb.) bags corn meal
1/2 can egg solids
1 box powdered milk

2 qt. sugar
1 c. baking powder
2 lb. shortening, melted
5 gal. water

Combine all ingredients and thin to right baking consistency with water and add a pinch of soda to each 2 quarts of dough. Also, add a dash of cinnamon and cook them.

THOUSAND ISLAND DRESSING

3/4 gal. salad dressing
1 c. sweet relish

4 c. French dressing

Combine all ingredients and shake well.

RUSSIAN DRESSING

Use the 1,000 Island Dressing above; add 6 chopped or ground hard-cooked eggs and shake well.

FRENCH DRESSING

1 can (46 oz.) tomato soup
2 c. sugar
2 c. vinegar

4 c. oil
1 T. garlic salt
2 t. pepper
1 large onion, grated

Combine all ingredients.

WILDERNESS CORN BREAD

3 lb. - 4 oz. granulated sugar
1 lb. shortening
2¼ oz. salt
4 lb. egg, or 1 quart whole
  eggs or 2 cups egg solids
1 lb. - 4 oz. dry milk solids

12 lb. - 8 oz. water (1 gallon
  and 2 quarts)
8 lb. - 12 oz. corn meal
7 lb. all-purpose flour
6 oz. baking powder
1/2 c. baking soda

Cream the shortening, sugar and salt together well. Sift together or mix very thoroughly all the dry ingredients and add them with the water to the creamed mixture. Pour into prepared pans and bake in a moderate oven, 350 degrees, until done. This recipe will fill three sheets, 16x24" or one sheet this size three times. Makes about 278 pieces.

CARROT AND RAISIN SALAD for 100

2 lb. raisins (soak to plump)
2 lb. carrots, peeled and ground

6 heads lettuce, shredded
2 T. flaked coconut
French dressing

Soak raisins to plump. Peel and grind carrots. Cover with cold water and let stand. Prepare lettuce and shred. When time to serve, drain raisins and carrots very well. Mix with shredded lettuce. Toss gently. Place in bowls; sprinkle with coconut and add French dressing over the top.

COLE SLAW FOR BARBECUE

35 lb. cabbage, shredded
1 gal. salad dressing

1 can (No. 10) pineapple tidbits,
  or crushed

Combine all ingredients and toss and serve. Cabbage can be prepared the day before.

SCRAMBLED EGGS FOR 175

12 doz. eggs, beaten
3 gal. white sauce (cooked)

1 c. salad mustard
3 T. salt

Break and mix eggs the night before needed. Cook medium white sauce. Blend with salad mustard and salt. In the morning, divide eggs into thirds and add 1 gallon white sauce to each third. Pour into greased pans. Bake in medium oven, 325-350 degrees. Set the egg pans into other pans with water in the bottom pan. Serve hot.

BUTTERSCOTCH PUDDING FOR 100

3 gal. water

4 lb. brown sugar

Bring to boil, thicken to fold with cornstarch. Set to cool. Add 1 lb. butter, then beat with 2 quarts ice cold water, 1 tablespoon Mapleine, 2 cups finely chopped nuts.

CHOW MEIN FOR 300

40 lb. meat, cooked, and
   ground through coarse grinder
5 large onions, chopped
20 lb. celery, diced
32 oz. flour made into a paste
   in 2 qt. water
40 lb. bean sprouts, drained
   and washed

1 qt. plus 1 pt. soy sauce
3 c. Chinese molasses
6 lb. cooked rice for 100 servings
   OR 30 lb. cooked rice for
   300 servings (salt the rice lightly
   and add a little oil to each batch
   for shine)

Combine all ingredients and blend thoroughly except the sprouts which are added last. Serve hot.

GINGERBREAD

1 c. shortening
1 c. sugar
6 eggs, beaten
5 c. flour
2 t. baking soda
2 c. hot water

2 c. molasses
4 t. cinnamon
2 t. cloves
2 t. ginger
1 t. salt

Cream sugar and shortening well; add beaten eggs and blend. Sift flour, salt and spices together. Dissolve baking soda in hot water with molasses. Add dry ingredients alternately with liquid mixture to creamed mixture and blend thoroughly. Pour into 11x22½" pan and bake in a moderate oven, 350 degrees, until done. This recipe can be doubled if necessary. Gingerbread freezes well if well-wrapped. Serve plain or ice if desired.

TEXAS CHILI FOR 300

60 lb. ground meat
12 qt. chopped onion
4 cans (No. 10) diced tomatoes
3 cans (No. 10) tomato puree
7 cans water (use No. 10 can)

1½ c. salt
2 c. chili powder
6 cans (No. 10) kidney beans
   or 10 lb. kidney beans
   soaked overnight

Combine all ingredients and mix well. Cook slowly until done. Serve hot.

SPANISH RICE FOR 100

5 lb. rice, cooked and drained
8 qt. tomatoes, diced
4 oz. salt
1 T. black pepper

4 lb. bacon, diced and browned
   and drained
10 lb. onions, diced
2 celery heads, cooked until
   tender

Combine all ingredients and bake at 350 degrees for 1 hour or until thoroughly hot and blended. Recipe can be doubled for 200 servings. Serve hot.

TUNA AND NOODLE HOT DISH FOR 100

Make a medium sauce of:

4 qt. reconstituted dry milk	8 oz. flour
2 oz. salt	1 lb. butter

Cook 5 pounds wide noodles until tender; blanch and drain. Flake 5 pounds tuna (or canned tuna to equal 5 lb.) and grate 3 large onions. Blend all together. Top with either crushed potato chips or 2 quarts buttered bread crumbs. Bake 1½ hours at 300 degrees.

WILDERNESS BISCUIT BLEND

8 lb. or 2 gal. flour	Dry milk (1½ lb. or 1½ qt.)
8 oz. or 1¼ c. baking powder	Shortening (3 lb. or 1¾ qt.)
Salt (2 oz. or 1/4 c.)	

Mix like coarse meal; rub with hands. Store in covered airtight containers in a cool place. To use: follow directions on a commercial biscuit box. Use water for liquid agent.

SLOPPY JOES FOR 200 BUNS

30 lb. hamburger	12 onions, chopped

Brown and crush. Season well with salt and pepper. Now add 1 quart flour through sifter and add enough hot water to hold meat together. Use a scoop to fill buns. This makes about a 3-oz. serving of protein. One quart of soaked bulgar can be used with the above.

SALISBURY STEAKS FOR 100

54 lb. hamburger	4 qt. water
12 T. salt	1 qt. finely ground onions
4 t. pepper	5 qt. dry bread crumbs

Combine all ingredients and shape with a No. 12 scoop. Place on cookie sheets and bake at 375 degrees until done. Save gravy from patties and make a good onion gravy to accompany steaks. Serve hot.

APPLE RAKE

10 lb. soft wheat flour	1 c. baking powder
3 lb. shortening, softened	8 lb. granulated sugar

Combine and rub to coarse meal texture. Add salt, 1½ gallons milk and 30 eggs, beaten. Lastly, add 2 pounds cornstarch. Bake in a moderate oven, 350 degrees, until set. Makes 3 large pans; cut each into 54 squares. Spread apple slices (canned) on top; sprinkle with cinnamon and sugar mixture to taste.

MEAT LOAF FOR 50 or 100 or 200

20 lb. hamburger
3 c. egg solids
2 qt. milk

1/4 c. salt
2 c. chopped onions
1 qt. soaked bulgar for binding

Mix well in mixer or very thoroughly by hand. Now is the opportunity to use ground leftover beef. You may substitute 10 pounds of cooked meat for 10 pounds of fresh meat. Double the recipe for 100 servings and re-double for 200 servings. Use dough arm for mixing in a commercial mixer. When serving, top with gravy heated with spicy tomatoes and onion.

HUNTER'S STEW FOR 100

24 lb. boneless beef cubes

6 oz. flour (or more)

Dredge meat with flour and season with salt and pepper and any other type of seasonings desired. Brown in oven in not too much fat. Place in deep roasting pan. Add 2 gallons hot water. Season with salt and pepper. Cook until tender at 350 degrees. Add 3 cans (No. 10) butter kernel whole potatoes, drained. In a separate heavy pot, cook 6 pounds carrots cut to 1 to 2" lengths and 5 pounds whole onions. Cook until tender. Add beef extender to liquid. Add to meat mixture. Ready to serve.

BEANS AND WIENERS FOR 200

Soak 3 cans (No. 10) good navy or nothern white beans overnight; add more water to cover. In the morning, bring beans to a good boil. Turn off heat. Cover. Divide between two large roasting pans (or more if necessary) and add 2 quarts chopped onion to each pan and 1 quart brown sugar to each pan. Cut up bacon ends and ham scraps. Molasses is added to each pan just to color beans. Add 1 large tablespoon pepper and 2 tablespoons salt to each pan. Place bacon rind on top. Bake in a slow oven for 6 to 8 hours or overnight. Keep moist but do not cover. One hour before serving, cut up 6 pounds of weiners in 1" pieces. Toss in pan to just brown. Mix into baked beans carefully. More wieners may be added for more protein and for eye appeal.

SOFT OATMEAL COOKIES

2 qt. white sugar
2 qt. brown sugar
3 c. soft shortening
1 c. egg solids
4 T. cinnamon
4 T. nutmeg
2 T. cloves

1 bag oatmeal (uncooked)
1 qt. buttermilk
10 lb. flour
2 T. baking soda
2 T. baking powder
1 qt. soaked raisins

Cream sugars and shortening. Sift dry ingredients except oats, together and then add oats. Add dry ingredients to creamed mixture alternately with milk. Fold in raisins. Drop by tablespoonfuls onto greased cookie sheets. Makes lots of good cookies.

WILDERNESS MOLASSES CAKE FOR 250

1¼ lb. fat
1¼ lb. sugar
7 c. molasses, unsulphured
4 lb. - 6 oz. flour
7 T. cinnamon
7 T. cloves

7 T. ginger
Salt
2 oz. baking soda dissolved in
   7 c. hot water
1½ c. egg solids
3 lb. raisins

Cream fat and sugar well. Add molasses. Sift flour, cinnamon, cloves, ginger and salt and add alternately with water and baking soda mixture. Add egg solids to mixture. Add raisins that have been moistened but not cooked. Bake in moderate oven, 350 degrees, until done. Bake in large baking pans. Dust with confectioners sugar or icing of your own choice if desired.

Betty Tucker
Regional Office

ONE OF THE 47 MINERAL HOT SPRINGS IN HOT SPRINGS NATIONAL PARK, ARKANSAS. (NPS photo).

HOLDING BACK THE WATER FOR LAKE MEAD NATIONAL RECREATION AREA IS 44 STORY HOOVER DAM NEAR BOULDER CITY, NEVADA. (NPS photo).

Miscellaneous

AN ALMOST-PREHISTORIC ATMOSPHERE AWAITS THE VISITOR TO BADLANDS NATIONAL PARK, SOUTH DAKOTA. (NPS photo by Jack Boucher.)

FRENCH DRESSING

1/2 c. olive oil
1 t. salt

1/4 c. lemon or lime juice
Dash of sugar

Place ingredients in covered jar. Chill and shake two minutes before adding to salad. (This dressing can be used for marinating meats or vegetables. Good to keep on hand in refrigerator.)

Virginia Duckett
Regional Office

MEXICAN HOT SAUCE

2 (10 cent pkg.) Chiltepinos
   (small pea size chiles)
Oregano to taste

1 can (No. 2½) tomatoes
3 cloves garlic (ajo)

Mash Chiltepinos and oregano. Cut up and mash in garlic. Add tomatoes; add more oregano and salt to taste, preferably 2 teaspoonfuls.

Cecilia Martin
Petrified Forest NP

CHILI SAUCE — HOT

1 can whole tomatoes,
   chopped
1 small onion, diced

1 t. chili tepin, mashed (do
   not use chili powder!)

Heat to boiling and add salt according to taste. (May substitute any hot pepper.)

Marilyn J. Scott
Kings Canyon NP

FRENCH DRESSING

1 c. Campbell's tomato soup
1 c. oil
1 c. vinegar
1 T. sugar
1 T. salt

1 t. pepper
1 t. onion salt
1 t. garlic salt
1 t. Worcestershire sauce

Combine all ingredients and shake well.

Dorothea Miehle
Regional Office

RUM SAUCE

1/2 c. butter
1 c. brown sugar, firmly
   packed

1/4 c. light cream
1 t. vanilla
Rum

Combine all ingredients thoroughly.

Elaine Hounsell
Lake Mead NRA

TACO SAUCE

This should be made up fresh for each meal, using fresh chiles since they lose their flavor as they get older. It will keep refrigerated for about a week. Use it on any food, it is a basic hot sauce. Hot means HOT!!!!! Wash your hands after handling chile tepins. If you should rub your eyes and get some tepin into them you will promptly regret it! With the "hot" comes the delicious flavor other chiles just don't have. Tepins are hard to find in some places but are worth the effort. If you have friends living near Mexico or in our bigger cities have them send you some. They resemble small shrivelled Spanish peanuts.

1 (8 oz.) can tomato sauce
1 (8 oz.) can water
1/3 t. garlic powder (1 fresh
   garlic clove is better)

1 heaping t. oregano
1 T. chile tepins (or Safeway's
   dried small whole hot red
   peppers)

Put all ingredients in your blender and mix until the sauce is the consistency of tomato soup. We serve this in a small cream pitcher and pour it liberally on tacos, enchiladas, etc. Serve it in a bowl if you like, this enables you to scoop up those extra hot seeds that often settle to the bottom.

Ed and Sue Jahns
Regional Office

SOUR CREAM DRESSING

1/2 c. sour cream
1/2 T. vinegar or lemon juice

1 T. sugar
Dash of salt

Beat cream until stiff, using an egg beater. Add vinegar or lemon juice, sugar and salt very slowly; continue beating.

Variations: Fold in 1 teaspoon onion juice, or fold in slightly beaten egg yolk and celery salt.

Virginia Duckett
Regional Office

CUCUMBER RELISH

12 large cucumbers (peel
   if wax-coated)
4 large onions
6 green peppers, stems and
   seeds removed
4 t. celery seed

4 t. mustard seed
1 t. salt
1/2 t. ground cloves
1 T. ground turmeric
3½ c. cider vinegar
2½ c. sugar

Put the cucumbers, onions and green peppers through a food chopper or chop until fine. In a 5 or 6 quart pan, combine all ingredients. Quickly, bring to boiling, stirring constantly; reduce heat and simmer for about 3 hours or until reduced to about 5 pints. Put in hot, sterilized jars and seal. Recipe first appeared in SUNSET MAGAZINE.

Chris McKinney
Grand Canyon NP

186 MISCELLANEOUS RECIPES

FRUIT DRESSING

2 eggs
1 c. sugar
2 T. flour

1/2 T. salt
1/2 c. lemon juice
2 c. pineapple juice

Mix together and cook in double boiler until thick. Very good on fruit salad.

Naidene McKay
Grand Canyon NP

FRITTER BATTER

1 c. flour
1/2 t. salt
1/2 t. baking powder

2 beaten eggs
1/2 c. milk

Add dry ingredients together and gradually add milk and eggs until blended. Dip fruits or vegetables into batter and coat well. Drop batter-covered fruit or vegetables into hot fat (over 400 degrees) and cook until golden brown. Drain; serve hot. If using fruit, sprinkle with powdered sugar, if desired. Vegetables can be served with a hot sauce.

Anonymous
Regional Office

NO COOK WHITE ICING

2 egg whites
3/4 c. white Karo syrup
1/4 c. sugar

1/4 t. salt
1¼ t. vanilla

Combine ingredients and beat with mixer until very thick. It should resemble 7-Minute Icing.

Clara Furnish
Petrified Forest NP

SPAGHETTI SAUCE

2 lb. ground beef
1 c. chopped onion (or large
   onion)
3 cloves garlic, chopped fine
1 large can tomato sauce
   (1 lb. 13 oz.)
1 large can tomatoes (1 lb. 13 oz.)

5 T. chopped parsley (dried)
2 T. marjoram
2 t. thyme
2 t. rosemary
Scant t. allspice
Salt and pepper to taste

Brown meat. Remove meat and brown onions and garlic. Combine meat, onions, garlic with tomato sauce and tomatoes and all seasonings in a Dutch oven. Simmer at least 1½ hours, preferably 3 to 4 hours. If sauce becomes too thick, thin with water or to desired consistency. Mushrooms may also be added. Serves 8 to 10 generously.

Dagmar Robinson
Channel Islands NM

MAPLE CREAMS

Use maple syrup and boil it as you would molasses. When it begins to thicken, add a small half cupful of sugar to each quart of syrup. When it is brittle, pour it out onto buttered container. Broken nuts and grated coconut may be added. (Recipe from NEEDLECRAFT magazine, December, 1919.)

Anonymous
Regional Office

RHUBARB CONSERVE

4 c. diced rhubarb
1 c. canned sour cherries,
   pitted and drained
1 c. diced pineapple, drained

1/4 c. lemon juice
1/4 c. orange juice
4 c. sugar

Mix all in a heavy saucepan. Cook over low heat, stirring frequently until thickened (about 1¼ hours). Pour into sterilized jars and seal. Makes approximately 2 pints. You may thin with equal amount of orange juice and heat for sauce.

Marilyn J. Scott
Kings Canyon NP

APRICOT-RASPBERRY JAM

4 lb. sound apricots
1/4 c. water
4½ c. sugar

1½ c. raspberries
  (1 basket)

Pit apricots and cut in pieces. Add the water, sugar and raspberries (hulled and washed). Cook in a large kettle, stirring to prevent sticking, until jam is of desired consistency, thick and clear. Pour into sterilized glasses and paraffin at once.

Dorothea Miehle
Regional Office

BARBECUE SAUCE FOR BEEF

1 c. ketchup
5 T. A-1 sauce
3/4 c. water
3/4 c. cooking oil
1 coarsely chopped onion (lg.)
5 T. Worcestershire sauce

1/3 c. sugar
1/2 c. vinegar
1 T. dry mustard
1 T. chili powder
1 t. black pepper
3 t. salt
1 T. allspice

Cook, stirring constantly, for 5 minutes (until sugar dissolves), then simmer 10 minutes. Slice thin, 4 to 5 pounds cold roast beef; press down into sauce and simmer, covered, for 2 hours. Serve on buns, sliced bread, over rice or with baked potatoes. This sauce is sufficient for basting six 1-pound sirloin steaks or three medium chickens. Keeps in refrigerator.

Bettie Black
Joshua Tree NM

SEVEN LAYER SANDWICH CAKE

21 slices white bread
  (crusts trimmed)
Softened butter
Tuna filling
Deviled ham filling

Chicken filling
1 pkg. (8 oz.) cream cheese
1/4 c. sour cream
Sweet gherkins, cherry tomatoes,
  radish roses, carrots and
  pimientos

Place 3 slices bread on plate, side by side, spread with butter and tuna filling. Spread 3 slices bread with butter, put this side down on top of first layer and spread with other fillings. Continue this process until all bread and fillings are used. Whip sour cream with cream cheese. Frost sides and top of cake and garnish with gherkins, tomatoes, radish roses, carrots and pimientos.

Tuna Filling:

1 can (6 oz.) tuna
1/3 c. sweet pickle relish
2 T. radish
1/4 t. celery seeds
1/4 c. mayonnaise

Deviled Ham Filling:

1 can deviled ham (4½ oz.)
1/3 c. sweet pickle relish
1 t. Parmesan cheese
1 t. catsup
1 T. mayonnaise

Chicken Filling:

1 c. cooked chicken
1/3 c. sweet pickle relish
1/4 c. pecans

1 T. onion
1/4 t. curry powder
1/4 c. mayonnaise

Marina Hoy
Fort Bowie NHS

BREAD AND BUTTER PICKLES

1 gal. small cucumbers (3")
8 small white onions

8 green peppers, seeded
1/2 c. salt

Slice very thin - I use an electric slicer for wafer-thin slices. Bury all in ice cubes or blocks for 3 to 4 hours before heating. Drain well. Heat thoroughly in syrup but do not boil. Pack immediately into sterilized jars, seal, and band and invert jars.

Syrup:

5 c. sugar
1/2 t. cloves
2 T. mustard seed

1½ t. turmeric
1 t. celery seed
5 c. brown vinegar

Heat ingredients well. But do not boil.

Peggy Rolandson
San Francisco Office

DIVINITY

2 c. sugar
1/2 c. white Karo syrup
1/2 c. maraschino cherry juice
Cherries and nuts

1/2 t. salt
2 egg whites
1 t. vanilla

Cook sugar, syrup, juice and salt to hard ball stage. Cool. Beat egg whites until very stiff. Add syrup slowly. Continue beating until it begins to lose its gloss. Add nuts and maraschino cherries. Drop by teaspoonful onto greased or oiled paper. Swirl each to a peak.

Olina Stout
Petrified Forest NP

TOMATO GRAVY

3 ripe tomatoes
1/3 cube butter
2 T. sugar

1/4 c. water
2/3 c. milk
2 T. flour
1/4 t. salt

Peel and cut tomatoes into small pieces. Cook gently in butter, water and sugar. When tomatoes are tender, make a white sauce (uncooked) of the flour, milk and salt. Add this to the cooked tomatoes and cook until the gravy is thick enough to please your taste. Enjoy with biscuits and butter.

Ken Patrick
Point Reyes NS

MESQUITE BEAN JELLY

3 qt. mesquite beans
  (to make 5 c. juice)

5 c. sugar
1 box pectin

Pick the beans when still red and before turning white. Cover mesquite beans with water and simmer until juice turns yellow. Strain. Follow recipe on pectin box for making jelly. Boil jelly a little longer than recipe directs and use spoon test to tell when it jells. Pour into sterilized jars and seal. This recipe was first published by New Mexico State Park and Recreation Commission.

Richard T. Hart
Casa Grande Ruins NM

MORMON GRAVY

2½ T. pork or bacon grease
4 T. flour
Parsley

4 c. milk
Salt and pepper

Melt bacon grease, add 3 cups milk; mix other cup of milk with flour until smooth. No lumps. Pour slowly into first mixture and cook thoroughly. Salt and pepper to taste. Sprinkle parsley over mixture. Use with vegetables, meat or fish.

Nick Weeks
Regional Office

SPICED WALNUTS

1 c. sugar	1/2 t. nutmeg
1/2 t. salt	1/4 t. cloves
2 t. cinnamon	2 c. walnuts (halves)

Combine sugar, salt, cinnamon, nutmeg and cloves with 1/2 cup water in medium saucepan. Cook over medium heat, stirring constantly, until sugar dissolves. Continue cooking without stirring to 235 degrees (on candy thermometer) or until soft ball stage. Remove from heat, add nuts, stir until creamy. Put on wax paper and separate with forks.

Kathryn M. Steele
Regional Office

KOSHER DILL PICKLES

4 lb. pickling cucumbers	1 T. allspice
1 Bell pepper, cut into pieces	1 T. peppercorns
2 stalks celery, cut up	4 or 5 bay leaves (crumbled)
1 t. dill seed	5 cloves garlic, cut into
2 tall sprigs fresh dill	small pieces
1 T. pickling spices	1/2 c. kosher (coarse) salt

Wash cucumbers and place in gallon glass jar. Dissolve salt in cold water and add to jar. Place ingredients in jar and fill with cold water to the top. Screw on cap and let stand for about 5 days. Then refrigerate.

Leonard Lebovitz
Regional Office

SPICE TEA MIX - Hot

1/2 c. instant tea	1 c. sugar
1/2 c. Tang	Dash of ground cloves
1/2 c. lemonade mix	

Mix thoroughly. Use two or more teaspoons to a cup. Use hot water.

Anonymous
Petrified Forest NP

PEANUT BRITTLE

2 c. sugar	2 T. butter
1 c. white syrup	2 t. baking soda
2 c. raw peanuts	1 t. vanilla

Bring 1/2 cup water to boil and add 2 cups sugar and 1 cup white syrup; stir until it is dissolved and boil it until it spins a thread; then add 2 cups peanuts and cook slowly over a fire until it turns a golden brown. Remove from fire and add 2 tablespoons butter and the 2 teaspoons baking soda and 1 teaspoon vanilla. Stir quickly and spread on 2 large cookie sheets that have been well oiled. Place in a cold area to cool. Then break into pieces.

Naidene McKay
Grand Canyon NP

PEANUT BUTTER BALLS

1 lb. margarine
3 lb. powdered sugar

1 qt. chunky peanut
butter

Work together and make into 1" balls. Chill 24 hours or more. Hold each ball with a toothpick while dipping into a mixture of 3 pkg. chocolate chips and 3/4 stick paraffin, melted together in a double boiler. Makes 120 balls.

Jan Shaver
Lake Mead NRA

SOMEMORES

While sitting at a campfire -- or your living room in front of a roaring fire, you can whip up this little dessert. On one graham cracker, place 4 squares of Hershey's chocolate candy. (It used to be the 5-cent size, but now I'm sure you'd have to use the 10-cent size to taste it!) Roast one marshmallow and place on chocolate -- cover with another graham cracker. It's gooey -- but tasty!

Mary and Forrest Benson
Regional Office

BLENDER DELIGHTS

Purple Cow:

1/4 c. grape juice
1/2 c. cold milk

2 scoops vanilla
ice cream

Blend all ingredients together. Pour into glasses. Makes 2 servings.

Banana Smoothie:

1 banana
1 c. orange juice

1 large scoop ice cream
Dash of nutmeg

Combine in blender and mix until banana is crushed. Sprinkle with nutmeg. Makes 1 serving.

Apricot Milk Shake:

1 can (12 oz.) apricot nectar
1 T. lemon juice
1/4 c. sugar

Dash of salt
3 c. cold milk

Combine all ingredients in blender and blend until sugar is dissolved.

Orange Nog:

1 egg
1/2 c. milk

1 T. sugar or honey
1/2 c. orange juice

Combine all ingredients until well blended.

Peggy Rolandson
San Francisco Office

OLDE ENGLISH MINCEMEAT

4 lb. ground beef
2 lb. beef suet
2 lb. sugar
2½ lb. raisins
2 lb. currants
4 lb. apples, chopped fine
1/2 lb. citron
1/2 lb. candied lemon peel,
   chopped
4 c. 100 proof whiskey or brandy

Grated peel from 2 oranges
Grated peel from 2 lemons
1 grated nutmeg
1 t. salt
1 T. ground cloves
10 T. cinnamon
1/2 c. orange juice
2 c. sherry
1/4 c. lemon juice

Boil ground beef and suet together until cooked. Let cool. Skim off fat. Combine all other ingredients in a huge bowl (restaurant size) and combine thoroughly with hands. Place mixture into large crock with cover and let stand until all ingredients have blended together. Can be packed into sterilized jars and sealed or placed in freezer containers and frozen. This is truly "mincemeat".

Peggy Rolandson
San Francisco Office

PEANUT BUTTER FUDGE

1 c. brown sugar
2 c. white sugar
1 c. milk

Vanilla
Salt
1 T. butter or margarine

Boil above ingredients to soft ball stage - 260 degrees. Remove from fire and add 1 cup peanut butter and 1/2 cup chopped nuts (optional for the nuts). Beat until smooth and pour into greased pan and cut into squares. (This recipe is a favorite of Betty's mother.)

Betty Tucker
Regional Office

SAVORY MEAT SAUCE

1/2 c. olive oil
2 medium onions, chopped
2 cloves garlic, minced
3 lb. ground beef
3 cans (No. 2) tomatoes
2 cans (6 oz. each) tomato
   paste
2 t. sugar
2 bay leaves

1/4 t. curry powder
1 T. chili powder
1/2 c. water
1/2 c. chopped celery
1/4 c. chopped parsley
1½ T. salt
1/4 t. pepper
1 t. dried basil

Saute onions and garlic in oil. Add ground beef and saute until brown, breaking up the meat. Add remaining ingredients and simmer 3 hours or until thick. Remove bay leaves. Store, covered, in refrigerator or freeze.

Marilyn J. Scott
Kings Canyon NP

IRISH JAMS — Various

The following recipes were obtained from THE KERRYMAN, published in Tralee, County Kerry, Ireland. They were issued by the County Kerry Committee of Agriculture:

BLACK CURRANT AND RHUBARB

8 lb. blackberries   4 lb. rhubarb
8 lb. sugar

Prepare fruits. Cut rhubarb into small pieces. Combine all ingredients and boil gently, stirring constantly, until desired thickness is obtained. Skim and ladle into sterilized glasses and seal.

CARROT AND BEETROOT JAM

Equal weights of carrots and beets, sugar and lemons. Boil carrots and beets separately and sieve. To each pint of puree allow 12 ounces sugar and 2 lemons. If you wish to keep this jam for a long time, put some brandy into each glass. Pour into sterilized glasses and seal. (Cook until desired thickness is obtained.)

ORANGE MARMALADE WITH HONEY

Oranges and honey. Boil the rinds until tender shredded finely. Remove the pith and pips; measure the pulp and to each pint allow 1 pound honey and 1/2 pound prepared rinds. Cook until desired thickness is obtained. Pour into sterilized glasses and seal.

TOMATO MARMALADE

7 lb. ripe tomatoes   8 lb. sugar
6 lemons   1 pt. water

Prepare fruits. Boil the sugar and water to syrup stage first and then add the fruits and continue in usual way.

VEGETABLE MARROW

Equal amounts of marrow and sugar. To each pound of marrow, allow 1/4 ounce of whole ginger and the grated rind and juice of half of lemon. Remember, with vegetable marrow, to boil very gently as this is the only jam that does not require rapid boiling. Proceed in the usual way.

Peggy Rolandson
San Francisco Office

CACTUS JELLY

1 c. cactus juice
3 c. sugar
1/3 c. lemon juice

1/2 bottle Certo
1 stick cinnamon

Follow directions on Certo bottle for jelly, boiling for 1 minute. Add Certo after the sugar. Remove cinnamon stick before pouring jelly into glasses. Cover with paraffin. Makes 7 glasses.

Marilyn's instruction for cactus collecting: Go armed with heavy gloves and kitchen tongs or forceps for gathering prickly pears. They are ripe when a deep purple. Always be on the lookout for rattlesnakes and watch the bending over to avoid cactus spines in the backside. I simply rinse the cactus apples in a colander and then boil until soft. Boiling softens the spines so up to this point, you should not have to touch the pears with your hands. Prickly pears are delicious when raw, and fun to eat while hiking through cactus country. Remove pear (or cactus apples) from the cacti with a sharp knife or stick. Spines can be singed off with a match. Peel and eat — a must for a first-timer to cacti country.

Marilyn J. Scott
Kings Canyon NP

FRENCH DRESSING

2 green peppers, chopped fine
1 can (7 oz.) pimiento,
   chopped fine
1 large onion, grated and use
   juice
1¾ c. vinegar

3 c. sugar
1 T. salt
1 can (42-46 oz.) tomato soup
1 T. celery seed
3 c. Mazola oil

Blend one hour in mixer or 10 minutes in blender. This recipe will make 2 pints.

Mary Adamson
Lake Mead NRA

PORT WINE JELLY

2 c. port wine
1/8 t. cinnamon
3 c. sugar

1 bottle (6 oz.) liquid fruit
   pectin (Certo)
1/8 t. cloves

Sterilize four 8-oz. jelly glasses and leave in hot water. In top of double boiler, combine port, sugar, cinnamon and cloves. Place over rapidly boiling water and heat 2 minutes, stirring constantly. Then, over direct heat, bring to a rolling boil and stir in pectin. Again, bring to a rolling boil and boil 1 minute, stirring constantly. Remove from heat. Skim off foam. Ladle jelly into hot glasses. Cover immediately with 1/8" hot paraffin. Let cool and cover with lids. (Excellent with meats, game meat, or on toast.)

Bunny Chew
Lake Mead NRA

FRENCH SALAD DRESSING

1 t. salt
1 t. sugar
1/4 t. dry mustard
1 T. paprika
1 pinch dried basil

1 T. Spice Island's Beau Monde
   seasoning
1/3 c. wine vinegar
1/3 c. salad oil
1/2 c. dry white wine
2 cloves garlic, pressed

Combine all ingredients and shake well.

Dave and Josephine Jones
San Francisco Office

PRICKLY PEAR CACTUS JELLY

About 30 of the ripe, purple prickly pear fruits (tunas) will make 2
cups of juice. You will need a pail with a handle, kitchen tongs and gloves—
and you'll need to be careful—when selecting fully ripe tunas. Taking them
with the tongs, lower them gently into the pail (sometimes they burst and
juice is lost). Put them in a colander and spray or pour water over them to
wash. Next, put the tunas in a kettle, DO NOT add water, and cook until
they burst, or until the juice is released when pricked with a fork. Then
strain through 3 to 5 folds of cloth (3 if the cloth is new, 5 if you use strips
of old sheeting as we sometimes do). Here's the jelly recipe:

1 c. juice
3 c. sugar

1/3 c. lemon juice
1/2 bottle Certo (add this last)

To the measured cactus and lemon juice in pan, add the exact amount
of sugar. Mix well. Place over high heat and bring to a boil, stirring constantly. At once, stir in Certo. Then bring to a full rolling boil and boil
hard one minute, stirring constantly. Remove from heat; skim off foam
with metal spoon and discard, and pour the jelly quickly into glasses. Cover
at once with hot paraffin.

NOTE: Only CERTO WILL JELL WITH THIS RECIPE — Sure
Jell, etc., just won't work. The original recipe appeared in the Southwest
Region Women's Organization newsletter "Smoke Signals". Substitute
homemade Thompson seedless grape wine for a unique fast treat. It has
won a blue ribbon at the county fair.

Richard T. Hart
Casa Grande Ruins NM

HERBED POPCORN

1/2 c. butter
2 T. minced chives or onions
1 t. basil

1/4 t. ground thyme
1/4 t. marjoram
1 t. salt
4 qt. warm unsalted popcorn

Melt butter; add chives and all other ingredients. Heat slowly; drizzle
over hot popped corn. Toss lightly to coat.

Peggy Rolandson
San Francisco Office

LIVER DUMPLINGS

4 slices day-old bread, cut into small pieces	1 medium onion, steamed in 2 T. butter
3/4 c. hot milk	About 1/2 lb. liver
3/4 c. dry bread crumbs	1 egg
Parsley	1 T. flour

Pour hot milk over bread cubes and let stand while onions steam. Scrape liver. Mix all ingredients and drop into boiling soup. Cook for 5 to 10 minutes. Serve hot.

Dorothea Miehle
Regional Office

COUNTRY PANCAKES

1½ c. self-rising flour	2 eggs
1 c. buttermilk	3 T. honey
3 T. fresh bacon grease	Small pinch salt

Combine all ingredients together and stir until mixed, but leave slightly lumpy. Fry on lightly greased HOT griddle until bubbles form on top of pancakes. Turn only once. Serve with desired topping.

Ken Patrick
Point Reyes NS

PINEAPPLE FUDGE

4 c. sugar	1 c. crushed pineapple (well drained)
1/2 c. syrup	1 t. ginger
1½ c. milk	

Combine all ingredients and bring to a boil. Cook slowly to soft ball stage. Remove from heat, cool to lukewarm. Beat until it loses its sheen. Add nuts and candied cherries, if desired.

DATE FUDGE

Add 1 lb. finely chopped dates instead of pineapple to above. Cook as above.

Olina Stout
Petrified Forest NP

CRISCO FROSTING

3 T. flour	1 c. Crisco
1 c. milk	1 T. vanilla
1 c. sugar	

Put flour and milk in double boiler and stir and cook until thick. Cream the sugar and Crisco together then add to paste and beat until sugar is dissolved. Add vanilla and stir well.

Naidene McKay
Grand Canyon NP

BUNNU KUKKU
(Serve this Finnish dish for breakfast or brunch.)

4 eggs	3 T. sugar
4 c. milk	Dash of salt
2 c. flour	1/4 lb. butter or oleo

Set oven for 350 degrees. Place butter in large baking pan and place in oven. Beat eggs in large bowl until light and fluffy. Add milk, flour, sugar and salt. Beat until mixture is smooth and well blended. Pour mixture into pan with melted butter. Bake one hour, until golden brown. Serve with maple syrup or jam. Makes 4-6 servings. For 2-3 servings, cut recipe in half.

Bonnie Pollock
Petrified Forest NP

RED PEPPER JELLY
(Spicy-sweet and brilliant red)

2½ lb. red Bell peppers (about 7 large ones)	10 c. sugar
2 c. cider vinegar	2/3 c. lemon juice
2 t. salt	1 bottle liquid pectin (6 oz.)
	2 t. chili powder

Cut peppers in halves; remove and discard stems and seeds. Cut peppers into pieces and whirl a few at a time in blender until very finely chopped, or force through the fine blade of a food chopper (you should have about 4 cups). In a large kettle, combine pepper pulp and all the juices, the vinegar, salt and chili powder. Over high heat, bring to boiling and boil rapidly for 10 minutes, stirring occasionally. Remove from heat and stir in the sugar and lemon juice. Return pan to heat and bring back to boiling. Stir in pectin and boil, stirring constantly, for exactly 1 minute. Reduce heat and skim off any foam; quickly ladle hot jelly into hot sterilized jars to within 1/8" of rim. Wipe rim of jar, place on hot, sterilized lid and band, and tighten band. Turn jar upside down and place on cloth or board to cool. When cool, turn right side up and check for strong seal. Makes about 7 pints. This recipe was taken from SUNSET MAGAZINE.

Chris McKinney
Grand Canyon NP

TART LEMON CURD

2 T. butter	1 t. grated lemon peel
2 eggs	1/4 c. lemon juice
1/3 c. sugar	

Melt butter in top of a double boiler, add eggs and sugar, beating well to blend; then add lemon peel and juice. Cook, stirring, over simmering water (double boiler) until thickened. Remove at once from heat and chill, covered; will keep for as long as a week. Serve over cheesecake or fruitcake. Makes 2/3 cup or 5-6 servings.

Elaine Hounsell
Lake Mead NRA

CHOCOLATE FUDGE

4½ c. sugar
1 (14½ oz.) can evaporated
   milk (1 2/3 cups)

3 (6 oz.) pkg. chocolate chips
1 c. butter or margarine
3 T. vanilla (yes, Tablespoons)

Combine sugar and milk in 3 quart heavy saucepan. Cook and stir over medium heat until mixture reaches a full rolling boil. Reduce heat if necessary, but keep mixture boiling steadily for 6 minutes. Stir as needed to prevent scorching.

Meanwhile, put chocolate chips, butter and vanilla in large bowl of electric mixer.

Pour hot mixture into bowl and beat at high speed until there is no butter on top. To tell when candy is ready to pour, lift beaters and let a little candy drop off them. If the drops do not sink into the candy, it is ready to pour. Pour into a lightly buttered 13x9x2" pan. Let cool several hours or overnight, or until firm, before cutting. Makes about 4 pounds and freezes well.

NOTE: If pools of butter form on top as the candy cools, beat it more.

Mary Chilton
Montezuma Castle NM

HOT CHOCOLATE MIX

1 c. cocoa
1½ c. powdered sugar
1 c. sugar

1 jar (6 oz.) dry coffee cream
11 c. dry milk

Sift cocoa and powdered sugar. Add sugar, coffee cream and dry milk. To serve: Use 1/3 - 1/2 cup of mix and fill cup with hot water. You may also add malted milk to increase food value.

Betty Berrett
Petrified Forest NP

PEAR RELISH

10 lb. firm ripe pears
6 green sweet peppers
6 red sweet peppers
3 small red hot peppers
6 to 8 medium size onions
1 T. salt

1 T. celery seed
1 T. mustard seed
2¾ c. sugar
4 c. vinegar (white)
1 c. water
1 oz. crystallized ginger

Core, peel and prepare vegetables and fruits. Cover with water while completing this phase to keep fresh. (Put pears into water with some lemon juice in it to prevent darkening.) Remove seeds from peppers. Grind all fruit and vegetables through coarse blade of food grinder. Mix with remaining ingredients (mix vinegar and water together first) into a large kettle and place over medium heat. Bring to full rolling boil, stirring often. Boil until desired thickness. Pack into hot sterilized jars and seal and band. Invert jars to cool. Makes about 10 pints.

Peggy Rolandson
San Francisco Office

SOUR CREAM DRESSING

1 qt. sour cream
1 T. Coleman's mustard
1 t. salt, pepper and Accent

1 egg
1 pt. milk (2 c.)
1 c. vinegar

Blend thoroughly. Age in freshly emptied gin bottles. This is good for salads, warm sauce for vegetables and meat and many other uses. Especially good with leftovers—just add near the end of cooling.

Fifi and Doug Cornell
Golden Gate NRA

ROQUEFORT SALAD DRESSING (A family recipe of Diana Jagoda)

3 oz. Roquefort or Blue cheese
1½ t. Worcestershire sauce
1 dash Tabasco sauce
1 t. A-1 sauce

3/4 t. garlic powder
1/2 t. Lawry's seasoned salt
1 pt. mayonnaise
1 pt. sour cream

Mash cheese at room temperature; add seasonings in order and mix well. Add mayonnaise and stir. Fold in sour cream. Makes approximately 1 quart.

Bunny Chew
Lake Mead NRA

TURKEY STUFFING

4 c. bread crumbs
1/2 c. celery
1/2 pkg. onion soup mix

3 eggs
1 lb. sausage
1 lb. uncooked popcorn

Combine all ingredients. Stuff turkey. Bake at 350 degrees for 3 hours. At the end of 3 hours, get the hell out of the kitchen as that popcorn is going to blow that bird to bits!

Elaine Hounsell
Lake Mead NRA

POPCORN CAKE

6 qt. freshly popped corn
   (not buttered)
2 c. sugar
2/3 c. white corn syrup

3/4 c. hot water
1/4 c. margarine
1/4 t. salt
Food coloring, if desired

Combine all ingredients except popped corn and boil to the soft ball stage. Pour over popped corn and mix well in large container. (Candy mints and/or peanuts may be added to popcorn before mixing with syrup.) When thoroughly mixed, press into buttered angel food pan. Remove right away. To serve, cut into slices.

Helen Cropper
Petrified Forest NP

CREAM CHEESE FROSTING

1 pkg. (3 oz.) cream cheese
2 T. light corn syrup

1/2 t. vanilla
2½ c. sifted confectioners
sugar

In a medium mixing bowl, stir together cream cheese and corn syrup until blended. Gradually stir in the sugar and vanilla, keeping the mixture smooth.

Yvonne Razo
Tumacacori NM

CARAMELS

2 c. sugar
1 c. coffee cream

1¾ c. white Karo syrup
1 c. butter

Combine and bring to a boil, add coffee cream and cook until waxy or like a caramel tried in water. Flavor with vanilla or 4 squares of chocolate. Beat until cool. Turn into greased pan. When set, cut into 1" squares and wrap in waxed paper or foil.

Mary and Forrest Benson
Regional Office

ICEBOX FUDGE

2 c. sugar
10 or 12 marshmallows
Small can milk

1/4 lb. oleo
Nuts
Chocolate chips (1 pkg.)

Combine sugar, marshmallows and milk. Boil slowly about 6 minutes. Pour over chocolate pieces and oleo. Add nuts; stir; pour into prepared pan and put in refrigerator to set.

Naidene McKay
Grand Canyon NP

HOW TO DRY BLACKBERRIES

Pick all you can! Wash them thoroughly. Shake out excess water. Spread berries on large platters or trays (single layers) that have been lined with clean brown paper. Dry berries thoroughly. Spread a single layer of cheesecloth over to protect from dirt and bugs. Bring trays in at night and put out each day in hot sun until dried. (Test by crumbling a berry between fingers.) When dry, pack into clean dry sterilized glass jars and seal or put into clean brown paper bags and seal tight. When ready to use, soak overnight in water, add necessary sugar (and cornstarch for thickening if for pies). (Recipe from NEEDLECRAFT magazine, August, 1920.)

Anonymous
Regional Office

DATE, FIG, RAISIN, OR PRUNE FILLING

2 c. dates, figs or raisins,
   finely cut or ground, or 2 c.
   mashed cooked prunes
   (2 2/3 c. uncooked)

3/4 c. sugar
3/4 c. water
1/2 c. chopped nuts

Cook fruit, sugar and water together slowly, stirring constantly, until thickened. Add nuts. Cool. About 2 1/3 cups filling.

Anonymous
Petrified Forest NP

NEARLY NO-CAL SAUCE

1 c. diet cottage cheese
1/2 c. yogurt
1/2 c. chopped chives

1/2 t. dry mustard
Garlic salt

Put all those things in a blender and whizz until smooth and a green color. Don't refrigerate. Serve at room temperature. Vary this by using parsley or other fresh herbs. For a thinner sauce, use some sherry. Good on baked potatoes or other vegetables.

Bob Cox
Regional Office

RHUBARB ORANGE CONSERVE

2 seedless oranges
2 c. seedless raisins
2 lb. rhubarb, cut into 1"
   pieces

1/2 c. water
1½ c. coarse walnut pieces
4½ c. sugar

Cut oranges into 1/4" slices, then into bits. Wash raisins and drain. Mix together with rhubarb. Add sugar and water. Bring to boil, stirring occasionally, and simmer until thickened (about 35-40 minutes). Add walnut pieces about 5 minutes before removing from heat. Pour into hot sterilized jars and seal at once. Yields about 4 pints.

Marilyn J. Scott
Kings Canyons NP

BARBECUE SAUCE

2 T. liquid smoke
1/3 bottle Worcestershire
   sauce
1/3 bottle of A-1 sauce
1/2 bottle Tabasco sauce

2 c. ketchup
1/2 c. cooking oil
1/2 c. vinegar
1 small jar mustard
Garlic to taste

Put all this in a quart fruit jar and stir well. Put in refrigerator, the unused portion; it will keep for months.

Mary and Forrest Benson
Regional Office

FURNITURE POLISH

A good furniture polish can be made of equal quantities of linseed oil and turpentine and vinegar. Mix first two ingredients thoroughly before adding the vinegar. Shake well before using. (Recipe from NEEDLE-CRAFT magazine, June, 1910 issue.)

Anonymous
Regional Office

KITCHEN PHILOSOPHY

"Remember that beans, badly boiled, kill more than bullets; and fat is more fatal than powder. In cooking, more than anything else in this world, always make haste slowly. One hour too much is vastly better than five minutes too little, with rare exceptions. A big fire scorches your soup, burns your face, and crisps your temper. Skim, simmer, and scour, are the true secrets of good cooking." Excerpt from MANUAL FOR ARMY COOKS - 1883.

Charles Hawkins
Fort Point NHS

HAPPINESS CAKE

1 c. good thoughts
1 c. kind deeds
2 c. well-beaten faults

1 c. consideration for others
2 c. sacrifice
3 c. forgiveness

Mix thoroughly. Add tears of joy, sorrow and sympathy. Flavor with love and kindly service. Fold in 4 cups of prayers and faith. Blend well. Fold into daily life. Bake well with the warmth of human kindness and serve with a smile any time. It will satisfy the hunger of starved souls. (From Dorothee Poulsen's column in ARIZONA REPUBLIC.)

Helen Cropper
Petrified Forest NP

THE COOK'S CREED

"Cleanliness is next to godliness, both in persons and kettles; be ever industrious, then, in scouring your pots. Much elbow grease, a few ashes, and a little water, are capital aids to the careful cook. Dirt and grease betray the poor cook, and destroy the poor soldier; whilst health, content, and good cheer should ever reward him who does his duty and keeps his kettles clean. In military life, punctuality is not only a duty, but a necessity, and the cook should always endeavor to be exact in time. Be sparing with sugar and salt, as a deficiency can be better remedied than an overplus." Excerpt from MANUAL FOR ARMY COOKS - 1883.

Charles Hawkins
Fort Point NHS

RECIPE FOR SAFETY

Take sensible, safe clothing.
Add special safety equipment.
Mix briskly with a solution of common sense.
Sprinkle well with each safety regulation.
Handle the recipe with daily care.
And continue its practice forevermore.
Live a long and happy life.

Vera Poston
Regional Office

JUST 35 MILES NORTHWEST OF SAN FRANCISCO LIES THE BEAUTIFUL BEACHES AND HIGH CLIFFS OF POINT REYES NATIONAL SEASHORE, CALIFORNIA. (NPS photo by Jack Boucher).

INDEX OF RECIPES--by type

SOUPS

SALADS

GAME

CAKES

COOKIES

MISCELLANEOUS

INDEX OF PARKS SUBMITTING RECIPES

INDEX OF COOKS SUBMITTING RECIPES

AN INVITATION TO CONTRIBUTE TO A NEW NATIONAL PARKS COOKBOOK

What's Cooking in Our National Parks remains popular for recipe ideas, for its nostalgic tie with cooks associated with the National Park Service, and for the scholarship funds it raises. Still, a new approach is planned that will associate recipes more closely with parks and/or NPS traditions. Anecdotes relating to park themes will be included for each recipe, and perhaps some with no recipes. "Recipes" could be for cleaning, medicine, too. Recipes would be listed by parks and/or regions, rather than by type of dish.

Will you participate and help this new cookbook do good works, too? Ideas are welcome from park employees, alumni, and park friends and visitors.

The new book may relate unusual aspects of park cooking: How far does a family living in a distant park go for supplies; what happens when they run out? Describe cooking on a wood stove, or the time when the bear or the visitor or the VIP came to dinner. What about use of local foods? Park traditions that involve food?— "Christmas" in summer, clam bakes, Founders' Day events? Most recipes will be usable in today's kitchens; some may be historic.

Examples that fit this approach would be fry bread from Canyon de Chelly, flautas from Chamizal, mountain cooking from Great Smoky Mountains, cod from Cape Cod, Army beans from Fort Union, pioneer trail bread from Scotts Bluff, prison fare from Alcatraz, backountry recipe from Kings Canyon. Illustrations relating recipes or traditions to sites, and a new cover, will be sought.

Send ideas to Vistabooks (address on page 2)—copies only; we cannot acknowledge or return materials. No copyrighted items or trade names. If we use an item, you will get credit in the new book and a free copy. As on the present cookbook, 5% of sales will go to the E&AA Education Trust Fund for families of park employees.—William R. Jones, Editor, Vistabooks

BACK COVER—Suspended 6000 feet above sea level in an ancient volcanic crater is the sparkling clean beautiful blue water of Crater Lake National Park. (NPS photo by Billy Newhold.)